George Rudé was a distinguished historian and renowned expert on 18th-century history. He taught in universities all over the world and held many top academic posts. In retirement he lived in Sussex until his death in 1992.

BY THE SAME AUTHOR

The Crowd in the French Revolution
Interpretations of the French Revolution
Wilkes and Liberty
The Crowd in History
Revolutionary Europe
Captain Swing (with Eric Hobsbawm)
Paris and London in the Eighteenth Century:
Studies in Social Protest
Hanoverian London
Debate on Europe
Europe in the Eighteenth Century:
Aristocracy and the Bourgeois Challenge
Robespierre: Portrait of a Revolutionary Democrat
Protest and Punishment
Ideology and Popular Protest
Criminal Victim: Crime and Society in
Nineteenth-Century England

as editor

The Eighteenth Century
Robespierre

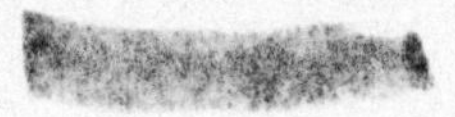

THE FRENCH REVOLUTION

George Rudé

PHŒNIX

A PHOENIX PAPERBACK

First published in Great Britain
by Weidenfeld and Nicolson in 1988
This paperback published in 1994
by Phoenix, a division of Orion Books Ltd,
Orion House, 5 Upper St Martin's Lane,
London WC2H 9EA

A catalogue record for this book is available
from the British Library.

ISBN: 1 85799 126 5

Printed and bound in Great Britain by
Butler & Tanner Ltd, Frome and London

Contents

PARIS in 1789

1. Madeleine
2. Champs Elysées
3. Tuileries Gardens
4. National Assembly
5. Jacobin Club
6. Palais Royal
7. Corn Market
8. Louvre
9. Châtelet
10. Temple
11. Hôtel de Ville
12. Place de Grève
13. Palais de Justice
14. Pont Neuf
15. Pont Royal
16. Cordeliers Club
17. Ile de la Cité
18. Notre Dame
19. Ile St. Louis
20. Bastille
21. Salpêtrière
22. Gobelins
23. Ste. Geneviève
24. Luxembourg
25. Invalides
26. Ecole Militaire
27. Champ de Mars

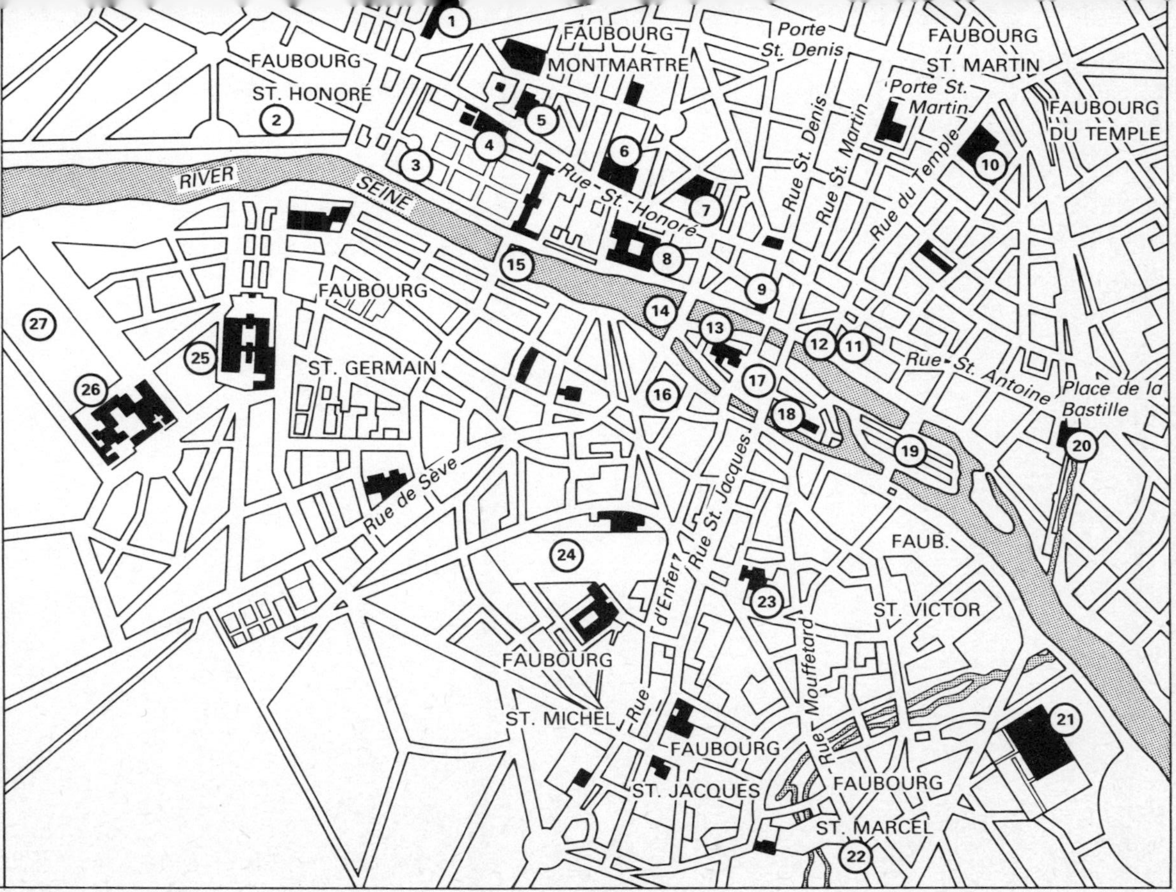

EUROPE in 1815
Boundary of the German Confederation
Moscow
RUSSIAN EMPIRE
Stockholm
KINGDOM OF NORWAY AND SWEDEN
BALTIC SEA
NORTH SEA
DENMARK
Copenhagen
PRUSSIA
Warsaw
POLAND
GREAT BRITAIN
Berlin
London
NETHER-LANDS
SAXONY
Prague
ATLANTIC
OCEAN
BAVARIA
AUSTRIA
HUNGARY
Paris
Vienna
Buda
Pest
AUSTRIAN EMPIRE
BLACK SEA
FRANCE
SWITZ
VENETIA
PAPAL STATES
OTTOMAN
EMPIRE
TUSCANY
KINGDOM OF SARDINIA
SPAIN
PORTUGAL
Lisbon
Madrid
Rome
Naples
THE TWO SICILIES
MEDITERRANEAN SEA

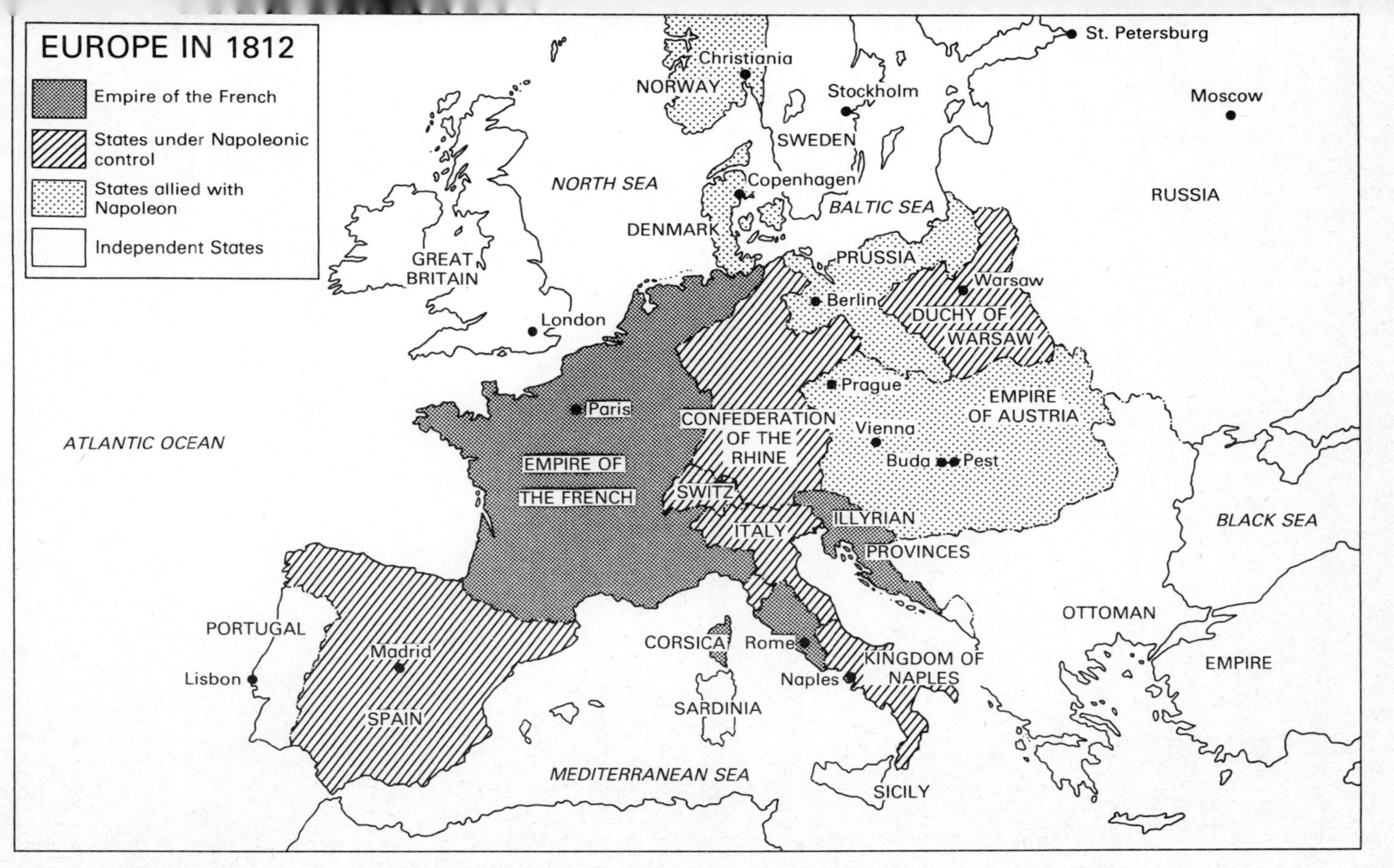
EUROPE IN 1812
Empire of the French
States under Napoleonic control
States allied with Napoleon
Independent States
St. Petersburg
Christiania
NORWAY
Stockholm
Moscow
SWEDEN
NORTH SEA
Copenhagen
RUSSIA
BALTIC SEA
DENMARK
GREAT BRITAIN
PRUSSIA
Warsaw
Berlin
DUCHY OF WARSAW
London
Prague
EMPIRE OF AUSTRIA
Paris
CONFEDERATION OF THE RHINE
ATLANTIC OCEAN
Vienna
EMPIRE OF THE FRENCH
Buda
Pest
SWITZ
ILLYRIAN PROVINCES
BLACK SEA
ITALY
OTTOMAN EMPIRE
PORTUGAL
Madrid
CORSICA
Rome
KINGDOM OF NAPLES
Lisbon
Naples
SARDINIA
SPAIN
MEDITERRANEAN SEA
SICILY

EUROPE in 1789
Kingdom of Prussia
Habsburg Dominions
St. Petersburg
SWEDEN
Christiania
Stockholm
RUSSIA
Moscow
NORTH SEA
KINGDOM OF NORWAY AND DENMARK
Copenhagen
BALTIC SEA
IRELAND
GREAT BRITAIN
Oldenburg
POLAND
HANOVER
PRUSSIA
Amsterdam
Hanover
Berlin
Warsaw
London
NETH
SAXONY
Brussels
Cologne
Bohemia
ATLANTIC OCEAN
Paris
Prague
Moravia
Mainz
HUNGARY
Yedisan
BAVARIA
Vienna
AUSTRIA
Buda
Pest
FRANCE
Tyrol
SWITZ
Trieste
Savoy
VENETIAN
Barat
Wallachia
BLACK SEA
Bosnia
Genoa
Serbia
PAPAL STATES
Bulgaria
TUSCANY
REPUBLIC
Constantinople
PORTUGAL
SPAIN
OTTOMAN
CORSICA
Rome
Montenegro
Lisbon
Madrid
Rumelia
EMPIRE
KINGDOM OF SARDINIA
Naples
THE TWO SICILIES
Levidia
MEDITERRANEAN SEA
Morea
Candia

PRE-REVOLUTIONARY FRANCE
Boundary of France
Boundaries of provinces
50
0
50
100
150
MILES
FLANDRE
Boulogne
Lille
ARTOIS
Douai
Abbeville
Arras
Amiens
PICARDIE
Rouen
Caen
Beauvois
Reims
ILE DE
NORMANDE
Versailles
Paris
FRANCE
Thionville
Verdun
Metz
Valmy
Nancy
Strasbourg
BRETAGNE
Rennes
MAINE
Chartres
CHAMPAGNE
Troyes
LORRAINE
Orleans
ORLEANS
ALSACE
Angers
Nantes
ANJOU
TOURAINE
Dijon
NIVERNAIS
FRANCHE-COMTÉ
Nevers
Poitiers
BERRY
Moulins
BOURGOGNE
AUNIS
POITOU
BOURBONNAIS
MARCHE
SAINTONGE
ANGOUNOIS
Limoges
LIMOUSIN
LYONNAIS
Lyon
St. Etienne
AUVERGNE
Grenoble
Bordeaux
GUYENNE
DAUPHINÉ
GASCOGNE
Toulouse
Avignon
COMTAT VENAISSIN
PROVENCE
BÉARN
LANGUEDOC
Fréjus
Marseille
Toulon
CTÉ DE FOIX
Pau
ROUSSILLON
Ajaccio
CORSICA on same scale

1 Introduction

1 *Why Was There a Revolution in France?*

Why was there a revolution in France in 1789 – and nowhere else in Europe? It is true enough that Belgium and Poland had waged something like national rebellions, against the Austrians and the Russians respectively. In the United Provinces (today's Holland) there was an attempted (though still-born) political revolution by the 'Patriots' and, in Geneva in 1768, a *coup d'état* by the city's Burghers which, for a year, redressed the balance of the constitution in their favour. But in none of these conflicts was there a decisive victory for any one social group over another; none was 'democratic', in so far as none transferred, or was intended to transfer, the weight of political authority to the nation at large; and none went on, by progressive stages, to effect a thorough transformation of existing society. This happened only in France; and while some of these countries, and certain others besides, later followed in the wake of the revolutionary changes taking place in France, this is not the question that concerns us here.

Why, then, was there a revolution of this kind in France? Historians, being adept at reading history backwards, have answered the question in different ways depending on their own prejudices or those of their contemporaries, and these we will consider in the next chapter. But let us begin with a brief introduction to French society of the *ancien régime*, together with its government and institutions, which will serve as a curtain-raiser to the dramatic events that began to unfold in 1789.

We may picture French eighteenth-century society as a kind of pyramid, whose apex was filled by the Court and aristocracy, its centre by the 'middling' classes or bourgeoisie, and its base by the 'lower orders' of peasants and urban tradesmen and craftsmen. This would, in itself, be nothing new: a similar model might fit the society of any other European country of the time. So, to find the distinguishing feature of French contemporary society, we must look for something else: the French social pyramid was riddled with contradictions both within and between its constituent parts. For it had a monarchy that, although absolute in theory, carried within it the seeds of its own decay; an aristocracy that, though privileged and mostly wealthy, was deeply resentful of its long exclusion from office; a bourgeoisie that, though enjoying increasing prosperity, was denied the social status and share in government commensurate with its wealth; and peasants who (in part at least) were becoming more literate and independent, yet were still regarded as a general beast of burden, despised and over-taxed. Moreover, these conflicts and the tensions they engendered were becoming sharper as the century went on.

Let us now look a little more closely at these problems, starting at the base of the pyramid and moving towards its apex. The peasants were, in general, by no means as impoverished and unfree as they were in many other European countries of the day. By the end of the *ancien régime*, perhaps one in four peasant families owned their land outright – comparatively few were prosperous *coqs de village* ('village roosters'), some were relatively prosperous *laboureurs* (yeomen farmers), and others, true enough (as Arthur Young, a contemporary English observer, noted in his *Travels in France*), were 'poor . . . and miserable, much arising from the minute division of their little farms among all children'. Half or more of the peasants were poor *métayers* (sharecroppers) who owned no capital and shared their produce with their landlords on a fifty–fifty basis; and a quarter or more were landless labourers or cottagers working for wages and renting tiny plots. Again, on the positive side of the equation, fewer than one in twenty – mainly on noble or ecclesiastical estates in the east – were serfs, though not fully tied to the land or deprived of royal justice. But, though his legal disabilities were less oppressive than in many other states, the French peasant bore a heavy burden of taxation: he paid tithe to the Church; *taille* (direct tax on income or land), *vingtième* (a 'twentieth' tax on income), *capitation* (income tax per head) and *gabelle* (salt tax) to the state; and to the *seigneur* (lord) of his manor, whether lay or ecclesiastical, he discharged a varying toll of obligations, services and payments ranging from the *corvée* (forced labour on roads) and the *cens* (feudal rent in cash) to the *champart* (rent in kind) and the *lods et ventes* (tax levied on transfer of property), or, if not owning his land outright, he might have to pay for the use of his lord's mill, wine-press or bakery. The heaviness of these burdens, like the status of the peasant himself, varied greatly from one region to the next – and in some areas they were not too onerous. But, in years of bad harvests and depression, they proved to be universally vexatious and intolerable, and this was to be a problem that grew more acute as the century went on – as were the grievances of the middle classes of which more will be said anon.

The nobility or aristocracy (for our purposes they amount to the same) fell into two main groups: the *noblesse d'épée* (the traditional nobility 'of the sword') and the *noblesse de robe*, formerly wealthy bourgeois who, from the seventeenth century on, had acquired hereditary deeds of nobility from their purchase of *charges*, or offices, in the royal bureaucracy. This allowed them to take such posts as secretaries or intendants, and gave them access to the Parlements – the great legal corporations that, in times of weak and divided governments and idle or incompetent rulers, were able to exercise political authority by refusing to register government edicts. Such offices had, since Louis XIV's time, been refused to the elder nobility as a punishment for the disruptive role they had played in the civil war of the Frondes in the late 1640s and early 1650s.

Though this older nobility continued to harbour resentments because of their exclusion from high office, they retained the privilege of occupying the senior army posts and, as owners of landed estates, exercising the rights of the old feudal lords of the manor: rights of local justice and surveillance, rights of monopoly, such as the exclusive right to hunt and maintain a mill, an oven or a wine-press (*banalités*), and, above all, the right to exact feudal rents and services from their peasants. In addition, members of the French nobility as a whole, whether of the 'robe' or the 'sword', enjoyed a considerable degree of freedom from direct taxation. They were virtually immune from payment of the principal and most onerous of these taxes, the notorious *taille* (levied on both estimated income and land), and in large measure, too, they evaded payment of their proper share of the *vingtième* and *capitation* which had been introduced to supplement the *taille* in the lean years at the end of Louis XIV's long reign, taxes to which both nobles and commoners were nominally subject. The clergy, whose upper ranks belonged almost without exception to the nobility, enjoyed even greater financial privileges: in addition to the income derived as landowners from rents and feudal dues, they drew tithe (which might amount to one-twelfth the yield of the land) and discharged their obligations to the exchequer by the payment of a relatively small percentage of their income in the form of a *don gratuit* or voluntary gift (admittedly, less 'voluntary' to some rulers than to others).

Of course, the degree of privilege that the privileged classes were able to enjoy depended in large measure on the degree of authority at the King's command. In theory, France's system of government was still the 'absolute' system that Louis XIV had built at Versailles a century before. But, under the Sun King's successors, that system had lost a great deal of its vigour and its ability to command the respect and loyalty of its subjects, whether privileged or not. This was due, in part, to the indolence and personal failings of Louis XV, to whom government was a painful chore, and, in part, to the tendency of the bureaucracy, staffed largely by privileged office-holders, to become almost a law unto itself. Meanwhile, the middle classes became more resentful of the extravagance, inefficiencies and tyranny of a court and government to whose upkeep they contributed heavily but over which they had no control. Louis XVI, after his father's long reign, was eager to bring about substantial reform in the administration, to reduce the expenditure of the Court, to free trade of petty restrictions, to ease the tax burden of the peasants and to promote a measure of self-government by means of local assemblies in the provinces. Unlike his predecessor, he had a high sense of personal responsibility. Besides, in his newly appointed Chief Minister, Turgot, he had a man who enjoyed the esteem and affection of both the 'enlightened' and the industrious middle classes. Yet the whole plan collapsed and Turgot was out of office in a couple of years. Why? Turgot's reforms, though welcome to the middle classes, ran counter to the vested interests of the Parlements, the upper clergy and aristocratic factions at Court. In this his experience was similar to that of reforming ministers such as Machault and Maupeou before him, and of Calonne, Brienne and Necker who followed. And it proved once more, as it was to prove a decade later, that no far-reaching measures of reform were possible, however well intentioned the monarch or honest and able his ministers, so long as the privileged orders were left in possession of their powers through the Parlements and their influence at Court to obstruct the operation. These were the limits beyond which reform could not go – sufficient to whet the appetite of some, to irritate others and satisfy none. Sufficient, too (and this was to prove an important consideration in the future), to draw further hatred on the privileged orders and contempt on the monarchy that appeared to protect them.

And the French middle classes, for all their expanding prosperity, had other grievances besides. Among them were the obstacles to the freer exercise of trade and manufacture created by onerous internal tolls and duties (exacted by both state and private interest) and the inquisitions of armies of government inspectors. Another was their growing failure to realize social and political ambitions commensurate with their wealth. It had long been the aim of merchantmen and financiers, enriched by banking, manufacture or commerce, to crown their careers by the purchase of hereditary offices of state or commissions in the army. Yet it has been argued – by Mathiez, Lefebvre and Godechot in France and by Ford and Barber in America[1] – that these avenues to preferment were becoming restricted in the latter half of the eighteenth century, in what has been termed a period of 'aristocratic' or 'feudal' reaction. An example that has often been cited is that of the Army Law (the *Loi Ségur*) of 1781, whereby promotions to the rank of captain and above were to be reserved for men of at least four 'quarters' of nobility, which excluded all commoners and those recently ennobled. During this period, too, several provincial Parlements, notably those of Aix, Nancy, Grenoble, Toulouse and Rennes, were slamming their doors on the 'intruders'. More generally, it appears that by 1789 noble status had become an almost indispensable requirement for high office not only in the army but in the Church and administration.[2] Thus, paradoxically, writes Jacques Godechot, 'the more numerous, the wealthier and better educated the French bourgeoisie became, the scarcer became the number of governmental and administrative posts to which they could aspire'.[3] While these views have been contested and the whole notion of an 'aristocratic' or 'feudal' reaction has been questioned,[4] it appears evident enough that the bourgeoisie, towards the end of the *ancien régime*, were suffering from an increasing sense of indignity and humiliation at the hands of government and aristocracy. It was not just a matter of doors to preferment being progressively closed – and the number of such doors may well be exaggerated – but of doors being closed at all, at a time when the bourgeoisie's rising wealth and perception of their social importance, not to mention their rising numbers, led them to believe that doors should be opened wider. The resentment and grievances were both genuine enough, and in history, as Tocqueville reminds us in *The Ancien Régime and the French Revolution*, it is often resentment that is the more important of the two. So it is perhaps all the more remarkable that the French bourgeoisie – if we except the writers, journalists and pamphleteers among them – waited so long before giving their resentment overt political expression. In fact, as we shall see, it was only when prodded by the Parlements, upper clergy and nobility, whose challenge preceded theirs, that they began seriously to lay claim to social equality rather than to a share in 'privilege', and to play an appropriate role in control of the state.

The resentments and grievances of the peasants were also compounded during these latter years of the *ancien régime*. For one thing, the increasing peasant prosperity was never universal. While one in four of French peasants owned their land, the majority of these rural proprietors held tiny plots that, even in years of good harvest, were quite insufficient for their family's needs. There were, too, the even greater numbers of sharecroppers and landless, who purchased their bread in the market and who could never, even in the most fruitful of seasons, hope to enjoy more than a meagre share of the general prosperity. Moreover, the small proprietors, poor tenants and cottagers, had the added grievance that 'improving' landlords and the more prosperous peasants, stimulated by the urge to increase their profits, were, as opportunity offered, enclosing fields and encroaching on the villagers' traditional rights of gleaning and pasture. A more general cause for discontent was the recent tendency of landlords (whether noble or bourgeois) to revive old privileges attaching to the land and to impose new or added obligations to those already exacted from their peasants. This is what the peasants – or, at least, the more vocal among them – in their 'notebooks of grievances' (*cahiers de doléances*) of 1789 called a revival of feudalism and what many French historians have termed a part of the 'feudal reaction'. Alfred Cobban, however, objected to the use of the term on the grounds that what landlords were doing was 'less a reversion to the past than the application to old relationships of new business techniques'.[5] There is some truth in this contention, though it overplays the element of a new spirit of 'capitalism' applied to rural production. But, even so, the peasants were not inclined to make such fine distinctions and to them 'feudalism' (as they saw it) appeared even more obnoxious when dressed up in a new and unfamiliar garb.

Furthermore – and this has only recently been brought to light – it was precisely in these closing years of the *ancien régime* that the general prosperity of agriculture was grinding to a halt. This developed in two main stages. After 1778, the year France entered the American Revolutionary War, there was a recession as a result of which prices fell, gradually in most industrial and farm products, but reaching crisis proportions in wines and textiles. During these years, the net profits of small tenant farmers, peasant proprietors and wine-growers tended, because of the heavy and sustained toll of tax, tithe and seigneurial exaction, to fall out of all proportion to the fall in prices; large landed proprietors were cushioned against loss by means of their seigneurial (or 'feudal') revenues. Then, on top of the cyclical depression, came the sudden catastrophe of 1787–9 which brought poor harvests and shortages, with the price of wheat doubling within two years in the north and in mid-summer 1789 reaching record levels in twenty-seven of the thirty-two *généralités*. The crisis hit the bulk of the peasantry both as consumers and producers: as wine-growers, dairy-farmers and wheat-growers. From agriculture it spread to industry; and unemployment, already developing due to a 'free-trade' treaty signed with Britain in 1786, reached disastrous proportions in Paris and the textile centres of

Lyons and the north. The wage-earners and small consumers, in both villages and towns, were compelled by the rapid rise in food prices to increase their daily expenditure on bread to levels far beyond their means. Thus peasants and urban craftsmen and workers – not to mention manufacturers – were drawn together in a common bond of hostility to government, landlords, merchants and speculators. These classes therefore entered the Revolution in a context of increasing shortage and hardship rather than one of 'prosperity'.[6]

But, of course, it needed more than economic hardship, social discontent and thwarted ambitions to make a revolution. To give cohesion to the discontents and aspirations of widely varying social classes there had to be some unifying body of ideas, a common vocabulary of hope and protest – something, in short, like a common 'revolutionary psychology'. In the revolutions of the past hundred years this ideological preparation has been the work of mass political parties, but eighteenth-century France had no such parties until long after the Revolution started; nor did she have them when revolutions occurred again between 1830 and 1871. So the ground had to be prepared by other means: in the first instance by the writers of the Enlightenment who, as Burke and Tocqueville were both quick to note, weakened the ideological defences of the *ancien régime*. The ideas of Montesquieu, Voltaire, Rousseau and many others were widely disseminated and were absorbed by an eager reading public, both aristocratic and plebeian. It had become fashionable, even among the clergy, to be sceptical and 'irreligious', and the writings of Voltaire had combined with the struggles within the Church itself (above all, the resentment of the parish clergy over the wealth and increasing authority of bishops) to expose the Church to indifference, contempt or hostility. Meanwhile, such terms as 'citizen', 'nation', 'social contract', 'general will' and the 'rights of man' – soon to be followed by 'third estate' – were entering into a common political vocabulary that became widely diffused. This was largely the work of the pamphleteers of 1788 and 1789, but, long before, the ground had been prepared by the tracts and remonstrances of the Parlements who, in their prolonged duel from the 1750s on, with ministerial 'despotism', quoted freely and often indiscriminately from the writings of Montesquieu and Rousseau and other 'philosophical' critics of the day. The new factor here was that the Parlements were not simply writing political tracts as the 'philosophers' had done, but were deliberately setting out to mould public opinion and to marshal active public support for their struggles with the Crown.

However, despite all this, it is still doubtful if (say) in January 1787 an intelligent Frenchman or foreign observer could have found good reason to predict that a revolution was close at hand, and still less to foretell the form that such a revolution would take. It is easy for us, with the knowledge gained by hindsight, to see that such reasons existed. Yet, even so, there was still an important element lacking: it still needed a spark or 'trigger' to cause an explosion of any kind, and it needed a further spark to bring about the particular alignments of 1789.

The first spark was provided by the French government's involvement with the revolution in America. The result had little to do with America's internal history: neither the Stamp Act riots nor the Boston Massacre made any great impact on what happened in France. Nor can it seriously be argued that the French Declaration of the Rights of Man (issued by the first French Revolutionary Assembly in 1789) owed anything of great substance to the Declaration of Independence proclaimed by the Americans in 1776. Both drew on a common stock of 'philosophical' ideas that were current at the time, and Thomas Jefferson, the author of the first draft of the American Declaration, was in Paris when the French were considering theirs (and may even have been consulted in the course of the discussions); but the two Declarations, though they share certain similarities in style, have little in common as to purpose and content. The real connection between the two revolutions can only be found in the consequences of France's decision to join the Americans in the war against England in 1778. For, though five years later France was victorious and England suffered defeat, England survived with her economic position relatively unimpaired while France, having overstretched her resources, was left financially crippled. And this was the spark, or trigger, that ignited the first of the explosions that led to the revolution in France.

Yet the gravity of the situation took time to develop. It was not until two years after the war was over that Calonne, the Controller-General (or Minister of Finance) faced with a deficit of a quarter of the nation's annual revenue, declared a state of bankruptcy and called for drastic remedies to overcome it. In the event, it was decided to abandon the traditional procedures and, in place of the obstreperous Parlements, to invite an assembly of handpicked 'Notables', thought to be more amenable to persuasion, to consider the crisis. The Notables, however, refused to endorse the ministerial reforms, largely because their own cherished fiscal immunities were threatened; they countered with a call that the States-General, a convocation representing all three Estates but held in abeyance for

175 years, should be consulted instead. The Ministry, however, turned this proposal down, thus provoking the 'aristocratic revolt' which tore the country apart for almost a year. The revolt ended with the defeat of the Ministry and a total victory for the Parlements and aristocracy. Above all, the government was forced to concede that the States-General (through which the 'privileged' hoped to solve the crisis at the commons' expense) should be summoned after all. So, in September 1788, as the Paris Parlement returned to the capital from enforced exile, it seemed as if the prophecy reported a few months before by Arthur Young, as he travelled round France, would be realized: that 'some great revolution in the government' would follow that was likely to 'add to the scale of the nobility and clergy'. So a belief in revolution, provoked by the nobility's challenge, was already in the air, but the form that it took proved to be of quite a different kind. Why was this? Briefly, because the promise of a States-General compelled the contending parties to define their aims and to take up new positions. The bourgeoisie, or Third Estate, hitherto divided into supporters and opponents of ministerial reform, now found it expedient, once the States-General was called, to close ranks and present a programme of its own. The Parlements and nobility, however, who entertained quite different hopes of the meeting of the Estates, were also obliged to put their cards on the table and to show that the reforms (or 'liberties') they had in mind were by no means the same as those voiced by the Third Estate or (increasingly) by the nation at large.[7]

In consequence, the aristocracy and clergy, far from gaining more recruits, began rapidly to lose them. Mallet du Pan, a Swiss observer accredited to the Court of Vienna, reported only four months after the revolt had ended that political alignments in France had radically changed: the question at issue, he wrote, was no longer a constitutional conflict between the King and the *privilégiés* but 'a war between the Third Estate and the other two Orders'. Alignments changed after the States-General met at Versailles in May 1789. Although hesitant as ever, when faced with the irreconcilable claims of nobility and Third Estate Louis chose to support the former. He called in troops to Versailles and prepared to dismiss the National Assembly (recently formed quite illegally by the third Estate and its allies) by force of arms. This *coup* was averted by the intervention of the people of Paris. The peasants, too, stirred by the economic and political crises, had begun to take action of their own; and it was a combination of these forces – middle classes, urban craftsmen and peasants, now united in a common purpose – that, with liberal–aristocratic and clerical support, in July–August 1789, carried through the first major stage of the revolution in France.

The French Revolution appears, then, to have been the outcome of both long-term and short-term factors, which arose from the social–political conditions and the conflicts of the *ancien régime*. The long-standing grievances of peasants, townsmen and bourgeoisie; the frustrations of rising hopes among wealthy and 'middling' bourgeois and peasants; the insolvency and breakdown of government; a real (or, at least, perceived) 'feudal reaction'; the claims and intransigence of a privileged aristocracy; the propagation of radical ideas among wide sections of the people; a sharp economic and financial crisis; and the successive 'triggers' of state bankruptcy, aristocratic revolt and popular rebellion: these all played a part. Were these explosive factors peculiar to France? Taken individually or in isolation, the answer must be no. If we exclude the ultimate 'triggers', similar tensions, crises and frustrations appeared, in one form or another – often complemented by a greater degree of poverty – in several other European countries at this time. Why, then, was there a revolution in France in 1789 and nowhere else? Or we may phrase the question differently and ask, as Jacques Godechot does after reviewing the riots and uprisings in large cities (including London, Brussels and Amsterdam, but not Paris) in the 1780s: 'Why was it that the riots which broke out in foreign capitals, notably in London, did not entail the collapse of the Old Régime or of the royal or aristocratic powers before the insurgent masses?'[8]

The short answer must be that, for a variety of reasons, the factors we have noted in eighteenth-century France did not appear in a similar *combination* in any other part of Europe. In some, mainly eastern, countries, two factors were conspicuously absent: a substantial and 'challenging' middle class and a widely circulated corpus of radical political ideas. But there was also another factor that set France apart from countries both east and west: Paris, even more than London, was a capital city that lay at the very heart of public affairs: at the centre of government and administration, of law, culture and education. It was a capital, moreover, that had a teeming population of bourgeois, lawyers and common people which, once the fuse was lit, was able to imprint its collective mark on the succession of dramatic events that followed.

Yet, once the Revolution had been launched in France, certain western countries and regions (the Rhineland and Piedmont as well as Holland, Belgium and Geneva) followed suit in the 1790s. In others – Germany (excluding Prussia), Poland, southern Italy and parts of Spain – revolutions, or near-revolutions, that followed resulted from French military occupation rather than from the mere force of the French example or of the Declaration of the Rights of Man.[9]

But this is another story which will be left to a later chapter. First, however, and before we are charged with begging too many questions in dispute, we must return to the problem only given the briefest mention before: the varying views of historians on what the Revolution was all about.

2 *Historians and the French Revolution*

So we come to the debate that has divided historians for the past 200 years – from the day when Edmund Burke, an Anglo-Irishman, first dipped his quill in vitriol to blast the Revolution at its birth. The debate has continued through various stages, raising new issues and sparking new conflicts as it went along. For example, during the first century of discussion – from 1790 to, say, 1900 – historians tended to consider the problems of the Revolution in largely political and ideological terms, without paying much attention to its social and economic foundations. Burke was no exception; he never made any serious attempt to study the society out of which the Revolution grew. Yet, flimsy as his evidence was, he found the old system by no means antipathetic: in fact, only a few minor adjustments were needed to put it right. The Revolution could not, therefore, in his opinion, be the outcome of a genuine and widespread desire for reform but was provoked rather by the ambitions and intrigues of a few. He cites, in particular, the clique of literary men and 'philosophers', who had long been sniping at the established Church, and the jumped-up moneyed interest, ever eager to settle accounts with the traditional nobility. And, in the wake of these, he argues, followed the 'mob' or 'swinish multitude', hungry for loot, given to crime and incapable of forming any judgements of their own. Thus the Revolution, having no roots in legitimate complaint, was the child of the conspiracy of a few.[1] This 'conspiracy thesis' has been taken up by many writers since that time: by the Abbé Barruel in the mid-1790s; by Hippolyte Taine, a liberal of the 1840s who became soured by the Commune of 1871; and, with different points of emphasis, by Augustin Cochin in the 1910s and 1920s[2] and J. L. Talmon in the early 1950s. In short, such an explanation has tended to find favour with many to whom the Revolution has appeared as an evil rather than as a good, and who have been inclined to fasten on to a variety of scapegoats in order to explain its origins and progress: whether freemasons, Jews, Committees of Thirty or disgruntled 'cabals' of unsuccessful lawyers or *literati*.

On the other hand, those who have favoured the Revolution, either in whole or in part, have naturally tended to explain it in somewhat different terms: either as a legitimate political protest against the shortcomings of the *ancien régime* or as a social protest of depressed or underprivileged classes. The liberal historians of the Restoration – writers like Thiers, Mignet and Madame de Staël – saw it mainly in the former light:[3] and the motives that prompted them, in the 1820s, to demand a more liberal constitution, or charter, from Louis XVIII and Charles X were basically the same as those which, a generation before, had prompted the revolutionaries of 1789 to draft a Declaration of the Rights of Man and to draw up the liberal Constitution of 1791. Thus such writers saw the Revolution essentially as a political movement 'from above', promoted by the 'respectable' classes of the nation – the liberal aristocracy and bourgeoisie – for the redress of longstanding grievances and the reform of outmoded institutions. 'When a reform becomes necessary,' wrote Mignet, 'and the movement to achieve it has arrived, nothing can stand in its way and everything serves its progress.'[4] This liberal or Whiggish explanation, too, with its emphasis on an almost inevitable forward-looking progression in political ideas and institutions, has found plenty of adherents down to the present day. So we find Francis Parkman, the American historian of the British settlement of Canada, in a history written in the early 1920s, describing the French society of the *ancien régime* as an 'aggregate of disjointed parts, held together by a meshwork of arbitrary power itself touched with decay', which was 'drifting slowly and unconsciously towards the cataclysm of the Revolution'.[5]

Jules Michelet, the great French historian of the 1840s, also sympathized with the revolutionaries of 1789; but being a Republican and a democrat, he saw the Revolution as a far more drastic surgical operation than did Mignet or Thiers. In his pages the Revolution becomes a spontaneous and regenerative upsurge of the whole French nation against the despotism, grinding poverty and injustice of the *ancien régime*: something, in fact, like the spontaneous outbreak of popular hope and hatred portrayed by Charles Dickens in the opening chapters of *A Tale of Two Cities*. For Michelet, the common people – the peasants and city poor, who have suffered most from the cruelty and injustice of kings and aristocrats – are far from being a passive instrument manipulated by other groups; they are the real and living heroes of the piece.[6] This view of the Revolution as a spontaneous, angry outburst of a whole people against poverty and oppression has, until recent times, probably been more influential than any other.

Alexis de Tocqueville, writing a few years later, held other views. Being a provincial aristocrat with strong Whiggish inclinations, it was natural enough that he should share Michelet's taste for liberty, but he firmly rejected his passion for equality and the 'people's' revolution. In fact, he wrote that the French Revolution 'was prepared by the most civilized, but carried out by the most barbarous and the rudest classes of the nation'. However, far from presenting the Revolution as an unfortunate break with a more glorious past (in the manner of Burke and the conservatives of the 1820s), Tocqueville stressed the continuity of institutions and ideas linking the Revolution and Empire with the *ancien régime*. 'The French Revolution', he wrote, 'will only be the darkness of night to those who merely regard itself; only the time which preceded it will give the light to illuminate it.'[7] And he goes on to argue that, while the Revolution and Empire strengthened the central authority, in terms of both the government and its agents, in doing so they merely added to or completed the measures already taken by their forerunners in the *ancien régime*. It was, in fact, in his opinion, little more than the logical sequel to the 'administrative revolution' launched by Louis XVI. He pointed to the extended powers that by the 1750s had been accorded to the Royal Council, the all-pervading activities of the Intendants, the progressive reduction in the independence of the local government and the *pays d'états**, the growing integration of the Gallican Church with the machinery of state, and the emergence of a whole new apparatus for the exercise of administrative justice. And not only that: France had the best roads in Europe; social welfare was being improved; torture was being abolished; and the system of issuing *lettres de cachet* ('sealed letters') to commit persons to prison without trial was falling into disuse (there were only 14,000 such 'letters' issued under Louis XVI, compared to the 150,000 under Louis XV). Moreover, the Bastille was being emptied of its prisoners, and only seven remained to be liberated in July 1789. But Tocqueville added with a remarkable flash of insight: 'The social order destroyed by a revolution is almost always better than that which immediately precedes it, and experience shows that the most dangerous moment for a bad government is generally that in which it sets about reform.' Thus it was not so much the absence of reform as the nature and tardiness of it which, in opening the eyes of men to better things, served to precipitate a revolution rather than to avert it.

Tocqueville adds a further dimension to the debate when he applies a similar argument in criticizing Michelet's notion of revolution as a spontaneous revolt of 'misery'. Was France, in fact, poor or becoming poorer? No, answers Tocqueville, her trade, her national income and the production of her industries and agriculture were rapidly expanding; the middle classes were becoming more

* Provinces recently attached to France.

prosperous; Paris was being rebuilt, largely by the enterprise of the wealthy bourgeoisie; and Bordeaux, on the eve of revolution, could outmatch the wealth and trade of Liverpool. The peasants, too, far from continuing to grovel in abject poverty, backwardness or unrelieved squalor, or to be bound by servitude to their lord's domain, were becoming literate and had already become proprietors of one-third of the land in France. Why, then, asks Tocqueville, was there a revolution in France and not in Austria, Prussia, Poland or Russia, where the people – and the peasants in particular – were far more impoverished and oppressed? It was precisely, he argues, because the middle classes were becoming richer and more conscious of their increased social importance and because the peasants were becoming free, literate and prosperous that the old feudal survivals and aristocratic privileges appeared all the more vexatious and intolerable. And he concludes, in a passage from which I have already quoted:

> It is not always from going from bad to worse that a society falls into a revolution. It happens most often that a people, which has supported without complaint, as if they were not felt, the most oppressive laws, throws them off as soon as their weight is lightened.... Feudalism at the height of its power had not inspired Frenchmen with so much hatred as it did on the eve of its disappearing. The slightest acts of arbitrary power under Louis XVI seemed less easy to endure than all the despotism of Louis XIV.[8]

Yet, for all his originality and brilliance and the respect he has won among later generations of scholars, Tocqueville left several questions unanswered, among them: if Louis XVI and his ministers were of so reforming a disposition, why did their reforms stop short – and *have* to stop short – of giving a more general satisfaction? And, more particularly, what were the actual circumstances – what was the spark or trigger – that provoked the outbreak; and how did a revolt of disgruntled and power-hungry magistrates and aristocrats – for this is how the floodgates were opened – become transformed into a revolution of the 'middling' and lower classes of town and countryside? (As the reader may remember, I have dealt with some of these questions in the previous chapter.)

But, meanwhile, the debate continued and other historians entered the fray, among them Alphonse Aulard, author of a four-volume *Political History* of the Revolution which appeared at the turn of the century. As Michelet's views were those of a Republican democrat and Tocqueville's of a liberal conservative of the 1840s and 1850s, and Taine in his turn reflected the views of an ex-liberal turned conservative by the events of 1871, so Aulard was a typical radical of the Third Republic which immediately followed. Like Tocqueville's *Ancien Régime*, Aulard's *Political History* blazed a new trail and marked a turning-point in the study of the French Revolution. On the one hand, it ushered in a new era as a work of exact and scrupulous scholarship: Aulard was, in fact, the first French historian to apply a rigorously systematic and critical use of sources to a work of modern history, taking as his models the German school of Ranke and the French medievalist tradition established by the École des Chartes. But Aulard's *History*, as its title suggests, still follows the nineteenth-century pattern of arguing about the Revolution in political and ideological terms. Though his *History* exhibits the great objectivity of the scholar trained in the use of original records, it has by no means eliminated the political bias of the citizen who like Michelet has been reared in the democratic–Republican tradition. This bias and his general conception of the Revolution are evident enough from the preface he wrote for his first edition:

> I wish to write the political history of the Revolution from the point of view of the origin and development of Democracy and Republicanism. Democracy is the logical consequence of the principle of equality. Republicanism is the logical consequence of the principle of national sovereignty. These two consequences did not ensue at once. In place of Democracy, the men of 1789 founded a middle-class government, a suffrage of property-owners. In place of the Republic, they organised a limited Monarchy. Not until September 22nd [1792] did they abolish the Monarchy and create the Republic. The republican form of government lasted ... until 1804 ... when the government of the Republic was confided to an emperor.[9]

Yet, for all the deep differences of social origin and outlook and political attachment that divide them, these earlier historians of the Revolution have certain significant characteristics in common. For one thing, they all (even Michelet) treated the Revolution 'from above' – that is, from the elevation of the Royal Court at Versailles, or the National Assembly, the Jacobin Club or the national press. In consequence, the Revolution becomes as a battle of ideas or of rival political factions in which the main contenders for power are the King and the Court party, the Parlements and aristocracy, and the Third Estate with its middle-class and liberal–aristocratic leaders. Even with Michelet and Tocqueville the peasants hardly appear in any corporeal sense (or with any degree of substance) let alone the urban lower classes (or *sans-culottes*); and, when they do, their thoughts and actions are merely made to mirror those of the aristocracy, the revolutionary bourgeoisie, or the orators and journalists of the Tuileries and the Palais Royal. This approach to the problem is as true of the liberal and radical historians as it is of the conservatives and monarchists – as true of Thiers, Michelet and Aulard as it is of Burke and Taine.

It is, in fact, this shift in focus from the predominantly political–ideological to the predominantly social and social–economic that has been the most significant innovation of the main school of revolutionary historians since Aulard's day. The peasantry and urban *sans-culottes* (particularly those in Paris, it is true) have been brought into the picture and studied in their own right – or 'from below' – as social classes and groups having their own identity, ideas and aspirations independent of those of the upper and middle classes. Accompanying this shift in focus is the tendency to present the conflicts of the Revolution in terms of a struggle of classes rather than of political ideas or ideologies. This reorientation of revolutionary studies clearly owes a great deal to Marx and to the spread of socialist ideas in Europe during the past hundred years, and to that extent it may be said to represent a new *socialist*, as well as a more generally *social*, interpretation of the French Revolution. But it is more than that, and it may perhaps be more accurately portrayed as a response to the new problems and social developments of the twentieth century which have widened the horizons of historians in general – such developments as universal suffrage, market research, the welfare state, working-class movements, mass political parties, the revolutions in Eastern Europe and Asia and the upheavals resulting from two world wars.

The first French historian to give this new direction to revolutionary studies was Jean Jaurès, the author of *L'Histoire socialiste de la Révolution française*, first published in four volumes in 1901–4. Jaurès was certainly a socialist, as the title of his work makes clear. But the book was by no means a party piece or a narrow political polemic, and Jaurès, as he acknowledged himself, owed as much to Michelet and to the narrative–biographical style of Plutarch as he did to Marx. Yet, in spite of this variety of influences, his *Histoire* is essentially an economic and social interpretation of the origins and course of the Revolution. In fact, he considered purely 'political' history to be 'a mere abstraction' and pointedly asked: 'How can [Aulard] fully understand the change that occurred during the Revolution from a bourgeois oligarchy to a democracy without conceiving of the social and political upheavals as intimately linked?'[10]

Jaurès' more particular innovation was to have probed far more deeply than his predecessors into the evident divisions within the Third Estate, and to have begun the systematic exploration of the role played by the peasants and *menu peuple*. And this tradition, once established, was carried on, during the next sixty years and more, by his principal successors in the field: Albert Mathiez, Georges Lefebvre and Albert Soboul. Mathiez dominated the study of the Revolution in the period between the two world wars, both at home and abroad; his main claim to fame for a long time rested on his rescue of Robespierre from the Chamber of Horrors in which the historians of the previous century (with some support from Aulard) had almost universally confined him. But, in the context of the 'social interpretation', his major achievement was probably his close scrutiny of the Parisian *sans-culottes* and their spokesmen and, in his *La Vie chère et le mouvement social sous la Terreur*, his clear distinction between the notion of 'freedom' held by the shopkeepers and merchants and that held by the small consumers or *sans-culottes*.[11]

No other historian of the Revolution, however, had an international reputation for scholarship equal to that of Georges Lefebvre, who was born in the same year as Mathiez (1874) but who long outlived him. His career also followed a quite distinctive course. In 1924 he published his great pioneering study *Les Paysans du Nord*, in which for the first time the peasants of the Revolution were presented not as a single undifferentiated class (as they had been by Tocqueville and others) but as a conglomeration of widely differing social groups. In spite of their common identity as a rural community, which enabled them to unite in a universal peasant rising in the summer of 1789, in more normal times they were deeply divided by conflicting interests within the village, which ranged small proprietors against landlords and speculators, and landless peasants and sharecroppers against large tenant farmers and what Lefebvre called the 'rural bourgeoisie'. These differences and conflicts were traced throughout the revolutionary years and measured in terms of social disorder, purchase of land, distribution of property and relations with government representatives 'on mission' and local authorities. But the Revolution, far from healing these differences by giving universal satisfaction, widened the breach and made them irreconcilable. For the 'rural bourgeois', both old and new, reaped substantial advantages both by shedding the burden of tithe and seigneurial levies and by the purchase of land at low prices, whereas the small and landless peasant, whose demand for controlled rents and the subdivision of properties went unheeded, remained poor and dissatisfied for generations to come.[12]

Lefebvre also broke fresh ground by making important studies of the rural panic (the 'Great Fear') of 1789 and of the social attitudes and behaviour of revolutionary crowds.[13] But it was left to his closest disciple, Albert Soboul, to make the decisive contribution to the study of the urban *sans-culottes*.[14] For, in spite of the pioneering work undertaken by Jaurès and Mathiez, until the publication (in 1958) of Soboul's thesis on the Parisian *sans-culottes* there had been no fully documented study of their everyday activities and way of life, their composition and organizations, their social and political ideas and aspirations, and their forms of behaviour. The result has been to give this considerable part of the urban population – accounting in Paris for about three persons in every four – that distinctive identity that Lefebvre had given the peasants, to bring them to the front of the stage as a vital revolutionary force, and in so doing to shed new light on the political history of the Revolution in one of its most critical phases. Like Aulard, Mathiez and Lefebvre before him, Soboul went on to occupy the Chair of the French Revolution at the University of Paris; and, until his death in 1982, he was the most prolific and influential of the French historians writing on the Revolution in the Republican–Marxist tradition.

Of course, as we have seen, many of the older traditions – whether liberal, conservative or avowedly counter-revolutionary – lingered on and the new direction given to revolutionary studies by the practitioners of a 'social interpretation' did not hold the field entirely to themselves. But there is little doubt that the 'new orthodoxy' (as it has been called), with its long history and its succession of brilliant scholars, came to dominate the teaching and study of the Revolution in French schools and universities. For long the critics – and there were many – held their fire, possibly inhibited by the scholarly record of their opponents. The first serious criticism came from the left, from Daniel Guèrin, a Marxist and author of the Trotskyist-inspired *La Lutte de classes sous la première République*, published in 1946. Guérin thought that the period of Jacobin rule (1793–4) praised by the Jaurès–Lefebvre–Soboul school was a fraud that, far from advancing the popular interest, was a dictatorship directed against the *sans-culotte* militants or *bras nus* (workers).[15] But Guérin found few convinced supporters and his duel with his fellow Marxists ended in a guarded reconciliation. He and Soboul in particular agreed that the Revolution, despite their differences over the respective roles of Jacobins and *sans-culottes*, remained 'notre mère à tous' (our common heritage).[16]

Critics from the right – whether conservative or liberal – have mounted a more sustained and fundamental challenge. This has gradually gained ground and momentum, finding support not only in France but in Western Europe, Britain and America. However, it was not in France but in England, soon followed by the United States, that the more serious phase of the assault began. After a preliminary skirmish in his *Myth of the French Revolution* in 1955, Alfred Cobban went on to publish his *Social Interpretation of the French Revolution* in 1964.[17] The book was written in a style characteristic of the author, as he laid about him with iconoclastic zest, slaying every would-be dragon or sacred cow that came within his sights. These included such time-honoured concepts as the overthrow of 'feudalism', the eighteenth-century 'feudal' or 'aristocratic' reaction, and a large part of the 'bourgeois' revolution as well; while the 'social interpretation' itself (he argued) was shot through with Marxist–Leninist political assumptions and so was virtually no 'social' interpretation at all. In so doing, Cobban virtualy denied the bourgeoisie any credit for the end of the seigneurial system in the summer of 1789, and he argued further that as a predominantly office-holding and landowning class the bourgeoisie could claim little credit either for the development of capitalism or, more specifically, for a capitalist industrial revolution. In fact, he insisted that the French Revolution, under the direction of its new landowning and ex-office-holding rulers, retarded this process rather than advanced it. In short, the Revolution was 'in essence a triumph for the conservative, propertied, landowning classes, large and small'.[18]

In France, Cobban's new thesis was at first ignored or met with scant approval; after all was *their* revolution that was at issue and not his! But in America, as in England, it drew a more enthusiastic response. Among American historians who accepted the new arguments with more or less unqualified praise were George Taylor, Elizabeth Eisenstein and (rather more reservedly) Robert Forster. Their views, or an important part of them, were published in the *American Historical Review* between 1963 and 1967. Taylor was able to show that a prosperous French bourgeois on the eve of revolution was as liable as any wealthy aristocrat or nobleman to invest his capital in 'proprietary' goods or 'conspicuous consumption', whether in the form of city *hôtels* or land or extravagant living. Forster argued, in a somewhat similar vein, that the provincial nobility (and he instanced, in particular, that of Toulouse) could claim as much, if not more, credit as the merchant or industrial capitalist for preparing the way for an industrial revolution. Eisenstein claimed that the 'bourgeois revolt' of 1788–9 was orchestrated by a committee whose members included more nobles and clergy than bourgeois.[19] And, in England, varying degrees of support have come from a number of scholars, notably (though not uncritically) from William

Doyle, of the University of Nottingham, whose *Origins of French Revolution* appeared in 1980. The title betrays the author's main preoccupation clearly enough, and he focuses rather on the Revolution's origins than on its course and its final results. He is doubtful about the term 'bourgeois revolution' (for, after all, weren't the more adventurous of the nobility also involved?) but he certainly does not deny that a combination of these Notables effectively destroyed, with the peasants' support, what remained of feudalism in late-eighteenth-century France. However, his major concern is to show that there was no settled *a priori* plan to do so on the part of any particular class or group; circumstances were, in fact, more powerful than any deliberate human agency in achieving the result. So he concludes his book as follows:

> Only now [he is writing about the last months of 1789] could France's new ruling elite begin to assess what they stood for and what they had achieved. As victors will, they soon convinced themselves that all had gone to plan from the start. But there was no plan and nobody capable of making one, in 1787. Nobody could have predicted that things would work out as they did. Hardly anybody would have been assured if they could. For the French Revolution had not been made by revolutionaries. It would be truer to say that the revolutionaries had been created by the Revolution.[20]

But more pointedly, he also concludes, after discussing the trends of recent research, that the 'old orthodoxies are not only dead but now in urgent need of burial'.[21]

By now, however, a more detailed and sustained attack on the school of 'social interpretation' had developed in France. Its principal and more prolific exponent has been François Furet, of the École Pratique des Hautes Études in Paris. It began with a two-volume history of the Revolution published by Furet and Denis Richet in 1965–6. It was a relatively restrained and muted beginning and in fact owed little to the new arguments advanced by Alfred Cobban in England. Indeed, there is little in its exposition of the Revolution's origins and its outbreak in the 'three revolutions of summer '89' (those of the deputies, the peasants and the urban *sans-culottes*) that basically differs from Lefebvre's. Nor do they present the outbreak of war, the fall of the monarchy, the struggle between the parties for control of the Assembly, the fall of Robespierre, the Thermidorian 'reaction' or the rise of Napoleon in other than the most 'orthodox' terms. But there is one fairly important exception, yet one so relatively unobtrusive that to some it must have passed unnoticed (though it was certainly picked up by Claude Mazauric, a vigilant critic):[22] it is the assertion that, with the fall of the monarchy, the Revolution (that is, the real or bourgeois revolution) was 'blown off course' and 'lost its bearings'. For it was now, as allies of the 'middling' bourgeoisie who took over control, that the *sans-culottes* were called upon to play a role for which, in the authors' view, they were singularly ill-prepared.[23]

Furet went on to mount a far more savage assault on the 'new orthodoxy' in 1971, when he published in the *Annales* in Paris an article entitled 'Le catéchisme révolutionnaire'. This time the attack, although implicitly directed against the 'Lefebvre school' as a whole, was more particularly focused on Soboul and Mazauric for being not only Marxists but Marxists of a special hue – 'neo-Jacobins', who based their assumptions (and here he follows Cobban) on a Marxist–Leninist philosophy compounded by the experience of the Jacobin government of 1793–4.[24] It was a bitter personal onslaught with few holds barred, which therefore temporarily slammed the door on any further serious debate.

However, by 1978, when Furet's next book appeared, some of the steam and venom had gone out of the attack. The bitter hostility engendered by dissensions within the left, expressed in 'desertions' involving Furet himself as well as Emmanuel Leroy Ladurie and several others, had, for the moment at least, abated; and this new atmosphere of a relative easing of tension was reflected in the publication of Furet's *Penser la Révolution française*.[25] In it he concedes that the French Revolution, by its very nature, was bound to inspire a variety of interpretations, ranging from left to right depending on the historian's political affiliation and therefore on the performances of actors in a drama that attracted or repelled him, for 'The French Revolution has its royalist, liberal, Jacobin, anarchist or libertarian histories'; and further: 'The event is so fundamentally rooted in contemporary French political consciousness that any attempt to consider it from an intellectual distance is immediately seen as hostility.' But Furet does not accept that such a variety of interpretations, while understandable, makes for universal rational enquiry; and here it is not the Marxist or 'social interpreter' that is most at fault, but the outright counter-revolutionary who closes his eyes not only to reality in terms of origins, but also to the nature of the actors and the sequence of events. But the Marxists, inevitably, do not escape unscathed. They are among those, for example, who fail 'to distinguish between the Revolution as a historical process, a set of causes and effects; and the Revolution as a mode of change, a specific dynamic of collective action'. More specifically, he adds: 'In examining the causes or the results of the Revolution the observer must go back far beyond 1789 on the one hand, and far ahead beyond 1794 or 1799 on the other. Yet the "story" of the Revolution is enclosed between 1789 and 1794 or 1799.' So there are two levels of analysis depending on the focus chosen. There is the short-term, mainly political, focus and the longer-term social and economic focus, and to confuse the two (as he charges the 'social interpreters' with doing) is to court disaster, or at least to invite a degree of ridicule.

> One may say, for example [Furet continues], that between 1789 and 1794 the entire political system of France was radically transformed because the old monarchy then came to an end. But the idea that between these same dates the social and economic fabric of the nation was renewed from top to bottom is obviously much less plausible.[26]

This confusion he attributes in large measure to the tendency of some historians to identify too closely with the actors in the 'event' who, through the intimacy of their experience, were inclined to endow it with a causal inevitability that it never possessed. The Marxist historian, mesmerized by October 1917, has in addition been inclined to see the bourgeois revolution in France as a stepping-stone to or a harbinger of the socialist revolution in Russia. So 'the Bolsheviks were given Jacobin ancestors and the Jacobins were made to anticipate the communists', as if the change in the historical setting were of scant importance.[27]

Yet, while accusing the 'Lefebvre school' of historians of allowing their political affiliations to warp their judgement, Furet concedes that their focus on the popular classes 'has brought advances in our knowledge of the role played by the peasants and urban masses'. So this, at least, is a bonus; and, for all the bitterness of the writer's earlier attacks on the Marxists, he now appears to believe that, with the advance of scholarship and the growing diversity of socialist beliefs, a certain 'cooling off' in the wrangles over the French Revolution may eventually come about.[28] And other scholars, too, less rigidly committed to simplistic interpretations, have expressed similar hopes that some new consensus may be found to bring the warring camps at least within measurable distance of a partial, if not a total, reconciliation.[29] Yet, as the Bicentenary of 1789 approaches, such hopes do not appear to be too rosy. While some daggers may have been less overtly displayed, others have been drawn afresh and threaten to stir up the embers into a more lively conflagration. A sign of the times is that one contestant from the right, Pierre Chaunu, has even claimed the 'genocide' of half a million victims of the Terror in the west of France alone – a statement which, apart from its tendentious formulation, inflates beyond the bounds of credibility all previous calculations of the kind.[30] Such pronouncements, set in the wider context of frequent bitter exchanges on television (I am writing in early 1987),[31] do not augur well, to say the least, for that wider consensus or 'new synthesis' of opposing views to which some scholars – and, no doubt, many students too – have begun to look forward.

II Opening Years

1 *How the Revolution Began*

So far we have examined the different ways in which successive generations of historians have interpreted the French Revolution; we have also discussed its origins and examined the question of why the Revolution broke out in France when it did. But, before we go on to relate in greater detail the *events* of the Revolution itself, we must also consider how the alignments of French society which gave rise to the Revolution came about, together with the ideas that informed them; and here we must pay particular attention to the ideology and attitudes of the common people, a subject that has been largely neglected by earlier writers and, notably, been given scant attention by the 'revisionist' historians of the last few years.

So it is not to these recent writers that we should look for guidance but rather to the historians of the 'orthodox' school that began with Jaurès at the turn of the century. For it was with Jaurès' *Histoire socialiste* that the first serious attempt was made to treat the problems, aspirations and movements of the peasant and urban masses in their own right and not simply as an echo of the speeches and actions of the revolutionary leaders in Paris. This approach, further developed by Jaurès' successors, has done more than merely throw a fresh light on the general causes and events of the Revolution. It has also made it possible to measure with greater accuracy the point of revolutionary outbreak and the part played in it by the peasants and urban *menu peuple*. The revolutionary explosion, therefore, no longer need appear as a more or less fortuitous climax to a succession of purely political, though interrelated, crises – such as the rejection of Calonne's proposals by the Notables, the convocation of the States-General at Versailles, and the dismissal of Necker from office – but rather as the collision of a complex of social, as well as political, forces at a moment when an explosion was imminent.

Yet the problem may still be where to begin and the picture may remain lopsided if one or other of the social forces involved in the crisis is not seen in its proper perspective. A familiar distortion is the idea that the revolutionary action of the peasants and urban masses was 'waiting upon' the action taken by the privileged classes or by the bourgeoisie. Mathiez, in particular, has made us familiar with the opening stages of the Revolution as a progressive 'unfolding' of minor revolutions: first the *révolte nobiliaire* involving the privileged orders, next the *révolution bourgeoise*, and finally the 'popular' revolution of the peasants and urban poor. While such a presentation is convenient and has more than a grain of truth in it, it tends, if taken too literally, to reduce the intervention of the masses to secondary importance and fails to show that the popular movement, while accelerated and intensified by the revolutionary crisis in the summer of 1789, had its origins deep in the *ancien régime* and, in fact, preceded the revolutionary activities of the middle classes by several months.

Another trend has been to present the revolutionary crisis almost exclusively in terms of economic factors. Thus Edouard Labrousse, noted for his important research into eighteenth-century prices and wages, has insisted on the primacy of 'natural' (or economic) over 'anthropomorphic' (or human) factors.[1] Fernand Braudel and his associates of the *Annales* school have gone further: by stressing the overriding importance of long-term over short-term factors (in their theory of *la longue durée*) they have been inclined to diminish the human (and therefore the popular) role in the chain of causes and events.

Daniel Guérin, on the other hand, has gone to the opposite extreme: by exaggerating the independence and the degree of coherence and maturity of the popular movement, he has made it anticipate the working-class movements of the nineteenth and twentieth centuries.[2] Here, of course, it is not so much the wage-earners and *sans-culottes* as the middle classes that cease to play an independent revolutionary role.

I will aim, however, to illustrate the range and diversity of the movements in town and countryside, in Paris and the provinces, in the years leading up to the French Revolution. I will attempt to place in their proper historical perspective both the revolt of the privileged orders in 1787–8 and the revolutionary activity of the bourgeoisie from the end of 1788. But, above all, I will try to trace the main stages and currents of the popular movement during the last years of the *ancien régime* up to the point where its 'merger' with that of the bourgeoisie touched off the revolutionary explosion.

To do so we must go back to the grain riots (or 'flour war') of 1775. There had, of course, been earlier movements provoked by hunger and the high cost of bread – in 1725, 1739–40, 1752 and 1768. But that of 1775 is not only the last of the great *spontaneous* food riots of the *ancien régime*, it is also the most extensive and the most fully documented and provides a convenient comparison with similar movements that occurred during the Revolution itself.

Turgot had been appointed Controller-General in August 1774 and he certainly started with no particular record of unpopularity as far as the common people or small consumers were concerned. In fact, he may well have appeared as a welcome change, for his predecessor, the Abbé Terray, had been burned in effigy in the Faubourg St Antoine. Yet, to the delight of Turgot's enemies at Court, he was soon to lose any semblance of popular favour by his haste in applying the free-trade notions of the Physiocrats to the trade in grain: an *arrêt* (judgement) of 13 September removed restrictions on the sale and purchase of grain and flour. This, combined with a bad harvest, led to an acute shortage and a rapid rise in the price of corn, flour and bread in the following spring and summer. The price of a 4-lb loaf in Paris (normally 8 or 9 sous though, in recent years, more often 10 or 11) rose to 11½ sous in early March, to 13½ at the end of April and to 14 sous in early May. Grain riots had already broken out in Bordeaux, Dijon, Metz, Tours, Rheims and Montauban, and in their wake sprang up that particular cluster of riots, centred in Paris and its adjoining provinces, known to history as *la guerre des farines* (or 'the flour war').

The movement spread from market to market and took the form of a popular price-control of wheat, flour and bread – the price of bread being generally fixed at 2 sous a pound, flour at 20 sous a bushel and wheat at 12 francs a *setier* (2 quintals).* Starting on 27 April at Beaumont-sur-Oise, to the north of the capital, it reached Pontoise on the 29th, St Germain on 1 May, Versailles on the 2nd and Paris on the 3rd. The riots then spread eastwards and northwards into Picardy and the Île-de-France and, having lingered for several days in the markets and villages of Brie, it reached Beaumont-sur-Gâtinais (fifty miles south of Paris) on the 9th and petered out at Melun on the 10th.[3]

It is instructive to note the main features of this remarkable event. It was essentially a spontaneous movement provoked by high prices and the fear of hunger. It saw the massive invasion of markets and farms by the small consumers of villages and towns and even by occasional farmers and well-to-do bourgeois. It was directed in the main against *laboureurs* or prosperous peasants, grain merchants, millers and bakers; and it aroused some sympathy among other classes – certain priests, for example, either encouraged their parishioners to take part in the movement or did little to restrain them, and more than one market official helped it along by setting a 'just' price on grain and flour. Moveover, the Parlement of Paris, ever

* There were 25 sous to the franc.

at odds with the government, gave the movement its conditional blessing.

Why, then, did a movement of such amplitude and, in certain respects, bearing a striking resemblance to later movements of the Revolution yield no tangible result? In the first place the food crisis itself, though severe, was overcome by the early autumn: prices began to fall in October. Secondly, Turgot managed to crush the movement by a combination of army and pulpit. Moreover, the bulk of the peasantry was not involved: the question of tithes, seigneurial dues or game laws did not arise, nor had the ideas generated by the Enlightenment – so important in 1789 – yet begun to circulate among the peasants and small urban consumers. Lastly, and perhaps most important of all, the bourgeoisie had not begun to challenge the existing order and were, in any case, likely to be hostile to a movement directed against the policies of a minister whose reforms – including freedom of the grain trade – they actively supported; in fact, in several towns the local militia was mustered in order to crush the revolt. In short, the main lesson of 1775 was that, in the conditions of eighteenth-century France, no isolated movement of wage-earners, craftsmen, shopkeepers and urban poor could hope to yield substantial results. This truth was to be realized on more than one occasion before and during the Revolution itself.

The twelve years that followed, despite the general sharpening of the economic crisis, were years of comparatively stable food prices and social peace. In Paris, at least, the price of bread remained remarkably steady: from the manuscript Journal of the Parisian bookseller Sébastien Hardy we learn that, whereas between 1767 and 1775 the price of the 4-lb loaf rarely fell below 11 sous (and, for a few days in November 1768, actually reached 16), in the later period the normal price was 8 or 9 sous, only rising to 10½ or 11 sous for brief spells in 1784.[4]

Popular movements during these years were scattered and sporadic, and due to a number of separate issues. There were bread riots at Toulouse and Grenoble in June 1778 and at Rennes in 1785. In 1784 and 1786, there were demonstrations in Paris against the ring of customs barriers encircling the city erected by the Farmers-General, a consortium of wealthy tax-farmers, to raise duty on the livestock, meat, wine and firewood that flowed through its gates. In Paris, too, there was a resurgence of popular anti-clerical feeling in the 1780s that recalled the hostility to the Jesuits in the 1720s and, in the early 1750s, to the Archbishop of Paris for refusing the sacrament to dying Jansenist priests.

Strikes, too, had some importance and occurred in both Paris and the provinces, involving journeymen in a considerable number of trades. In the case of the Lyons silk-workers they assumed, on two occasions, almost insurrectionary proportions. Yet it must be noted that, in eighteenth-century France, when strikes were illegal and generally suppressed, such disputes were more likely to break out at times of comparative plenty and stable prices than when food was short or prices were high. This was as true of the large-scale Paris builders' strikes of 1785 and 1786 as it was of the general strike of printers and book-binders for a fourteen-hour day in 1776. It was true, as well, of the dispute involving the organized porters and carriers in January 1786, when seven to eight hundred of them gave their strike an almost political dimension by marching to Versailles to place their grievances before the King.[5] Yet, with all this activity, it is doubtful if these labour disputes gave more than a minimal impetus to the widespread and varied popular movement that arose in the revolutionary crisis of 1788–9.

This was to open with the *revolte nobiliaire*, the aristocratic challenge which ended in the victory of the Parlements and their allies and the resounding defeat of the government. The 'revolt' fell into two main stages. After the first, ending in September 1787, the Parlement of Paris returned in triumph to the capital amid wild scenes of some jubilation on the Île de la Cité. Calonne, then still Controller-General, was burned in effigy, bonfires were lit on the Pont Neuf and fireworks and squibs were let off at the Guards. During this stage, the main body of demonstrators was formed by the clerks of the Palais de Justice and the apprentices of the luxury trades of the Place Dauphine. However, the following year brought the breakdown of further negotiations, widespread riots in the provinces when Parlements were again exiled, and a second and total victory for the privileged orders. The scene changed dramatically; there was not only the royal promise that the States-General would be summoned to Versailles in May 1789 – a concession of major importance in itself – but also a sudden and dramatic rise in the price of bread. The 4-lb loaf, having long remained at 8 to 9 sous, rose to 9½ sous on 17 August (on the eve of the Parlement's return to Paris), to 10 sous on the 20th and to 11 sous on 7 September. Under this stimulus, the inhabitants of the great popular Faubourgs of St Antoine and St Marcel joined in the 'welcoming' riots on 29 August and transformed their character. Riots now spread beyond the Place Dauphine and the Pont Neuf to the markets and the University Quarter, continued with short lulls until the end of September, and suffered a heavy toll in casualties and arrests; the latter were mainly of craftsmen and wage-earners of widely scattered districts and trades.[6]

An even more significant development was the transformation that now began to take place in the ideas and attitudes of the Parisian *menu peuple*. Troops were brought into the two popular Faubourgs on 5 September and Sébastien Hardy noted that the purpose was 'to subdue their inhabitants ... and to prevent the outbreak of riots which were expected to follow the rise in the price of bread'. He noted, too, that the common people were now beginning to be drawn into the political movement, no longer as marionettes manipulated by the Parlement but in order to challenge the authorities – including the King at Versailles – in a cause that was peculiarly their own.[7] We can follow this process in two entries in Hardy's Journal for 25 November 1788 and 13 February 1789. In the first, when the price of the 4-lb loaf rose to 12½ sous, he noted that a working housewife had declared in a baker's shop 'that it was monstrous to allow the poor to starve in this way' and 'that they should go and set fire to the four corners of the château at Versailles'; and, in the second, when the price of bread rose to a peak of 14½ sous, he noted further that 'some people were heard to say that the Princes had hoarded the grain supply the better to overthrow M. Necker whose removal from office they so ardently desired'.[8] So popular consciousness had acquired a new dimension, one completely absent in the riots of 1775: the conviction that to defend their daily bread they must engage in a *political* struggle, directed not merely against merchants and bakers but against the government itself. It was an important development, but the small consumers and *sans-culottes* still lacked firm allies among the peasants and bourgeoisie. The revolutionary crisis that brought them together was yet to come.

The crisis developed further in the winter of 1788–9 and found expression in both economic and political issues. The harvest was generally bad and, in the Paris region, crops had been flattened by a freak hailstorm in the previous July. There followed a winter of phenomenal severity which threw thousands out of work and brought further thousands of villagers flocking to the capital; in December, Hardy wrote of 80,000 unemployed.[9] Meanwhile, as we saw, prices continued to rise and the food crisis was compounded by a crisis in industry which, following a 'free-trade' treaty signed with England in 1786, threw many more out of work in every textile centre. According to the reports of the industrial inspectors for September 1788 to January 1789, there were 46,000 unemployed at Amiens, 10,000 at Rouen, 30,000 at Carcassonne and 25,000 at Lyons, while at Lille and Troyes half the looms were idle.[10]

Against this background and faced with the threat posed by the recent victory of the aristocracy, the bourgeoisie as spokesman for the Third Estate now united its forces and prepared to enter on a revolutionary course. It was prompted to do so for other, longer-term, reasons as well. These deeper causes sprang from the social and economic conditions of the *ancien régime*. While colonial trade, land values and luxury spending had substantially increased in the course of the century, capital investment and expansion of manufacture were everywhere impeded by the restrictions imposed on the production and circulation of goods by privileged corporations, 'feudal' landowners (not all of them noble) and government inspectors. Yet, while such collisions ensured deeper and more enduring antagonisms, the clash between bourgeois and *privilégiés* arose more immediately over the dual problem of representation and voting at the pending States-General. The Paris Parlement had already lost credibility as a spokesman for popular 'liberties' by its insistence that the Estates should be constituted as in the past – i.e. that each order should have equal representation and vote as a separate Estate, thus ensuring that the Third could never outvote the two other orders combined. Necker, the Minister of Finance, however, prevailed on the Council to allow the Third Estate double representation, though the bourgeois demand to vote 'by head' and not 'by order' was not conceded. So the central issue in dispute remained unresolved and the conflict continued – a conflict that Mallet du Pan caled 'a war of the Third Estate with the two other orders'. A month later, in February 1789, the 'war' was raised to a higher pitch by the publication of the Abbé Sieyès' pamphlet, *Qu'est-ce que le Tiers État?* (*What is the Third Estate?*), in which the bourgeoisie for the first time laid claim to control the destinies of the nation irrespective of the privileges or wishes of the other orders.

With these developments it is not surprising that the winter of 1788–9 should see the beginning of a popular movement of an altogether vaster scope and intensity than those of the preceding years. This movement had other, even more significant, features. It became a continuous movement that did not cease until the outbreak of revolution. It grew, as we saw, from a movement basically concerned with economic ends into one informed by more or less clearly defined political objectives. It developed a common bond of interest between the wage-earners, craftsmen, wine-growers and small tradesmen of town and countryside against monopolists, hoarders and speculators. This movement, in turn, began to 'merge' with that of the small peasant proprietors and tenants against feudal game laws, tithes and dues, and, finally (though not always in time), the movement of townsmen and villagers 'merged' with the political action of the bourgeoisie against seigneurial privilege and absolute monarchy.

The nationwide revolt against shortage and rising prices started in the last days of December 1788 and is recorded in the reports of the Intendants of several provinces. It took a variety of forms: pillaging of grain barges and granaries; enforcing price-control on bread, flour and wheat; rioting in bakers' shops and markets and outside town halls; assaults on customs officers, dealers and farmers; and the widespread destruction of property. In late December and in January reports came in from Brittany and Touraine. In March and April reports arrived from Burgundy, the Île-de-France, Languedoc, Nivernais, Orléanais, Picardy, Poitou, Provence and Touraine; followed by news from the Limousin and Lyonnais in May and June, and from Champagne and Normandy in July. Meanwhile, Hardy recorded bread riots at Rheims in March and at Nancy and Toulouse in April.[11]

In the countryside north of Paris, the fight against shortage developed into a movement directed against the game laws and hunting rights of the nobility. On the estates of the Prince de Conti at Cergy, Pontoise, l'Île-Adam and Beaumont, peasants and farm-workers, having reaped no harvest following the ravages of hail, set out to trap and destroy the rabbits infesting their fields. At Oisy in the Artois, peasants from a dozen villages banded together to exterminate the Count of Oisy's game and refused to pay him the traditional *soyeté* or *terrage*. More violent clashes occurred near Corbeil and at Chatou; south and west of the capital whole parishes, suspected of poaching on royal and aristocratic preserves, were disarmed in June. In Lorraine and the Hainault, landless peasants and small *laboureurs* joined forces in opposition to enclosure edicts and land-clearance schemes. Meanwhile, peasant revolt against royal taxes and seigneurial exactions had broken out in Dauphiné in February, in Provence in March and April, and in the Cambrésis and Picardy in May. This movement led in turn into that far vaster movement of July and August which, spreading over regions as widely scattered as Alsace, Normandy, the Hainault, Mâconnais and Franche-Comté, left in its wake the widespread destruction of *châteaux* and manorial rolls. Yet peasant hostility to enclosure and encroachments on the right of pasture led also to attacks on capitalist farmers; and, on more than one occasion, the *milice bourgeoise* (militia) joined with the *maréchaussée* (rural police) to repress peasant disorder.

But, in spite of such a conflict of loyalties, as the crisis deepened, bourgeois and *sans-culottes*, and even peasants, were drawn by the logic of events (as nowhere else in Europe) into a closer partnership and joint opposition to the privileged orders and the absolutist regime. The urban and rural masses never fully accepted the bourgeois notion of 'freedom' – this remained a serious bone of contention throughout the revolutionary years – but it was in their common interest to remove the fetters on production and the high cost of food occasioned by internal customs duties and fiscal charges; to clip the wings of (if not to dispossess entirely) the tithe-owner and the extractor of the more onerous feudal obligations; to compel the *privilégiés* to make a more generous contribution to the national exchequer; to curb the monopolists and Farmers-General; to destroy such relics of ancient tyrannies as the Bastille, the *lettres de cachet* and the vexatious inquisitions of the Parlements. It is precisely such demands – on occasions veiled, it is true – that were voiced in the *cahiers de doléances* which began to be drawn up in the early months of 1789. Although usually drafted by professional bourgeois such as lawyers and doctors, the *cahiers* were endorsed by meetings of peasants, small shopkeepers and workshop masters and even, though more rarely (as at Rheims, Marseilles, Troyes and Lyons) by guilds of journeymen or *maîtres-ouvriers*.[12]

The States-General raised such ardent hopes – 'la grande espérance' as Lefebvre called it – because it was widely believed that, cleared of the obstruction and domination of the privileged orders, it could realize a radical programme of reform. From this hope stemmed the enthusiastic adoption of the slogan 'Vive le tiers état!' with which Arthur Young was challenged on his journey through Alsace, and the passionate belief, after the Court party had threatened to dash these hopes, in the existence of an 'aristocratic plot'. And it was in direct response to this stimulus that the Parisian journeymen, labourers, shopkeepers and workshop masters – already stirred to action by the ruinous cost of bread, meat and wine – rallied to the call of the revolutionary leadership installed at the Palais Royal. More hesitantly, it is true, it rallied to the Electors of the Third Estate who were based in the City Hall. Furthermore, the belief that the Court was preparing to disperse the Estates and to subdue Paris with the aid of foreign troops won over the main body of the Paris garrison – though they had been recently engaged in shooting down rioters in the Faubourg St Antoine – to the side of the Revolution. So, when Necker, the currently popular chief minister, was dismissed on 12 July, the people of the Faubourgs and markets joined with the bourgeoisie and disaffected troops to mount an insurrection under arms – the first great popular uprising of the Revolution. The gunsmiths' arsenals and religious houses were raided for weapons, the hated customs *barrières* were burned down, a National Guard (including journeymen but not 'vagrants' and unemployed) was enrolled, a revolutionary government was established at the City Hall and, finally, the Bastille was taken by storm. The popular movement had not fully 'merged' with that of the revolutionary bourgeoisie; the example, where not already forestalled, was quickly followed in other parts of France.

But, before we conclude this chapter, one very relevant question remains to be asked: What of France's provincial cities? Did the common people there have a pre-revolutionary history similar to that of Paris or did they simply claim, as Arthur Young was told in reply to such a question at Nancy on the morrow of the Bastille's capture: 'We are a provincial town; we must await news of what is happening in Paris'? (Admittedly, Young's informants added that, in view of the rising price of bread, 'we must expect the worst from the common people' who were 'on the point of riot'.)[13] Jaurès, who was the first historian to give this matter serious attention, certainly believed that Lyons, France's greatest industrial city, had a pre-revolutionary history of its own that affected, in particular, its silk-workers and their employers. 'I do not believe', he wrote, 'that any other city in France was so violently torn by social conflict in the course of the eighteenth century.' Like later historians of the city, he pointed to the great industrial disputes of 1744 and 1786 which tore the industry apart, speculating about why the silk-workers' leaders, after excluding the merchant-manufacturers (as happened nowhere else in France) from the assemblies convened to draft the industry's *cahiers de doléances*, proved quite incapable, when it came to the point, of voicing demands intended radically to improve the conditions of the workers. Why was this? Paradoxically it was (as Jaurès and, later, Soboul understood) because, due to their particular experience, the Lyonnais workers had in one important respect gone beyond the scope of a purely bourgeois revolution: their conflicts with the employers had already begun to divide the industry on strictly class lines to a degree that had not yet been experienced in Paris or any other industrial centre in France.[14]

But what about other cities, such as Dijon, Rennes, Grenoble, Strasbourg, Bordeaux, Rouen or Marseilles; how far did they contribute before the event to the revolutionary crisis of July 1789? Some of them – Rennes, Dijon and Grenoble – had, like Paris, Parlements of their own and, through the tumultuous events of 1787 and 1788, must have seen developing among the common people a new political awareness or *prise de conscience*. Yet there is no certain evidence that this attained the level that we noted among Parisians in the early months of 1789. There is, however, the possible exception of Rennes and a small number of other towns in Brittany, including St Malo and Nantes, where the 'jeunes gens' (composed of law students, office-workers and the sons of notaries and shopkeepers – therefore predominantly petty-bourgeois rather than *sans-culottes*) began from December 1788 onwards to riot and engage in armed rebellion against the nobility in the name of the Third Estate. At Rennes, at least, further outbreaks occurred in January and February 1789.[15]

It is surprising perhaps that so little information of this kind emerges from the numerous local and regional histories that have been written since Jaurès' time. Such writing most certainly included studies, in addition to those already mentioned, of Strasbourg, Marseilles, Bordeaux, Rouen, Montauban, Rheims and Troyes. In all there is evidence enough of social unrest expressed in food riots and industrial disputes, but there appears to be no clear record of any heightening of political awareness or of political action on the part of the common people before the summer of 1789. Admittedly, this is not conclusive as the relevant questions may not have been directly posed. We must suspend a final judgement until further enquiries have been made. Yet we must assume for the present that, in the weeks and months before the revolutionary outbreak, the independent political activity of small shopkeepers and craftsmen was confined to Paris, Lyons and a handful of towns in the west; and that elsewhere, as with Arthur Young's informants at Nancy, local activity awaited rather than anticipated the news of the Parisians' example.

2 *1789: The 'Bourgeois' Revolution*

As we saw, the aristocracy, including the Parlements and upper clergy, made a bid for an extension of power in the *révolte nobiliaire* of 1787–8. This challenge had a two-fold result: it ended in an aristocratic victory over the Crown, but it also provoked the Third Estate, fearing its rivals' intentions, to abandon the neutrality it had hitherto observed, to unite its own forces and to make a bid for a share of government in its turn. So, by 1789 – '*l'année cruciale*', as a French historian has called it – the main thrust of the 'aristocratic revolt' was past and it was now time for the two other contenders – the bourgeoisie and the common people (peasants and *sans-culottes*) – to make their own distinct contribution to the revolution that now took place, based on a broad bourgeois–popular alliance, between July and October of that year. It is therefore convenient, though not strictly exact, to treat them as two separate developments in the two chapters that follow.

Some historians – notably Elizabeth Eisenstein in the *American Historical Review* – have denied that there was a specific 'bourgeois' component, as distinct from a common 'patriot' front in which liberal aristocrats often played a determining role, in the concerted challenge to privilege and absolute government which led, through the pamphlet warfare of 1788–9 and the States-General's meetings at Versailles, to the revolutionary outbreak in late summer 1789.[1] It is true that the bourgeoisie was slow to react, preferring to wait upon the events of 1787–8 before staking a claim of its own; but the challenge, once made in the winter of 1788, was conceived to promote a broadly 'bourgeois' interest in which lawyers, doctors and merchants – rather than their liberal–aristocratic and clerical allies – called the tune. And this will become more evident as we follow the course of events of the spring, summer and autumn of 1789.

After the initial skirmishes of November–December 1788, as the Third Estate began to react to the extravagant claims of aristocracy, the first decisive step in the campaign was taken in late January 1789, when the Abbé Sieyès – admittedly only a bourgeois by adoption – published his famous pamphlet *Qu'est-ce que le Tiers État?* The Abbé answered his question in two terse words: 'the Nation'; and by 'the Nation' he meant not only the twenty-four million represented by the Third Estate, let alone the small minority of 200,000 *privilégiés* (including their families), but the whole nation at large. So he was not yet demanding that power should be vested in the Third Estate alone but he was insisting, in a closely argued case, that if the privileged orders refused to accede to the Third's request to join them in a common deliberative assembly, then the commons, who accounted for such an overwhelming proportion of the country's population, would be perfectly justified – and not only justified but willing – to ignore the obstruction of a paltry minority and take the direction of the nation's affairs into its own hands. And in the conditions prevailing in France in 1789, this meant that in practice the bourgeoisie, as the leaders of the *tiers*, was making its first bid to take over the conduct of government itself. While this was not yet the general view among commoners, it was already a clear statement of ultimate intent.

Meanwhile, the preparations for the States-General's first meeting, now called for 5 May, went forward. On 24 January, regulations were issued governing the election of deputies and the drafting of *cahiers de doléances*, or lists of grievances, to guide the Estates in their deliberations. In general, electoral districts were formed from the ancient subdivisions used for administering justice, the *bailliages* in the north and *sénéchaussées* in the south. Paris was treated as a separate electoral division and the recently revived regional Estates of Dauphiné were, as another exception, accorded the right to appoint their own deputies. Otherwise, deputies were to be elected by their own Estates meeting in separate assemblies. The privileged orders enjoyed direct male adult suffrage, while deputies of the Third Estate were chosen by a rather more restricted franchise as well as by a more complicated system of indirect election. Except in Paris, where the suffrage was limited to those paying six livres a year in *capitation*, French commoners of twenty-five and over, whose names were entered (for however small an amount) on the taxation rolls, were eligible to vote in their primary assembly, either of their parish or of their urban guild. In brief, all male adult commoners had the vote with the exception of domestic servants, non-householders (*non-domiciliés*), sons living in their father's house, the poorest labourers and downright paupers. But the finally elected representatives of their Estate emerged only after two, three or four stages of the electoral process depending (among other factors) on whether the constituency was urban or rural and upon the type of property held by the electors.

Whatever the government's intention, the system most certainly favoured the urban and professional bourgeoisie who dominated discussion and voting in the assemblies of the Third Estate. They took full advantage of their practical monopoly of literacy and verbal expression, and enjoyed the means and leisure to concert common action among 'patriots', to print circulars and pamphlets, and to conduct electoral campaigns denied to the rural craftsmen and peasants, let alone to the labourers and village poor. It is, therefore, no accident that the urban bourgeoisie captured the great bulk of the seats among the deputies of the Third Estate: of the 610 that went to represent their order at Versailles, some 25 per cent were lawyers, 5 per cent were professional men, 13 per cent were industrialists, merchants and bankers; at most 7 to 9 per cent were agriculturalists and, of these, only a handful were peasants.[2]

Meanwhile, a 'patriot' party had been emerging among the promoters of constitutional reform. Though mainly voicing the hopes of the Third Estate, it included such wealthy aristocrats as the Marquis de Lafayette and the Duke of La Rochefoucauld, and noted *parlementaires* such as Adrien Duport, Hérault de Séchelles and Lepeletier de Saint-Fargeau; some had taken part, on the liberal wing, in the 'aristocratic revolt' and all were to play a prominent role in the Revolution. Some belonged to masonic lodges, others to the Committee of Thirty, which met at Duport's house and was composed of lawyers, liberal aristocrats and clerics (Talleyrand and Sieyès among them). Others, again, such as Sieyès and Mirabeau, acted as links between 'the Thirty' and the Duke of Orleans, who as a near-claimant to the throne conducted his own separate campaign. Such facts have led some historians to lay too much stress on the existence of a central direction for all revolutionary agitation and to exaggerate the part played by freemasons and 'the Thirty', whose operations have been represented as evidence of a concerted conspiracy to undermine the institutions of the *ancien régime*. Yet it must be remembered that the masonic lodges, while generally suspect to the established Church, recruited men of every shade of opinion, and that communications were not yet sufficiently developed to allow for a highly organized direction by comparatively unknown men. Even so, it is certainly true that leaders were now beginning to appear from among both bourgeois and liberal aristocrats, able to give some guidance to the nationwide discussion and to impress their ideas and personalities on the spontaneous action of many thousands that broadly shared their views, or were willing to adopt them, in every part of the country.

The electors, meanwhile, had been drawing up their *cahiers de doléances*. They were of two kinds: those drafted in the preliminary assemblies of the parishes and guilds for submission to the assemblies of the *bailliages*, and those drawn up by the *bailliages* for direct submission to the States-General. Of the latter most have survived and are fairly evenly divided among the three Estates. As might be expected, the *cahiers* of the clergy and nobility generally stress their attachment to traditional privileges and immunities, though they frequently concede the principle that they should pay a larger share of the taxes. At the same time, they join with those of the Third Estate in demanding the removal of the more oppressive and wasteful abuses of the absolute monarchy. They roundly condemn fiscal abuses and extravagance, the arbitrary acts of ministers, the system of *lettres de cachet* (involving detention without trial), the anomalies and vexations of the internal customs, and the prevailing chaotic system of weights and measures. More positively, they demand freedom of the press and the individual (though not yet freedom of conscience) and a constitution that, while upholding the traditional authority of the monarchy, will invest a periodically convened States-General with the right to frame laws and vote taxes, whose assessment and collection shall be entrusted to elective provincial and municipal assemblies. In short, there was a considerable measure of agreement among the three Estates on matters affecting political and administrative reform.

But the general *cahiers* of the Third Estate, drawn up in nearly every case by spokesmen for the bourgeoisie, go much further. They not only demand freedom of speech, writing and assembly, freedom of trade and freedom from arbitrary arrest; they generally also insist on the complete civil equality of all three Estates – that is, that the clergy and nobility must not only surrender such utterly discredited survivals as serfdom, but they must also give up age-old privileges like tithe, *banalités* (manorial monopolies), *champart* (feudal rent in kind), hunting rights and seigneurial jurisdiction. This much the bourgeoisie had learned, if not from their own experience, at least from a study of peasant grievances; but the most urgent peasant need of all – for more land – is seldom, if ever, addressed in these *cahiers*.

Of the local *cahiers* a far smaller proportion has survived. Some are set pieces based on circulated models and therefore tell us little of the real intentions of their reputed authors. Others (and there are several among the parish 'notebooks') are genuine enough and illustrate two truths: one, that the villagers taking part in the debates supported bourgeois criticisms of the absolute monarchy and of feudal survivals in land-tenure and justice; and the other, that they often had social claims of their own which, in some respects, divided them sharply from the 'capitalists' and large proprietors of the Third

Estate.[3] We shall return to these demands in the following chapter.

The States-General met at Versailles on 5 May against a background of mounting crisis and popular unrest. In Paris, the price of bread was at almost twice its normal level; there had been bloody riots in the Faubourg St Antoine; and in the countryside the peasants had passed from words to deeds and were stopping food-convoys, raiding markets and destroying game reserves. As the great assembly opened, nothing was done to spare the commons' susceptibilities or to hold out any promise of far-reaching reform. They were ordered to wear the traditional black and to enter by a side door and were in every way made mindful of their inferior status. The Royal Council, though it had agreed to grant the commons double representation, had refused to concede their further demand to deliberate jointly with the other Estates. Necker was sympathetic but, being strongly opposed within the Council by Barentin, the Keeper of the Seals, felt unable to give a lead. He merely advised the Third Estate to be patient while inviting the *privilégiés* to make a voluntary sacrifice of their fiscal immunities. Meanwhile, the Estates were ordered to meet in separate assemblies and to recommend which subjects should be discussed and voted in common. The King had no settled policy and was pulled from one side to the other. But to the commons it seemed that he had already decided to throw in his lot with the nobility and clergy, for double representation would be a hollow victory unless accompanied by a union of the Estates: without the support of like-minded deputies from the other orders, they could always be outvoted by the combined strength of their opponents. So they refused to deliberate as a separate assembly and demanded a joint session to consider the validity of mandates, as a first step to holding common sessions on more fundamental issues. The bishops and nobles naturally saw the danger and resisted the suggestion, though the bishops had difficulty in dissuading the parish priests (who outnumbered them by five to one) from joining their fellow commoners. Behind this five-week wrangle over procedure lay a struggle over a basic principle.

On 10 June, encouraged by the support it was receiving from outside, the Third Estate decided to take the bull by the horns. It invited the other orders to join in a common session to establish a common authority; if they refused to comply it would (following Sieyès' earlier argument) be ready to proceed without them. Joined by a few parish priests, it completed a check of election returns, elected two secretaries and Jean-Sylvain Bailly as President; on 17 June, by a majority of 491 to 89 votes, it arrogated to itself the title of National Assembly. This first revolutionary act of the bourgeoisie was followed by the issue of two decrees: one provided that a dissolution of the new Assembly, for whatever cause, would invalidate all existing taxes; the other, that, as soon as a constitution had been determined, the public debt, instead of being levied locally, should be consolidated and underwritten by the nation as a whole. On 20 June, a further challenge was thrown down when the Assembly found itself – accidentally, it seems – locked out of its usual meeting hall. Following President Bailly into an adjoining tennis court, every deputy except one took a solemn oath that the National Assembly should not disperse until the constitution had been firmly established. By this time the clergy had, by a narrow majority, decided to throw in its lot with the new Assembly; 150 clerical deputies, headed by two archbishops, joined it a few days later.

Even before this last act of defiance by the Third Estate, Necker had urged the King to reassert his authority, break the deadlock between the orders and take the initiative in legislative form. To this end, he suggested that a *séance royale* should be held, where it should be announced that such matters as the future constitution of the States-General be discussed in common, whereas matters affecting the particular interests of individual Estates should continue to be separately considered. After bitter arguments within the Council, a first decision was taken on 19 June to hold the *séance* on the 22nd, presumably on the basis of Necker's proposals. But, meanwhile, the King, indecisive as ever, had been prevailed upon by other counsel. Surrounded by a group of courtiers led by his younger brother, the Comte d'Artois (who was supported by the Queen), he was persuaded to quash the self-styled Assembly's decrees of 17 June, to refer discussion of the future organization of the States-General to each of the separate orders, and to overawe the Third Estate by a show of force. It was at this time that the secret decision to remove Necker from office was made.

When the *séance royale*, deferred for a day, assembled on 23 June, efforts were made to intimidate the Third Estate: it was kept waiting in the rain while the *privilégiés* took their seats, the hall was ringed with troops, and the proceedings had all the arbitrary atmosphere of a *lit de justice*.* The main business was conducted by Barentin, a nominee of the Queen's, who read two royal declarations. The first pronounced the National Assembly's resolutions null and void and, while recommending the acceptance of the principle of common sessions for matters of common concern, expressly reserved for

* A session of the Parlement of Paris, specially convened to hear the King's judgement on its 'remonstrances'. He lay stretched on his '*lit de justice*' and his verdict was imposed without further discussion.

separate deliberation all questions relating to the special privileges and immunities of the First and Second Estates. The second declaration outlined the Council's legislative programme. It provided, broadly, for a reform of the institutions of the *ancien régime* along the lines already advocated in the *cahiers* of all three Estates, but the social fabric of the old order was to remain intact: it was categorically stated that tithes and seigneurial dues were to be treated as property rights and that no surrender of fiscal privilege would be called for without the consent of the parties most directly concerned. Finally, the Estates were ordered to disperse and to resume discussion in their separate chambers on the morrow.

Yet the plans of the Court party miscarried. Thousands of Parisians, responding to its counter-revolutionary challenge, flocked to Versailles to demand that Necker be retained in office. Soldiers under the command of the Prince de Conti refused to obey the order to fire, and the deputies of the Third Estate, having declined to disperse at the end of the *séance*, were rallied by Mirabeau in a militant speech. The King was compelled to yield. Necker remained in office and not only was the National Assembly (whose numbers had risen to 830 deputies) left in possession of its chamber but, on 27 June, the remnants of the other orders were expressly commanded to join it.

Until now the revolutionary temper already developing in Paris had been without effective leadership. With the latest news from Versailles, however, the professional and commercial classes of the capital, who had been prepared to await events and had viewed with scant sympathy the rumblings in the Faubourgs and markets, began to give a direction to affairs. Without their leadership the July insurrection could hardly have taken place. From now on the journalists and pamphleteers in the entourage of the Duke of Orleans (they included both Danton and Desmoulins) began to establish a permanent headquarters at the Palais Royal. Here thousands congregated nightly and acquired the slogans and directions of what the diarist Sébastien Hardy called 'the extreme revolutionary party'. Also, at this time, the 407 electors of the Paris Third Estate, whose task it had been to appoint the Parisian delegates to represent them at Versailles, began to meet regularly at the City Hall. These two bodies were to play distinct yet complementary roles in the events that followed. In the earlier days, however, it was the Palais Royal alone, with its ample supply of talents and funds, that gave a positive direction to the popular movement. Whereas the City Hall contented itself with drafting paper schemes for a citizens' militia, the Palais Royal took steps, by public agitation and liberal expenditure, to win over the troops – above all, the Gardes Françaises – from their loyalty to the Court. Tracts supporting the stand of the Third Estate were distributed among the Paris garrisons, and by the end of June the Guards, who had loyally shot down rioters two months before in the Faubourg St Antoine, were parading the streets of Paris to shouts of 'Long live the Third Estate! We are the soldiers of the Nation!' On 10 July, eighty artillerymen who had broken out of their barracks in the Hôtel des Invalides were publicly fêted in the Palais Royal and the Champs Elysées.

Responding to these developments, the Court, which had been steadily summoning loyal Swiss and German troops to Versailles, attempted a further showdown. On 11 July, Necker was sent into exile and replaced by the Baron de Breteuil, a nominee of the Queen. This proved to be the spark that touched off the popular insurrection in Paris which, from the point of view of the Committee of Electors installed at the City Hall, threatened to get out of hand. So, on the morning of 13 July, they made a firm bid to gain control. They formed a permanent committee to act as a provisional government of the city and determined to put a stop to the indiscriminate arming of the whole population which had already begun. The bands of homeless and unemployed, most of whom had flocked in from the surrounding countryside, were, they felt, as great a menace to the security and property of the citizens as the Court and privileged orders conspiring at Versailles. So it was with both threats in mind that they now set about seriously organizing a citizens' militia or National Guard, and it is hardly surprising that it was on the former score alone that the King was induced, the next day, to give his consent. Householders were summoned to attend meetings in the sixty electoral districts into which Paris had been divided. Each district was to provide 200 (later 800) men. Barnave wrote, the same evening, to his constituents in Dauphiné that there were already 13,200 citizens registered and equipped. From this body all vagrants and homeless persons (*gens sans aveu*), and even a large part of the settled wage-earners, were excluded: the Guard was in fact intended, as Barnave wrote, to be 'bonne bourgeoise'. Yet arms continued to fall into unauthorized hands as long as the insurrection continued. To limit their distribution, the electors deputed one of their number, the Abbé Lefevre, to guard the stocks of weapons and powder assembled in the vaults of the City Hall. But so great was the pressure of the crowds surging round the building that he was compelled to hand out the powder, at least, with more speed and less discrimination than had been intended.

And it was from this frantic search for arms that, on the 14th, the cry went up, 'to the Bastille!'. The story of its capture, however, being part of the 'popular' rather than of the 'bourgeois' revolution, will be deferred until the next chapter. Yet the electors – and this, too, is important – played a part in the operation, though they would have preferred to have negotiated its surrender by making a deal with its governor, de Launay. But the plan misfired and the fortress was only taken by a frontal attack in which the Gardes Françaises, so recently enlisted for revolution by the Palais Royal, played a crucial role. Its fall had dramatic and far-reaching consequences that proved of particular advantage to the 'patriot' leaders. The National Assembly, for the time being at least, was safe. The Court party began to disintegrate as Artois, Condé and Breteuil went into exile, while Necker, their victim, was recalled. In the capital, power passed into the hands of the electors who set up a municipal council (or *Commune*) with Bailly as mayor and Lafayette as commander of its National Guard. The King himself three days later made the journey to Paris, escorted by fifty deputies, and was received with acclaim at the City Hall where, in token of acquiescence to the turn of events, he donned the red, white and blue cockade of the Revolution. So it seemed as if the National Assembly might now proceed quietly with its plan to give France a constitution.

The provinces, however, had yet to have their say, having mainly waited, as Arthur Young was told at Nancy in mid-July, to hear 'what was done in Paris'. Yet there were, of course, exceptions to this general rule, as at Rennes and other Breton towns; at Dijon, the people sprang to arms and formed the nucleus of a National Guard on 15 July, anticipating by three days the receipt of the news from Paris that the Bastille had fallen. Most often, however, it was this news, conveyed by word of mouth, or by letter, that in the following seven to fourteen days spurred the provinces into action in more or less close imitation of the great events in Paris. 'The Parisian spirit of commotion,' wrote Arthur Young from Strasbourg on 21 July, 'spreads quickly'; and it had almost instantaneous results, the speed of reaction generally depending – though by no means always – on the distance from the capital. Thus Angers reacted as soon as 17 July, Bordeaux on the 19th, Lille and Strasbourg on the 21st, and Toulouse on the 27th. In nearly every case the news led to a 'municipal revolution' in which the wealthy bourgeoisie usually played the leading role. Yet this took a variety of forms, depending on the recent history of such matters as social and political conflicts or the incidence of shortages and riots. Thus, in maritime Flanders, the old town corporation merely broadened its composition, adopted the tricolour cockade and carried on as before. Sometimes, as at

Bordeaux, it closely followed the example of Paris and made way for the electors of the Third Estate. More often – as at Lille, Rouen, Cherbourg, Dijon, Rheims, Rennes, Lyons and Montauban – the old authorities were brushed aside or overthrown by force and replaced by new committees of more dedicated citizens often pledged to reduce the price of bread. In nearly every case, the transfer of authority was accompanied by the creation of a National Guard on the Parisian model, of which a major object was, as in the capital, to meet the double danger of popular 'licence' and aristocratic obstruction of reform.[4] Meanwhile, the Intendants, the old rulers in the provinces, quietly disappeared.

There is little doubt that such developments, following closely after the Paris events, increased the status and esteem of the National Assembly. Yet its position was far from secure. As long as the Court and King remained at Versailles and an active minority of deputies were able, in alliance with the Court, to frustrate the wishes of the majority, effective power remained divided in an unstable balance between the revolutionary bourgeoisie, supported by a minority of aristocrats and bishops, and the adherents of the *ancien régime*. The gains so far made, substantial as they appeared to be, were precarious. Louis refused to endorse some of the Assembly's most urgent demands, such as the Declaration of the Rights of Man; there were repeated royalist or aristocratic intrigues to abduct the King to a safe distance from the capital; and, in August, determined attempts were made to persuade the Assembly to adopt a conservative English-style constitution by granting the King an absolute 'veto' on legislation and by creating an Upper Chamber.

These proposals were put forward by the so-called *Monarchiens* or 'English party', a group led by Mounier and Malouet among the commons and Lally Tollendal among the nobility. Their aims were to frame a 'mixed' constitution on the English model, where powers would be divided, in more or less equal proportions, between King, nobility and commons, and one in which only property-owners of substance would have the vote and the rebellious peasants and urban *menu peuple* would be kept in their proper place. The proposal for an Upper Chamber found little support: not only were the left and centre opposed to it, but it was also opposed by the provincial *noblesse* who feared their virtual exclusion from a Chamber dominated by the Court aristocracy. The 'veto' proposal, however, was tenaciously upheld and created sharp divisions both within and outside the Assembly. The Parisian 'patriots', established at the City Hall, called for its complete rejection; but Barnave, who spoke for the left at Versailles, was prepared to negotiate with the centre, who favoured acceptance. When, at the end of August, negotiations broke down, the Parisians' position was strengthened, and an attempt was made by a group of Palais Royal journalists (including Desmoulins) to induce their fellow citizens to march to Versailles and fetch the King back to his capital. The attempt, however, failed because Barnave and his colleagues, fearing a trap, opposed it, and because Parisians had not yet become convinced of its necessity.

They would become so, however, five weeks later as the food crisis deepened and as the Court party engaged in a new wave of provocation which, arising in mid-September, brought the 'patriots' back into the picture. On 11 September Barnave, renewing his attempt to negotiate a settlement, persuaded the Assembly to urge the King to adopt a more conciliatory attitude towards the majority's proposals, and it was in direct response to this insistence that the Court decided on a further resort to military force. On the 15th Louis, having rejected the moderates' advice to move the Court to the greater safety of a provincial town, ordered the Flanders Regiment to Versailles. The news was welcomed with a banquet given by the royal Gardes-du-Corps (Life Guards) in the course of which the new tricolour cockade was trampled underfoot and the Queen and her children were received with almost mystical fervour. The incident was widely reported in the Parisian press and provoked an almost immediate response among both the people and the 'patriot' leaders of the National Assembly. This time Barnave, outraged by the new development, withdrew his objection to a resort to force. Danton carried a resolution in the Cordeliers Club in which he urged Parisians to march to Versailles with an ultimatum for the King, and Desmoulins repeated from the Palais Royal his call to Parisians to fetch the King to Paris.

Parisians now responded in what has been called the October 'days'; and it was the people, rather than the 'patriots' or the bourgeoisie, who became most actively engaged in their operation.

3 *The 'Popular' Revolution*

The 'popular' revolution of 1789 quite naturally falls into two main parts; that associated with the peasants and that with the urban *sans-culottes*. Though sharing a common political background, each had its own distinctive origin and mode of behaviour, and its own short and long-term results. The two movements overlapped but the peasant movement was the first to begin and the first to come (at least temporarily) to an end.

As we observed in an earlier chapter, the origins of peasant unrest lay in the economic and political conditions of the *ancien régime* and it was nourished by grievances over taxes and the seigneurial exaction of dues, services and obligations going back to medieval times. In addition, the poorer peasants – being purchasers rather than producers of wheat and bread – also suffered as small consumers from the frequent rises in the price of food. And this was the initial issue in what became a continuous and protracted peasant movement that began in the winter of 1788, developing by the spring of 1789 into a more widespread revolt against game-laws, hunting rights, royal taxes, tithes and seigneurial dues. The peasant revolt (or 'revolution', as Lefebvre called it) had an identity and a momentum all its own and did not, like the urban outbreaks in the provinces, wait upon the 'news from Paris' before it began. Yet this news did give it a new stimulus, particularly because of the rumours accompanying it: not only that the Court and aristocracy had attempted to disperse the new Assembly (on which the peasants pinned great hopes) by force of arms, but also that the royalist troops disbanded after the fall of the Bastille were really 'brigands' who were preparing to seize their land and destroy their crops. So 'fear bred fear' (to quote Lefebvre again) and gave a new dimension to peasant unrest which, in the latter part of July, became generalized and spread over the greater part of France. It had precise objectives and never took the form of a free-for-all *jacquerie*, as peasant outbreaks had often done before. It was directed against carefully selected targets, stopped short of cities and sought out the hated manorial rolls and the *châteaux* in which they were known to be housed. Whole villages, sometimes led by their local officials, went on the march and hundreds of *châteaux* went up in flames; both rumour and the distribution of leaflets supported the widely held belief that this was done in the name – if not by direct order – of the King. There was no indiscriminate disorder and only four *seigneurs* (both noble and bourgeois) are known to have been killed. There were few criminals among the assailants and, as one magistrate said of two dozen men whom he sentenced to prison or execution: 'They seem to have gathered by common consent with the intention of destroying châteaux and mansions, and freeing themselves from their rents by destroying their charters.'

It was out of this general peasant revolt, whose main thrust was directed against *châteaux* and seigneurial charters, that there developed at the end of July that strange and quite particular phenomenon known as the 'Great Fear', a phenomenon which had, as Lefebvre has always insisted, quite particular features of its own. Fear (he claimed) was a continuing element, but it was no longer simply a fear that 'brigands' were on the march; now there was 'a total certainty' that they were actually at the door and ready to break in. It was no longer a case of scattered pockets of fear spread far and wide over the length and breadth of the country; panic had now become focused within well-defined regions and, within each, it spread by a process of chain-reaction and contagion from one town or village to the next. The Great Fear had precise boundaries of time and place: the riots began on 20 July and ended on 6 August, were limited to half a dozen regions and bypassed some of the main areas of peasant revolt. Brittany, for example, was virtually untouched, as were Alsace, the Mâconnais (north of Lyons), the Landes and Basque country to the south-west, and the Norman woodlands to the north-west, while two of the most rebellious regions in the north, Hainault and Cambrésis, were hardly touched at all. There was no longer a single starting-point in Paris, as with the more generalized fear; now there were half a dozen starting-points, as many as there were currents, or waves, within its sphere of operations. Near Nantes, where the Great Fear started, rumour spread – and rapidly gained the villages around – that a detachment of dragoons was marching on the town. At Clermont, near the centre, the Fear sprang from a fight between poachers and gamekeepers; near Angoulême, in the south-west, from a fear of beggars and vagrants on the eve of the harvest; and so on. Lefebvre sums up the progression of each of the Great Fear's half-a-dozen currents as follows:

> The Great Fear of Les Mauges and Poitou started in Nantes on the 20th; that in Maine, in the east of the province, on the 20th or 21st; the Fear in the Franche-Comté, which set the entire East and South-East in a panic, on the 22nd; in southern Champagne it began on the 24th; in the Clermontois and the Soissonnais on the 26th; it crossed the South-West from a starting-point in Ruffec [north of Angoulême] on the 28th; it reached Barjols in Provence on 4 August and Lourdes, at the foot of the Pyrenees, on the 6th of the same month.[1]

But with all the confusion and irrationality that attended it, the Great Fear had quite positive features and results. It forced the towns and newly created militias to organize themselves in a more efficient manner; it linked the towns and villages and thus laid the basis for the Federation of the future; and it stoked up a more intense hatred of the nobility which, in turn, gave an impetus to the progress of the Revolution in the provinces. In only one region did the Fear precede the general peasant revolt. This was in Dauphiné, where the attack on the *châteaux* and charters flowed directly from the arming of the peasants to meet the 'brigands' whom the Great Fear had conjured up.

Moreover, as part of the general peasants' revolt, the Fear contributed to results that were even more far-reaching and enduring. For early in August the National Assembly was compelled by the continuing rural unrest to pay immediate attention to the survivals of feudal privilege and to the pressing needs of the rebellious peasants. So, while still meeting at Versailles, it made important concessions in order to bring the conflagration to an end. These took the spectacular form of the surrender, on the night of 4 August, of those seigneurial rights still considered to be 'feudal' and the long cherished and stubbornly defended fiscal immunities. But the Assembly's claim that thereby 'the feudal regime had been utterly destroyed' was misleading: while the remnants of serfdom, the *corvée* (unpaid labour on roads), ecclesiastical tithe, and *banalités* were abolished outright, some of the more onerous privileges and obligations – the *cens*, quit-rent, *champart* and *lods et ventes* among them – were only made redeemable (or so it was intended) by compensation paid by the peasants to their landlords. The landlords never got their money (the total compensation has been assessed at 4,000 million livres), which was due less to the foresight and generosity of the legislators, both bourgeois and aristocratic, than to the continued – though temporarily abated – resistance of the peasants, who were not prepared to draw such a fine distinction between what was 'feudal' and what was not. So Alfred Cobban is right in arguing that the arrangement arrived at in what became known as the 'August Decrees' reflected the particular advantages that bourgeois landowners hoped to gain.[2] Yet peasant resistance eventually proved too strong to hold the line where it had been drawn in August 1789: and it was a combination of peasant militancy and the Jacobin need for a wider degree of national unity at a time of political crisis that induced the Jacobin Convention, by a decree of June 1793, to bring the 'feudal regime' to its final conclusion.[3]

The contribution made by the *sans-culottes*, if less enduring, was equally dramatic. Their constant intervention on the streets helped to carry the Revolution forward through all its successive stages. The revolt of the *sans-culottes* began with the struggle for physical survival. All through the eighteenth century, the most constant concern of the urban *menu peuple* – the wage-earners, small shopkeepers, craftsmen and housewives – was for the provision of cheap and plentiful bread. Popular protest over bread began to acquire a new political dimension some time between November 1788 and February 1789, a crucial turning-point marked by the end of the 'aristocratic revolt' and the bid for power by the Third Estate. Under this impetus the 'politicization' of the *menu peuple* – above all, but not exclusively, in Paris – grew apace.

The Réveillon riots broke out in the Faubourg St Antoine at the end of April. They have been called the first great popular outbreak of the Revolution in Paris though they may perhaps with equal justice be called the last of the *ancien régime* or (perhaps more accurately still) be seen as a point of transition between the two. Réveillon was a successful manufacturer of wallpaper, whose main factory off the Rue du Faubourg St Antoine employed 350 workers. He was wealthy: his library housed 50,000 volumes, and his furniture was said to be worth 50,000 livres. He had the reputation of being a good employer who paid none of his workers less than 25 sous a day at a time when it was common for a labourer to be paid no more than 20, and it is certainly significant that not one of his own workers was among those killed or wounded in the affair or among those picked up later by the police. Why, then, did such a solid citizen, good employer and respected member of his local Electoral Assembly become the target for the destructive violence of the journeymen and labourers of the St Antoine district?

On 23 April Réveillon made a speech in the Assembly of the Ste Marguerite district, in which he regretted the rising costs of production and the burden imposed on industry by the high level of wages. He appears to have mourned for the days when workers could make do on only 15 sous a day. Similar views were expressed on the same day by Henriot, a powder manufacturer in a neighbouring district. So much is well attested, and that it was these remarks, whatever their intention, that aroused the immediate and spontaneous fury of the wage-earners of the Faubourg is evident from a report prepared for the government the next morning by the Lieutenant of Police.

After a lull the storm broke on the 27th; being a Monday (*saint-lundi*) it was a workers' rest-day and therefore well suited to the occasion. At three o'clock in the afternoon, ran the police report, five or six hundred working men gathered near the Bastille and, having hanged Réveillon in effigy, paraded dummy figures of the two manufacturers around different parts of the city. That same afternoon Hardy, whose bookshop off the Rue St Jacques was admirably placed to witness such processions, noted in his Journal that the 'insurrection' had spread to the Nôtre-Dame district. Later, he encountered several hundred workers, armed with sticks and headed by a drummer, in the Rue de la Montagne–Ste Geneviève. Having recruited reinforcements in the Faubourg St Marcel, they returned to the City Hall some 3,000 strong.[4] A first attempt, however, to assault Réveillon's factory in the Rue de Montreuil was foiled by the presence of troops, so the crowds changed course and made for Henriot's house in the nearby Rue de Cotte, destroying his furniture and personal effects. Meanwhile, more troops were called in and it appeared that the crisis was over.

But early the next morning the movement started up again and extended over a wider area. No work was done in the docks that day, and more factory workers and workshop journeymen, many recruited by the itinerant bands, came out in the early afternoon and joined them. The climax came that evening at six, when Réveillon's house was stormed. Fifty protective Guards of the Royal Cravate Regiment were brushed aside, and the destruction of the previous night was repeated on a greater scale. The Duc du Châtelet, commanding the Gardes Françaises, gave the order to fire. Many were killed (the exact number is not known), but the crowd fought back with shouts of 'Liberty ... we shall not yield!' Others shouted (and this was a significant indication of the popular mood), 'Long live the Third Estate!', also 'Long live the King!' and 'Long live M. Necker!' The battle lasted until eight, when the crowds – both besiegers and onlookers – dispersed. Hardy feared a repetition the next day and noted that, before dispersing, the rioters had warned 'that on the morrow they would make a big disturbance to force down the price of bread'.[5] But, apart from the post-mortems and the judicial reckoning (one man was hanged, five were exhibited in stocks and twenty-six – including a woman – were imprisoned for short terms), this was the end of the affair.

What, then, was this violent disturbance all about? It was certainly not a strike, in spite of the overwhelming proportion of wage-earners among those taking part; for how else had Réveillon's own workpeople not become involved? It is Hardy's last observation that gives us a clue: behind the anger with Réveillon and Henriot over their injudicious remarks about wages lay a deeper and more abiding concern – the price of bread. It is significant that the crowds, on dispersing, attempted to break into two neighbouring food shops. There was evidently a degree of political motivation as well, a sure indication that the workers were well aware that the States-General were to meet at Versailles a week later. Here the two shouted slogans are important: 'Long live the Third Estate!', appropriate enough if we consider the new meaning being given to the term in popular ideology. (Réveillon and Henriot, though prominent members of their electoral assemblies, had evidently by their behaviour shown themselves to be unworthy of the title.) Equally appropriate, and more readily understandable, were 'Long live the King!' and 'Long live M. Necker!' They were both still considered to be champions of the Third Estate on the eve of the eventful proceedings about to take place at Versailles.[6]

Meanwhile, both peasants and *sans-culottes* had had some say (though rarely a decisive one) in drafting the preparatory *cahiers* in the parishes and guilds. We have noted that some of these 'popular' *cahiers* were highly critical of the 'capitalists' and wealthy proprietors in the Third Estate. The voice of the wage earners, however, is rarely heard, least of all in Paris where none but the most prosperous merchant guilds were invited to air their grievances. Elsewhere, too, the *compagnons*, or journeymen, were generally excluded from the assemblies of the master craftsmen. There were exceptions, as at Rheims, Troyes, Marseilles and Lyons, where the workers protested against the rise in prices but otherwise accepted the lead given by their masters. Some wage-earners and craftsmen or petty tradesmen, however, were more explicit in the grievances they voiced against merchants and employers. From Concarneau, near Quimper, for instance, came two *cahiers*, drafted by fishermen in the one case and by mariners in the other, complaining of the encroachments on their fishing rights by selfish boat-owners and 'monopolists'. Journeymen hatters in Orleans bitterly complained of the low prices paid for their work by unscrupulous merchants; and the craftsmen of Pont l'Abbé (Brittany) demanded that municipal office be open not only to 'bourgeois' but to craftsmen and small peasant proprietors as well.[7]

Peasant *cahiers* are more abundant and tend to be more outspoken and even more explicit. In addition to the grievances of the whole rural community (which includes, of course, what Lefebvre has called a 'rural bourgeoisie'), we occasionally hear the particular complaints of the small proprietor, sharecropper or labourer. In the Rouen district, where the price of the 4-lb loaf had risen to 16 sous, villagers demanded that it be reduced by half. In Brittany, small peasants around Rennes complained that the burdens of taxes and seigneurial dues were so onerous that a strip of land with a gross yield of 40 livres per annum scarcely brought its owner a net income of one quarter of that sum. In Lorraine and Hainault, landless peasants and small proprietors (*laboureurs*) joined forces in opposing enclosure edicts and land-clearance schemes promoted by the more prosperous members of their community. In the Vosges, on the other hand, a parish *cahier* protested that the allocation of land to landless labourers, following a decision of the commons, disturbed the harmonious relations existing hitherto between labourers and proprietors.[8] In short, the parish *cahiers* reflect both the common bonds of interest linking all members of the peasant community in opposition to royal tax-collector, tithe-owner and landlord, and the further divisions within the community itself separating small consumer from large producer, and landless labourer and sharecropper from tenant farmer and substantial *laboureur*. The revolution in the village reflected all these elements and would continue to do so long after the dramatic events of the summer of 1789.

The contribution of the *sans-culottes*, though minor in May and June, was of far greater importance to the course and outcome of the revolutionary events that followed in July and October. The first of these events began when the news of Necker's dismissal reached Paris on 12 July. Parisians flocked to the Palais Royal, where orators – Camille Desmoulins among them – gave the call to arms. Groups of marchers quickly formed and paraded the busts of Necker and Orléans, the heroes of the hour, on the Boulevards; theatres were closed as a sign of mourning; in the Place Louis XV (today's Place de la Concorde), demonstrators clashed with the cavalry commanded by the Prince de Lambesc who had been ordered to clear the Tuileries Gardens. Besenval, commander of the Parison garrison, withdrew to the Champ de Mars. The capital was in the hands of the people.

As the tocsin sounded the alarm, bands of insurgents joined those who had, two days earlier – on their own initiative or on that of the Palais Royal – already begun to burn down the hated *barrières*, or customs posts, that ringed the city. While the Palais Royal almost certainly had a direct hand in the operation – it was reported that two posts belonging to the Duke of Orleans were deliberately spared by the incendiaries – the common people of Paris had their own account to settle with an institution which levied a toll on all wines, meat, vegetables and firewood that entered the capital. During the night, too, armed civilians, Gardes Françaises and local poor broke into the monastery of St Lazare on the northern fringe of the city, searched it for arms known to be hidden there, released prisoners and removed fifty-two cartloads of corn and flour to the central grain market. But the main feature of that night was a frantic search for weapons. Religious houses were visited and gunsmiths, armourers and harness-makers were raided all over the capital. In fact, the Parisian gunsmiths later submitted to the National Assembly a statement of their losses, amounting to more than 115,000 livres (a little over £9,000) which they do not appear to have recovered. The next morning the search continued and 30,000 muskets were removed from the Hôtel des Invalides. It was from here that the cry was raised, 'To the Bastille!'

Royalist historians have scoffed at the picture of thousands of Parisians hurling themselves at the Bastille to release a handful of prisoners (only seven were still kept there). But such criticism falls somewhat wide of the mark. The immediate aim was to find the powder which had been sent there from the Arsenal – all the more urgent after the large haul of muskets taken from the Invalides. Other motives no doubt played a part. It was believed that the fortress was heavily manned; its guns, which that morning were trained on the Rue St Antoine, could play havoc among the crowded tenements; besides, it was rumoured that during the night troops had marched into the Faubourg and had already begun to slaughter its citizens. Moreover, though it had ceased to harbour more than a trickle of state prisoners, the Bastille was widely hated as a symbol of ministerial 'despotism': the Parisian *cahiers* of all three Estates bear witness to this. Yet there was no intention to take it by force, least of all on the part of the Permanent Committee of Electors who directed operations, with fumbling uncertainty, from the City Hall. They had made their intentions clear from the start: to negotiate with the governor for the surrender of the gunpowder in his keeping and for the withdrawal of the guns from his battlements. To this effect they sent a deputation – later followed by another – to parley with him at ten o'clock that morning. De Launay received them courteously, invited them to dine and, while refusing to surrender the fortress, promised not to fire unless he was attacked.

However, negotiations stalled after the crowds, surging round the fortress and fearing a trap when the deputation took so long to reappear, lowered the drawbridge (unaccountably left unguarded) that led into the inner courtyard. Believing a frontal attack to be imminent, de Launay gave the order to fire. In the affray that followed, the besiegers lost ninety-eight dead and seventy-three wounded. At this point the electors abandoned their efforts and the crowd took over. The decisive blow was struck by two detachments of the Gardes Françaises who, responding to the summons of Hulin, a former non-commissioned officer, marched to the fortress with five cannon removed that morning from the Invalides. Supported by a few hundred armed civilians, they trained their cannon on the main gate. De Launay threatened to blow up the fortress but, being dissuaded by his garrison, lowered the main drawbridge and surrendered to his assailants. He himself and six of the 110 defenders were slaughtered – a small number of victims, it must be said, when compared with the far heavier losses suffered by the besiegers. So the Bastille fell, with political consequences that were briefly noted before.

But one question remains to be answered: who, in fact, were the besiegers? Among the many legends surrounding the Bastille's capture there have been few as persistent as that which depicts its captors as vagabonds, criminals or a mercenary rabble hired in the wine-shops of the St Antoine quarter. Yet all available evidence refutes this view. From lists of the accredited *vainqueurs de la Bastille*, subsequently drawn up by the National Assembly, we know the occupations, ages and addresses of the great majority of the civilians – some 600 in number – who took a direct part in the surrender. Most of them, far from being vagrants or down-and-outs, were settled residents of the Faubourg St Antoine and its adjoining parishes; their average age was thirty-four; nearly all were fathers of families and most, again, were members of the newly formed citizens' militia from which such elements as vagrants and *gens sans aveu* had been rigorously excluded. Among them appear the names of a handful of men who were to distinguish themselves in the course of the Revolution – such as Jean Rossignol, goldsmith and later general of the Revolution, and Antoine-Joseph Santerre, wealthy brewer and commander-in-chief of the militia that overthrew the monarchy in August 1792. But most were men of no particular distinction, drawn from the typical crafts and occupations of the Faubourg and its adjacent districts: joiners and cabinetmakers, locksmiths and cobblers (these alone accounting for more than a quarter of the civilian captors), shopkeepers, gauzemakers, sculptors, riverside workers and labourers, among whom the craftsmen and shopkeepers far outnumber the wage-earners, reflecting a reasonably faithful picture of the Faubourg's working population.[9]

Yet, in a wider sense, we may perhaps agree with Michelet that the capture of the Bastille was the affair not of a few hundred citizens of the St Antoine quarter alone, but of the people of Paris as a whole. It has been said that on that day between 180,000 and 300,000 Parisians were under arms. Taking an even broader view, we should not ignore the part played, though less conspicuously, by the great mass of Parisian petty craftsmen, tradesmen and wage-earners – in the Faubourg St Antoine and elsewhere – whose revolutionary temper had been moulded over many months by high living costs and, as the political crisis deepened, by the growing conviction that the hopes raised by the calling of the States-General were being thwarted by an 'aristocratic plot'.

And it was the same conviction, further sharpened by the rising price of bread, that stimulated popular participation in the provincial 'commotions' that generally followed the example set by Paris. We have already mentioned such outbreaks at Dijon, Angers, Lille and Toulouse; there were others at Nancy and Douai, and Arthur Young reported on similar manifestations from Strasbourg and Belfort towards the end of July. Vovelle, a modern historian, relating such incidents in Provence (at Aix, Marseilles, Toulon), notes that at Marseilles the composition of the crowd, with its predominance of craftsmen, conformed to a pattern broadly similar to that recorded at the Bastille.[10]

We have seen, too, that the fear of an 'aristocratic plot' played an important part in inciting Parisians to march to Versailles in October. The movement had been well prepared – not least by a development in popular revolutionary ideology during August and September. That the common people of the capital were becoming deeply influenced by the currents of advanced opinion had been evident during the electoral campaign, and they continued to be so. The debates at Versailles in July and August were relayed with amazing speed to crowds in the Palais Royal and the Place de Grève. The term *tiers état* was already being voiced by craftsmen, on the eve of the Réveillon affair, in the third week of April. On 24 August, even before the Declaration of Rights was adopted, a journeyman gunsmith, when arrested by the police for abusing Lafayette, insisted that 'le droit de l'homme' entitled him to a fair hearing. Malouet reports that *chaise*-bearers standing at the gate of the National Assembly were discussing the rights and wrongs of the royal 'veto'; and in mid-September, the unemployed workers of the *ateliers de charité* stated their intention to go to Versailles to fetch the royal family to Paris.

Yet, once more, it was the food crisis that gave a particular edge to popular agitation. The price of the 4-lb loaf had, a week after the fall of the Bastille, been reduced from 14½ to 13½ sous and, a fortnight later, after demonstrations at the City Hall, to 12. But the calm that followed was short-lived. The harvest had been good, but a prolonged drought made it impossible for millers to grind sufficient corn. The shortage of flour and bread that resulted was a boon to speculators but a matter of deep concern to bakers, who were the most ready targets of popular vengeance. During August and September there were constant bread riots in Paris and Versailles and at St Denis, in the course of which a baker and a municipal officer were killed by angry crowds while others were threatened with hanging from the dreaded *lanterne*. It was noted by Hardy that, from mid-September, a leading part in the agitation was played by women of the markets and Faubourgs, and it was they who took the initiative and gave a lead to their menfolk in the march to Versailles.[11]

But it was the men in the circle of the Duke of Orleans who gave the call to action which, as on the previous 12 July, was echoed in the gardens of the Palais Royal. Early in the morning of 5 October, women from the central markets and the Faubourg St Antoine invaded the City Hall, calling for bread and searching for arms. Outside the building they were joined by Stanislas Maillard, a sheriff's officer and captain of the Bastille Volunteers, whom they persuaded to lead them to Versailles to present their demands to the King and the National Assembly. So, headed by Maillard, they marched to Versailles six or seven thousand strong, 'armed with broomsticks, lances, pitchforks, swords, pistols and muskets', through Chaillot and crossing the Seine at Sèvres.[12] As they marched, they chanted (or so tradition has it), 'Let us fetch the baker, the baker's wife and the little baker's boy.' They were followed a few hours later by 20,000 National Guardsmen of the Paris districts, who had compelled the reluctant Lafayette to place himself at their head, and a motley band of civilians armed with muskets, sticks and pikes. Faced with this impressive array, the King needed little persuasion to give orders for the provisioning of the capital and to sanction the long-obstructed August Decrees and the Declaration of Rights. But these concessions were not enough to satisfy the insurgents, and the next day the King and his family, having thrown away their last chance of seeking refuge in flight, were compelled to accompany the marchers back to Paris, where they were joined ten days later by the National Assembly. So the French monarchy, after an absence of over a hundred years, returned for a brief sojourn to its ancestral home.

By this second intervention of the people of Paris the gains of the July revolution – both 'popular' and 'bourgeois' – were consolidated. The King came under the watchful eye of the Assembly, the Paris city government and districts; the 'English' party, with its more conservative programme, was now finally discredited and its leaders followed Artois and Condé into exile; and power passed firmly into the hands of the 'constitutional' monarchists. Yet they had only survived because, under the pressing compulsion of events, they had been willing to make common cause with the people who, though having aims and grievances of their own, shared their fears and suspicions of aristocracy. In this sense, the revolution of 1789 resulted from an alliance that would leave its mark on the whole course of the Revolution in France.

Yet the alliance of bourgeoisie and people was by no means an easy, stable or unchequered one. Even among the victors of October, there were many who, not sharing Barnave's enthusiasm for the Parisians' role, viewed it with misgivings; and once the insurrection had served its purpose, the Assembly was persuaded to take measures to curb the revolutionary energies of the Parisian *menu peuple* by imposing martial law, the death penalty for rebellion and a censorship on the radical press. The first victim of these restraints on liberty, Michel Adrien, a Bastille labourer, was hanged on 21 October for attempting to provoke a 'sedition' in the Faubourg St Antoine, and Marat, the popular journalist of the *Ami du peuple*, came under close surveillance. For, having won its victory over 'privilege' and 'despotism', the bourgeoisie now wanted peace and quiet in order to proceed with its task of giving France a constitution.

III Constitutional Monarchy

1 *The 'Principles of '89'*

The constitution-makers of 1789 to 1791 were by no means starry-eyed 'ideologues' or total renovators as Burke and others have portrayed them. The Constituents, or constitutional monarchists, were essentially the lawyers, merchants, former government officials and landed proprietors of the old Third Estate, shorn of a small minority of 'monarchists'. Their numbers were swollen by the addition of fifty 'patriot' nobles, forty-four bishops and about 200 parish clergy (most of whom were endowed with a fairly strong sense of which side their bread was buttered). Their new leaders, after the departure of the right in October, were men of the former left and centre – the triumvirate of Barnave, Duport and Charles Lameth; with Sieyès and Mirabeau playing an important, relatively independent, role and with a left opposition formed by a small group of democrats that included Pétion and Robespierre. Owing to circumstances not entirely within the Assembly's control, the *ancien régime* of aristocratic privilege and royal absolutism had collapsed and something had to be put in its place. The constitution and the laws they enacted within the next two years of comparative social peace bore, like the earlier Declaration of Rights, the stamp of the current philosophy, but they were also conceived in the legislators' own decidedly 'bourgeois' image.

The Declaration of the Rights of Man was adopted by the National Assembly, before its move to Paris, on 27 August 1789. These 'principles of '89', which were later to enthral or divide the whole of Europe, were the outcome of hard bargaining between different groups of deputies. Both Mounier and Lafayette, respectively of the right and centre, played an important part in their drafting. But even the presence of Thomas Jefferson in Paris and their close kinship with the Virginian Declaration of 1776 do not prove that they owed their inspiration largely to American influence: it is more reasonable to conclude that both Americans and Frenchmen owed a common debt to the 'natural law' school of philosophy, in particular to Locke, Montesquieu and Rousseau. The 1789 Declaration of Rights, moreover, is remarkable in that it neatly balances a statement of universal principles with an evident concern for the interests of the bourgeoisie. In general, it voices the basic claims of the Third

Estate, as expressed in their *cahiers de doléances*: protection of property; freedom of conscience, freedom of the press and freedom from arbitrary arrest; equality before the law; equal taxation and equal eligibility for office; and, to show the deputies' appreciation of practical realities, it implicitly sanctioned – *post factum* – the right of rebellion.

On the other hand, the Declaration's omissions and reservations are equally significant. Nothing is said about economic freedom, and the Assembly was still divided over the future of the guilds, and the resistance of small consumers to the 'freedom' of the market was not yet a burning issue. Equality is presented in largely political terms; economic equality does not yet arise. Property is 'a sacred and inalienable right', and no attempt is made as yet to define it or circumscribe it. Nor is there any mention of the State's obligation to provide work or relief for the poor and unpropertied. There is silence, too, on the rights of assembly, petition and association. Law is stated to be 'the expression of the general will', but there is no guarantee that all citizens will have an equal share in its enactment – least of all in the colonies: no mention is made of slavery and the slave trade. In matters of religion, Protestants and Jews are entitled to their opinions, 'provided their manifestation does not disturb the political order'; there can be no question of complete and untrammelled liberty of public worship as long as the Roman Catholic Church retains the sole and unchallenged blessing of the state. The Declaration, for all its nobility of language and its proclamation of universal truths, is essentially a manifesto of the revolutionary bourgeoisie and its clerical and liberal–aristocratic allies. As such, it sounded the death-knell of the *ancien régime* in France, while preparing the public for further developments and elaborations in laws that were yet to come.[1]

2 *Constitution of 1791*

The greater part of the first National Assembly's legislation became incorporated in the Constitution of 1791. Running through its text is the concern of the nation's new rulers that the system to be devised should be adequately protected against the triple danger of royal 'despotism', aristocratic 'privilege' and popular 'licentiousness'. There were no declared Republicans in the Assembly as yet, and it was generally agreed that the monarchy should remain; but it was to be a new constitutional monarchy, stripped of its former absolute control over government, legislation, army and justice. The 'King of the French' should hold hereditary office, be granted a civil list of 25 million livres as the first servant of the state, and have the right to appoint his own ministers (from outside the Assembly), his ambassadors and military commanders. By a so-called 'suspensive veto', he would have the power to suspend or delay all laws initiated and adopted by the Assembly for a period of up to four years, or for the duration of two consecutive Parlements. But he would have no power to dissolve the Chamber; ministers would be virtually answerable not to him but to the Assembly and its numerous committees; and, while he might take the first steps in declaring war or making peace, such measures would be subject to the approval of Parlement. The armed forces, meanwhile, had already been largely removed from royal control: a great many of the old aristocratic officers had been purged, often by the troops themselves; commissions were declared open to all; all ranks were called upon to take an oath of allegiance to the nation as well as to the King; and local authorities were to have the disposal of their own militia or National Guard. So those leaders on both right and left who, for differing reasons, wanted a strong executive with an absolute power of veto failed in the attempt.

The real power in the land was, in fact, to be the National Assembly itself. It was to be a unicameral body, untrammelled by 'checks and balances' on the English or American model, armed with unlimited powers over taxation and with initiative and authority in all legislative matters, restricted only by the obligation to hold elections every two years. The majority took care besides to ensure that, if not they themselves, at least like-minded deputies should be returned at each subsequent election. Prompted by Sieyés, they adopted a formula whereby only citizens of some substance and property should be entitled to vote in two electoral stages. Though the Declaration of Rights had proclaimed the right of all citizens 'to take part, in person or through their representatives, in the making of laws', it had been silent on the specific right of suffrage. Citizens were now to be divided into 'active' and 'passive', of whom the 'active' alone would have the vote. To qualify for active citizenship one had to be a male twenty-five years old or more, domiciled for a year, not engaged in domestic service, and paying a direct tax equivalent to the value of three days' unskilled labour. Such citizens might select the candidates of their choice in the primary assemblies - that is, at the first stage of the electoral process. But the secondary assemblies, which actually elected the deputies, excluded all but those who paid a direct tax equivalent to the value of ten days' labour. Finally, to qualify as a deputy, a citizen had to pay a silver mark, or 52 livres, in taxes. What limitations this system actually imposed, or was intended to impose, on the right to vote and representation has been hotly disputed by historians. It is a difficult question to resolve and all the more so because, in August 1791, the Assembly considerably tightened up the provisions governing access to the electoral assemblies, while easing those relating to deputies. Formally, Professor Palmer may be right in concluding that, up to August 1791, almost seventy in a hundred citizens had the right to vote at the primary stage, about ten in a hundred might qualify as electors, and one in a hundred might qualify as a national deputy.[1] Yet published lists indicate that, in practice, both 'active' citizens and electors – particularly the latter – tended to be men of greater substance than these figures suggest. Even so, it is undeniably true that these restrictions on the right to vote or govern were far less stringent than those imposed by the unreformed Parliament of Britain: French bourgeois society of 1789–92 was decidedly more democratic than aristocratic society across the Channel.

The royal authority was further weakened by the reform of administration and local government. The old hereditary offices, acquired by purchase, were swept away and their holders compensated: it could hardly be otherwise, as two in five of the Assembly's members were previous office-holders. A similar fate befell the old complicated system of *généralités* and *intendances*, *bailliages* and *sénéchaussées*, *pays d'états* and *pays d'élections*, privileged corporations and the surviving pockets of ecclesiastical and seigneurial jurisdiction. Following the Declaration of Rights, public office was made open, by election or appointment, to talent. In place of the old patchwork of local authorities a uniform system was devised based on departments, districts, cantons and communes which, in its essentials, has survived to the present day. There were to be eighty-three departments of more or less equal size, whose boundaries were, however, drawn with careful attention to geography: in fact their names, like those of the months in the later Revolutionary Calendar, were derived from natural phenomena – in this case, mainly from rivers, mountains and seas. The departments and their subdivisions, the districts and cantons, were no longer, as under the old royal absolutist system, to be run by nominated officials but by committees elected from below. The base of the pyramid was formed by some 44,000 communes (or municipalities), whose mayors and councillors were elected by the active citizens and exercised considerable powers of local administration. Paris was to have its own municipal council and to be further subdivided into forty-eight sections (replacing the sixty electoral districts of 1789) armed with the authority to elect officials, and control of the police and the administration of justice. Thus not only absolute monarchy but the whole system of centralized government was dismantled; and France, at this stage of the Revolution, became virtually a federation of elective departments and municipalities enjoying a wide measure of local autonomy and held together, at the centre, by a strong legislature but a weak executive.

The same considerations governed the reform of justice and the judicial system. In the new bourgeois state, justice could no longer be subject to the royal prerogative or be dispensed by a local aristocracy of the sword, mitre or robe. So Parlements, 'sealed letters' and seigneurial and ecclesiastical courts followed the Bastille and the old venal offices into oblivion. As in England and America, the judiciary was declared to be independent of the executive: it was to become dependent on the 'nation' (that is, on the enfranchised citizens) instead. Justice was made free and equal for all; a network of tribunals was created at municipal, departmental and national level, with elective judges and with juries elected to serve in criminal cases. At the apex were two national tribunals – a Court of Appeal and a High Court – of which the latter, concerned with the trial of ministers, public officials and enemies of the state, looked forward to the Revolutionary Tribunal of 1793. And in due course (after March 1792) the guillotine, the great leveller, would replace the aristocratic sword or axe and the plebeian noose as the single instrument of execution for all capital offenders.

The old fiscal system had been largely destroyed in the summer of 1789; then the hated *taille* and *gabelle*, as well as tithes, customs barriers, fiscal immunities and the authority of the Farmers-General had been swept away by the nation under arms. In replacing them the Constituents were faced with one of their knottiest problems. To meet immediate requirements a land tax was introduced, assessed on all properties and calculated to raise 240 million livres a year. Further taxes were to be levied on personal incomes and movable property, and on commercial and industrial revenues; in addition, a 'patriotic' contribution, proposed by Mirabeau, raised another 100 million livres. But these measures were quite insufficient to meet the mounting toll of debt, compensation payments and current expenditure, and they provoked violent hostility – particularly from the peasants who, complaining that they were still being over-taxed, declared in many districts what amounted to a tax-payers' strike. So exceptional remedies had to be found, of which by far the most important was the decision to nationalize the estates of the Church and put them up for public auction. To finance the operation, interest-bearing bonds termed *assignats* were issued, which gradually came to be accepted as banknotes and, after 1790, suffered steady depreciation. The *assignat* was a salutary shot in the arm and saved the Assembly from its momentary difficulties, but the inflation that it eventually brought in its train – under the impact of war and speculation – was to exact a heavy toll in terms of human suffering and popular disturbance.[2]

The nobility had, as we saw, lost their rights of private justice, fiscal exemptions and feudal dues and privileges. In addition, titles and hereditary nobility were abolished and the aristocracy ceased to exist, with other corporations, as an estate of the realm. The abolition of titles by reducing the former nobleman to the simple status of citizen, satisfied the commoners' demand for social equality. But more far-reaching in its consequences was the removal of feudal burdens from the land in 1789 when, as discussed above, the Assembly distinguished between one type of feudal obligation and another, thus betraying the deputies' anxiety not to transgress more than absolutely necessary against their own declared principle of the inviolability of property. They accepted the contention of Merlin of Douai, an accepted legal authority, that certain rights had been usurped or established by violence: among these were the rights of conducting manorial courts, hunting and fishing rights, the right to maintain warrens, dovecotes, mills and wine-presses, to collect tolls and market fines, to levy personal taxes and compulsory service labour (*corvée*) and, above all, to keep peasants in personal bondage. But others, though often a heavier burden on the peasantry, were declared to be lawful rights of property: these were the various payments made in respect of the holding or transfer of land, such as the *cens* and *champart* (rents paid in cash and in kind) and *lods et ventes* (tax on the sale of land). Such redemptions, or discharge of obligations, could be paid off at a rate of 5 per cent of their capital value in the case of payments made in cash, and 4 per cent for those made in kind. The peasants, however, as we noted before, failed to appreciate the nicety of these distinctions and refused to pay any compensation whatsoever – until the Jacobin Convention, four years later, declared the debt to be null and void.

The abolition of tithe also benefited the peasant proprietor, but there remained the great mass of sharecroppers and landless labourers who were largely untouched by these arrangements. The nationalization and sale of Church lands provided a possible solution, but sale by auction tended, in most cases, to favour large purchasers, and little was done by the Constituent Assembly to sell land in small lots or to encourage the rural population to combine resources. In this respect, their Jacobin successors, though their intentions were more generous, did little better. So an important part of the agrarian problem remained unsolved and would continue to be so even after the Revolution ended.

As befitted an Assembly in which middle-class commercial interests played so large a part, the Constituents were more consistent and thorough in their handling of commercial and industrial reforms. These, however, were omitted from the Declaration of Rights. Meanwhile, opinion had hardened against the anomalies and controls of the *ancien régime*, and the Assembly passed a number of laws that, in large measure, removed past restrictions on the nation's economy and introduced free trade in the internal market. A unitary system of weights and measures was introduced; local tolls on roads and rivers were abolished and customs posts rolled back to the national frontiers; and the guilds and controls on manufactured goods (a controversial issue in the *cahiers* of the Third Estate) were finally suppressed in February 1791. In matters relating to external trade, their policy was less decisive and betrayed a clash of opposing interests. Thus the India Company lost its monopoly, trade beyond the Cape of Good Hope was released from controls, and Marseilles lost its privileges in trade with the Levant. But freedom of trade was another matter when it came to commercial relations with other European countries: tariffs were maintained to protect French industries, though manufacturers failed, for the present, to persuade the Assembly to repudiate the 'free trade' treaty signed with England in 1786. However, all parties closed ranks when faced with the problems of labour. In June 1791 the Constituents, for fear of unruliness among the unemployed, closed down the public workshops (*ateliers de charité*) set up to absorb and employ the workless in 1789. The same month they passed the famous Le Chapelier law, by which 'coalitions' of workers (or unions) were once more declared illegal, a law that was all the more strictly enforced as food prices, for lack of controls, were liable to rise. The measure followed strikes of carpenters and other tradesmen in Paris and was passed in response to the protesting petitions of manufacturers. No one in the Assembly, not even Robespierre, objected, and trade unions remained proscribed throughout the Revolution. The law was not finally repealed until 1884.

Most intractable of all the problems tackled by the Constituents, and most fateful in its consequences, was their settlement of the affairs of the Catholic Church. The solution that they found was not determined by philosophical contempt for religion, by ingrained anti-Catholic bias or by particular considerations of class; the deep divisions and hostility that the settlement provoked were due, in part at least, to circumstances outside the Constituents' control. It had been generally accepted – not least by bishops and parish clergy – that the Church was in grave need of reform. As a corporative body, the Church of the *ancien régime* had enjoyed immense wealth, privileges and authority: the value of its properties, yielding an annual income of between 50 and 100 million livres, represented something between two-fifths and one-half of the landed wealth in every province of the realm; and it was exempt from all taxation other than what it voluntarily offered to the Treasury in the form of a *don gratuit*. A large part of these properties was held, not by the secular clergy, but by monasteries and chapters which, as impropriators of tithe and other revenues, often paid a yearly stipend, known as the *portion congrue*, to the practising priest and chaplain, and whose own services to religion were being increasingly called into question by clergy and laymen alike. So little regard was in fact shown for the contemplative orders that, after an enquiry in 1768, no fewer than 1,000 communities had been disbanded and their properties transferred to secular uses. A social gulf separated the higher clergy of aristocratic bishops and abbots from the common run of parish priests: while a bishop of Strasbourg drew revenues of 400,000 livres and a wealthy abbot of Angers 50,000 livres, a humble *curé* might be expected to subsist on a income from tithe or *portion congrue* of 1,000 or 700 livres a year. Other diversions, too, had arisen: Gallican bishops, universities and Parlements had combined in 1762 to disband and expel the Jesuits; Jansenism, though a declining force after mid-century, persisted to confuse preacher and parishioner on matters of doctrine; and – most significant of all –

the parish priests resentful of increasing episcopal pretensions, had begun to voice the insistent demand that the Church should be governed, not merely by bishops and canons, but by the whole company of its pastors.[3]

So the Church had been swept into the Revolution as a divided force, though by no means as a disinterested observer. While bishops and abbots had supported the 'aristocratic revolt' and called for the convocation of the States-General, the parish clergy saw their opportunity of settling old scores when the Royal Council's intructions of January 1789 granted them the right to attend the electoral assemblies in person, while monks and canons might only send representatives. Taking full advantage of this dispensation, the parish clergy called in their separate *cahiers* for extensive reforms, including Church self-government that would allow their voices to be heard and even the right to elect their own bishops. Such claims could not be too easily ignored when they came, in point of numbers, to dominate the assemblies of their order at Versailles. Here, as we have seen, it was they who gave the warmest support to the demands of the Third Estate, and their defection from their clerical superiors played no small part in deciding the King, against his own inclinations, to order the two higher Estates to join the self-styled National Assembly. So it was not altogether surprising that the Assembly should receive support, rather than discouragement, from the main body of the clergy when, in August 1789, it decreed the abolition of tithe, annates and plurality of offices, and ended the old corporative status of the Church and its right of self-taxation. Nor was the clergy unduly alarmed when, as proposed by Talleyrand (then Bishop of Autun), it was decided to nationalize Church properties and put them up for auction. Again, when in February 1790 the Assembly dissolved, or regrouped, the monastic orders, few tears were shed except by those most immediately affected. It was not in fact any of these measures that brought Church and Revolution into serious conflict; this happened only when the Assembly, anxious to control the Church more fully, went on to adopt the Civil Constitution of the Clergy in the following July.

Yet, even now, the collision was not immediate and might perhaps have been averted. Several of the Constitution's provisions were acceptable enough to the main body of the clergy: neither bishops nor parish clergy had any particular objection to becoming salaried servants of the state; the priests, at least, were to be paid more generously than before; and the Constituents, though granting fuller freedom of worship to Protestants (and later to Jews) had no intention of disestablishing the Catholic Church or of ending its privileged status as the single state Church of France. Again, the clergy was prepared to accept a long-overdue redrafting of diocesan and parochial boundaries; but the drastic reduction of bishoprics from 135 to 83 (to accord with the number of departments) meant that several bishops – and many more parish priests – would be deprived of their livings. More serious still was the refusal of the Assembly to submit the Constitution, before it became law, to a synod of the Church for its sanction: thus both bishops and parish clergy might have been appeased. But 'corporations' had been abolished, and to refer to an assembly of the Church that which it was the sole duty of the 'nation' to decide upon would, it was objected (by Robespierre among others), be to subject the 'general will', as interpreted by the nation's representatives, to the overriding veto of a single corporative body. On this point the Assembly, apart from its clerical members, remained adamant. So canonical sanction (if any) had to be sought from the Pope. But Pope Pius VI, although known to be hostile to the Revolution, was engaged in delicate negotiations concerning the future status of the old papal enclave of Avignon and, fearing to prejudice his temporal interests by an over-hasty decision on a matter of doctrine, delayed his answer for several months. The Assembly, however, was in a hurry: sees and livings were falling vacant and, for lack of firm guidance and authority, the clergy was becoming confused and divided.

So, in November 1790, the Assembly decided to wait no longer and burned its bridges. It declared the Civil Constitution to be in force and ordered clerics holding office to take an oath of allegiance to the constitution of the kingdom (and therefore, by implication, to the Constitution of the Clergy as well). The lay deputies, firmly convinced that an agreement would be reached, were appalled by the result: only two of the Assembly's forty-four bishops and one-third of its clerical members complied. The clergy at large became divided into two more or less evenly balanced opposing blocs of 'jurors' and 'non-jurors' – a division that became all the more irrevocable when Pius at last, in March-April 1791, slammed the door on any compromise by condemning the Civil Constitution as a whole, suspending the conformist bishops (Talleyrand and Gobel) and expressly instructing all clergy to withhold, or to withdraw, their allegiance to the new Church settlement. So, once the Pope had spoken in these terms, those who acknowledged his authority or merely followed their own conscience in refusing the oath, became by inevitable stages the declared opponents not only of the Civil Constitution but of the Revolution itself and, as such, were identified by 'patriots' with aristocracy and counter-revolution. From this followed, in turn, the tragic and fateful sequence of emigration, proscription and even massacre of 'refractory' priests, the civil war in the west, terror and counter-terror. Another consequence was that, in time, the new Constitutional Church itself, whose doctrine was the same as that of the proscribed 'fanatics', also lost credibility, was separated from the state, persecuted in the days of 'de Christianization', and followed by cults of Reason, of the Supreme Being and Theophilanthrophy – until the old Church was re-established on new foundations by Bonaparte's Concordat of 1801.

But this, of course, is to anticipate events lying far beyond the tenure of the Constituent Assembly. It is also a reminder that the Constituents, though possibly the most significant, were not the only legislators that played a part in rebuilding France and in shaping her future after the overthrow of the *ancien régime*. Inevitably, important changes took place as the nation passed through the successive stages of a constitutional monarchy, a first republic, a consulate and empire. These political developments and their consequences – some ephemeral, others more enduring – we will consider in later chapters.

IV The Struggle for Power

1 *Fall of the Monarchy*

In proclaiming the Constitution on 28 September 1791 and in commending it to Frenchmen with a stirring plea for national unity, Louis XVI solemnly declared: 'The Revolution is over.' It was a hope that was shared, far more sincerely, by the Assembly's majority and even by some of the democratic opposition. Yet, within a year, the Constitution had been brushed aside, the King had lost his throne, leading constitutional monarchists were being proscribed or had gone into exile, and the Revolution, far from being completed, was entering a new and decisive phase.

Why had the situation changed so abruptly? In the first place, the King had only accepted the Constitution with his tongue in his cheek: long before it had been signed, he had made an unsuccessful bid to seek safety in flight and, having been returned ignominiously to his capital, he continued to intrigue with the rulers of Sweden, Prussia and Austria for the restoration of his old authority by force of arms. So the King – and still more the Queen – could not be trusted, and their desertion and treachery made it impossible for the constitutional monarchists to continue to govern or to achieve the sort of compromise that their Constitution had envisaged.

Again, only a minority of the nobility had willingly accepted the surrender of their old rights and privileges. Many had followed Artois and Breteuil into exile, or joined Condé's *émigré* army at Coblenz and Worms; however, these men never accounted for more than one in twelve of the former noble families of France. Another, smaller, minority actively opposed the Revolution from within and some 1,250 of these, it has been recorded, fell victim to the guillotine.[1] Some came to terms with the Revolution and numerous former aristocrats took part in the work of the assemblies, committees and tribunals even at the height of the Terror: the National Convention in 1793 included twenty-three ex-nobles, of whom seven were marquises and one a prince of the blood. But these were, of course, not typical. The great majority, though remaining in France and surviving the Terror, were never reconciled to the new order; they formed a constant focal point of dissension, sullen resentment and suspicion, and provoked the revolutionary authorities to take ever harsher measures to restrain their liberties and keep them in check.

More serious perhaps was the division caused among the clergy by the new Church settlement. By alienating many of the parish priests, the revolutionaries of 1790 had embarked on a course that was to drive considerable numbers of the clergy and of their flocks among the devout and socially backward peasantry of the west and south-west into the arms of counter-revolution. There followed the bitter civil and guerrilla warfare of the Vendée in the west, and in parts of the south and south-west, which was to drain the future Republic of its manpower and resources and provoke ever harsher measures of repression.

These dissensions would, in themselves, have made it impossible to arrest the course of the Revolution and to stabilize its gains on the basis of the settlement of 1791. Yet it was not only the opposition of forces having more to lose than to gain by the Revolution that drove it onwards, but, perhaps even more, the intervention of classes that had looked to the outbreak of 1789 for a solution to their problems and whose initial hopes had, in the outcome, been disappointed or only partially fulfilled. The peasants, as we have seen, had been freed from the tithe and the more oppressive taxes and feudal obligations, but few had satisfied their hunger for land, and the burden of debt still remained. Small and landless peasants and sharecroppers suffered, like townsmen, from rising food prices, and they had received little or no protection from the encroachments on their old communal rights by enterprising farmers (the so-called *coqs de village*) and landowners. So the Revolution in the village continued, though no longer with the explosive force of 1789, and served in its own way to stoke up the factional warfare of rival political groups. Again, among small urban proprietors and professional men, there were many who had been debarred from voting – and many more were disallowed their right to sit in the Assembly – by the restrictions imposed, on Sieyès' suggestion, in October and December 1789. Such men would play a leading part in the campaign to end the distinction between active and passive citizens and the qualification of the 'silver mark' (52 livres).

Above all, there was the continued and increasing dissatisfaction of the bulk of the urban *sans-culottes* – the small shopkeepers, workshop masters and wage-earners – particularly those in Paris, who had ensured the success of the Revolution of 1789 and had yet received no substantial reward, in the form either of political rights or of the material benefits of higher wages or cheaper and more adequate supplies of food. Their particular grievances and aspirations were of long standing, but in the context of revolution they had been given a new content and a sharper definition by their own participation in events and by their acquisition of the new infectious slogans and ideas of the 'rights of man' and the 'sovereignty of the people'. Thus, by stages, the *sans-culottes* became a political force to be reckoned with and, by finding allies and champions among the political factions contending for power, served to deepen the antagonism among the bourgeois groups and to drive the Revolution leftwards along courses neither intended nor desired by the men of 1789.

Yet, had France remained at peace with the rest of Europe, it is possible that, in spite of such disruption, the Revolution might have stopped its course or, at least, not been carried far beyond the settlement of 1791. But war broke out in April 1792 and, by the violence of its impact, immeasurably sharpened all existing tensions. As Engels wrote to Victor Adler a century after the event: 'The whole French Revolution is dominated by the War of Coalition; all its pulsations depend upon it.'[2] Inevitably, war gave fresh encouragement to those wishing to destroy the Revolution from within and without, and provoked in turn exceptional measures against counter-revolution, aristocracy and 'fanaticism'. It exposed the duplicity and treachery of the Court and brought about the downfall of the monarchy. It led to inflation and rising food prices, and hence to vigorous resistance and agitation by the urban *sans-culottes*. Through inflation, treachery, defeat and social disturbance, it compelled the Assembly, contrary to its own cherished principles, to set up a strong 'revolutionary' government, to institute the Terror, to control prices and to mobilize the nation for war. It was against this background of initial peace followed by war and social conflict that leaders and parties contended for power and the Revolution moved on through new phases, alliances and political experiments.

The year 1790 had been one of comparative social peace. The price of bread had fallen temporarily to its normal, pre-Revolutionary level, popular disturbance was in abeyance, and the Assembly was able to proceed, almost undisturbed, with its constitution-making. But the opening months of 1791 witnessed a revival of agitation. The Parisian democrats of the Cordeliers Club, lying to the south of the river, had begun to interest themselves in the plight of the unemployed, whose workshops were being closed down, and to give some support to striking workers. They had taken up the fight against the *marc d'argent* ('silver mark') and the disfranchisement of passive citizens, and were enrolling wage-earners and craftsmen in 'fraternal' societies affiliated to the parent-club. This deliberate indoctrination of the *sans-culottes* by the democrats was to yield a rich harvest in the future, but it might have taken longer to show results had it not been for the King's attempt to escape across the imperial border. To cover up his intentions Louis had instructed his minister, the Comte de Montmorin, to send out to foreign courts in April 1791 a letter extolling the virtues of the Revolution (described as 'only the destruction of a multitude of abuses accumulated over centuries through the errors of the people or the power of the ministers'). But both before and since he had, in secret correspondence with Spain, Sweden and Austria, repudiated all concessions made to the Third Estate and Constituents as having been extracted by force, and, since the end of 1790, the plan of escape that took place in June 1791 had been worked out with the Queen's devoted knight-errant, the Swedish Count Fersen. The plan was to leave Paris in disguise by night and to join the Austrians at the eastern frontier-town of Malmédy, whence a call would be made to Europe's rulers to intervene against the Revolution. Owing to the bungling of the King and his companions and the vigilance of a village postmaster, the plan miscarried and, on 25 June, the royal family was brought back from Varennes to Paris under heavy military guard and civilian escort (with Barnave in attendance).

The episode had an electrifying effect and destroyed many illusions. For fear of an invasion, troops were mobilized at the frontiers, the Paris clubs intensified their agitation, and demonstrations called for Louis' abdication and the proclamation of a republic. The Constituent Assembly was divided, but agreed on a compromise: the King was suspended from office but, having given a pledge to accept the pending Constitution, he was reinstated and the story was put out that he had been 'abducted' by enemies of the Revolution. The democrats and Republican journalists of the 'popular' Cordeliers Club, and even many of the more sedate sister club of the Jacobins, refused to accept the verdict and organized a series of protesting petitions. The last of these, while not specifically demanding a Republic, called for Louis' abdication and was supported by a large crowd in the Champ de Mars in Paris. Some 6,000 had already signed (or put their crosses on) the petition displayed on the *autel de la patrie*, when the Paris Commune led by Mayor Bailly decided to proscribe the demonstration, declared martial law and sent Lafayette, commander of the Paris militia, with 10,000 National Guardsmen to disperse it. Meeting opposition, the Guards opened fire, killing and wounding some sixty petitioners; a further 200 were arrested, while the Cordeliers Club leaders – including Danton – sought refuge in flight. It was a fateful episode, not so much because it won new recruits for the Republican movement (as yet in its infancy) as because from now on the old Third Estate of 1789 was irrevocably split. Three weeks before, to mark their disapproval of the democrats' agitation to remove the King from office, the majority of constitutional monarchists, headed by Barnave and the brothers Lameth, had broken with the Jacobin Club, in which deputies of both left and centre had hitherto been united, to form their own society, the Club des Feuillants. Thus the Jacobins, among whom Robespierre, the deputy for Arras, was playing an increasingly active role, emerged as the acknowledged leaders of the left within the Assembly and of the popular movement outside; and Jacobins, Cordeliers Club democrats and *sans-culottes* (the name was just beginning to stick) were drawn together in common opposition to the majority of Constituents, now held responsible not only for denying the humbler citizens the vote but for shedding their blood as well.

The King's flight, though its immediate effects were masked by the Assembly's attempts to forgive and forget and to unite the nation around the new Constitution, had other far-reaching consequences. It played its part in the series of developments leading up to the outbreak of war with Prussia and Austria on 20 April 1792. Though urged by Artois and the *émigrés* to intervene firmly against the Revolution, the 'liberal' and one-time 'enlightened' Austrian Emperor Leopold II, who had succeeded to his brother Joseph's throne in 1790, had resolutely refused to take action. He no doubt regretted the indignities suffered by his sister, Marie Antoinette, but he had pressing problems to attend to within his own dominions and, like Pitt's government in England, he was inclined to welcome some measure of constitutional reform in France. The picture was changed by Louis' flight from Paris and his subsequent suspension from office; and, believing the French royal family to be in physical danger, Leopold issued the Padua Circular on 5 July, inviting Europe's rulers to restore 'the liberty and honour of the Most Christian King'. This threat, however was considerably toned down in the Declaration of Pillnitz issued jointly by Austria and Prussia on 27 August: by this time Louis had been recalled to office, the Constitution was on its way and, besides, the response of the other powers to the Circular had been distinctly chilly or lukewarm. Consequently, the Declaration was more of a face-saver than a threat of war and merely invited the powers, *if* they could all agree, to prepare to unite and restore order in France. There was no suggestion of an immediate armed intervention. Yet, whatever its intentions, the Declaration was a provocation which both served to unite the counter-revolution at home and abroad by giving it a programme, and provided the war party in France with a further pretext for banging the martial drums.

For, quite apart from the alleged crimes of the Revolution, the possibility of armed conflict between France and Austria already existed. The Emperor's *protégé*, the Elector of Treves, had allowed Condé's army of *émigré* nobles to train and arm within his territories at Coblenz, and the German princes holding estates in Alsace had refused to accept the abolition or redemption of their feudal dues as decreed by the French Assembly in August 1789. Treves in the end submitted to French coercion and agreed to disband the counter-revolutionary force at Coblenz, and negotiations on the princes' claims might, in spite of the support given them by the Emperor and his Diet at Frankfurt, have ended in agreed settlement if there had been a reasonable measure of goodwill on either side. But this proved impossible, because of both the growing belligerency of the Imperial Court (Leopold was succeeded in March 1792 by the more aggressive Francis II) and the emergence of a strangely assorted, but highly vocal, war party in France. On the one hand there was the Court itself which, encouraged by the Austrian-born Queen and her advisers, began to count on France's military defeat as the best means to restore its own authority. Closely associated with the Court was the War Minister, Narbonne, current lover of Necker's daughter Madame de Staël, whose plan (though he never made it explicit) seemingly was to provoke a limited war with a view to strengthening the power of the Crown by way of a military dictatorship.

However, the most effective voice of all in rousing the country to a state of warlike fervour came from the new left in the Legislative Assembly (which had succeeded the Constituents on 1 October 1791). It was that of Jacques Pierre Brissot, deputy for the Eure et Loir, who was closely associated with a group of deputies, several of them from the south-western department of the Gironde.[3] From October 1791 on, Brissot preached an armed crusade against the crowned heads of Europe, in the course of which the peoples, liberated by their own endeavours or by the victory of French arms, would rally to the flag of revolution, while the King would be compelled to call on Brissot's supporters to take office. Brissot carried the argument from the floor of the Assembly to the Jacobin Club where, in December, a heated debate took place between himself and Robespierre. Robespierre alone of the Jacobin leaders at this time opposed Brissot's plan for a military crusade on the grounds that, far from promoting the cause of revolution abroad, it would serve to promote Narbonne's aim of a military dictatorship at home. But Brissot won the day and the main body of Jacobins, the Parisian sections and clubs, and the great majority of the deputies of the Legislative Assembly rallied to his view. After negotiations with the

Emperor and the German princes broke down in March, France declared war on Austria on 20 April and soon faced the combined armies of Austria and Prussia, led by Frederick the Great's old general, the Duke of Brunswick (now, admittedly, rather long in the tooth).

But Brissot's triumph was short-lived and it was Robespierre who in the long run proved to be correct; his party, not Brissot's, was to reap the harvest. Yet at first things appeared to go Brissot's way: even before war broke out, the agitation in the Paris sections was so pronounced that the King was compelled to dismiss Narbonne and his Feuillant ministers and call to office men of the Brissot connexion – Dumouriez, a professional soldier and spokesman for the anti-Austrian party, Claviere, a Swiss financier, and Roland, a civil servant and husband of a more famous wife. But the French forces, far from acting as 'armed missionaries', were quite unprepared for battle (still less for an offensive) and fled in disorder from Brunswick's armies, leaving France open to the enemy. Armed counter-revolution broke out in the south. The *assignat*, the newly adopted banknote, had fallen to 63 per cent of its face value in January and grain riots followed in the provinces. In Paris, as the result of civil war in the West Indian colonies, the price of sugar had trebled and provision shops in the Faubourgs were broken into by angry citizens, who compelled grocers to sell their wares at the former price. Treachery in high places added further fuel to the flames: the Queen's intrigues with the Austrian Court were becoming widely suspected and the conviction grew, and was ably exploited, that an 'Austrian Committee' was planning to restore the absolute monarchy with the aid of foreign arms. Brissot had boasted that such treasonable practices would redound to the advantage of his own party ('*il nous faut de grandes trahisons*,' he had claimed), and he and his associates did not hesitate to inflame popular passions against the Court. So much so that Louis felt obliged to dismiss the Brissotin ministers – an action that provoked a popular demonstration in Paris on 20 June, in the course of which the small shopkeepers and craftsmen of the two revolutionary Faubourgs of St Antoine and St Marcel paraded in arms before the Assembly and broke into the Tuileries palace, where they obliged the reluctant Louis to don the Cap of Liberty and drink with them to the health of the nation.

This proved to be a dress-rehearsal for the greater and more violent insurrection of 10 August that captured the Tuileries and overthrew the monarchy. Yet the Brissotin party, though it had stoked the flames and its ministers had been reinstated in office, derived no profit from the demonstration. In fact by this time they had surrendered the leadership of the popular movement to Robespierre and their Jacobin rivals. The truth is that, like the sorcerer's apprentice of legend and many other parties before and since, they were not prepared to face up to the consequences of the storm they had unleashed. Having demagogically aroused the sections and Faubourgs to demonstrate against the monarchy and having threatened to overthrow it, they now drew back in support of the King: they had not bargained for a republic that would be at the mercy of the votes and weapons of the hitherto 'passive' citizens, or *sans-culottes*. So the Jacobins, who had had little to do with the demonstration of 20 June, stepped into the breach. Pétion, who had succeeded Bailly as Mayor of Paris and was associated with Brissot and the Gironde, was still the hero of the day when the annual Festival of the Federation was celebrated on 14 July. But, by the end of the month, the mood had changed and forty-seven of the capital's forty-eight sections had declared for the King's abdication – by this time, Sieyès' old distinctions had broken down and passive citizens had been invited to attend the sectional assemblies. Yet, even now, Robespierre was arguing that the future of the monarchy, as of the Constitution itself, should be decided by a popularly elected Convention rather than by a resort to arms. But the genuine fears of a counter-revolutionary *coup* (the air was thick with rumours of plots and General Lafayette had recently deserted the front in order to urge the Assembly to introduce drastic measures against the democrats) and the pressure of the sections and clubs persuaded the Jacobin leaders to promote an armed insurrection. Preparations were already underway when popular fears and hatreds were given a sharper edge by the Duke of Brunswick's Manifesto of 1 August, which threatened the Parisian sections and National Guard combined under the direction of a newly formed 'revolutionary' commune to capture the Tuileries by force of arms and drive the King to seek refuge in the Legislative Assembly. He was deposed six weeks later by the National Convention, which succeeded the Legislative in September, and the Republic was proclaimed soon after.

In the wake of the 'revolution' of 10 August 1792 followed the grisly episode known as the September Massacres, when the prisons of Paris were entered by armed bands who set up hastily improvised 'people's' tribunals and executed some 1,000 to 1,400 of their inmates – priests and political prisoners among them, but mainly common law offenders: thieves, prostitutes, forgers and vagrants.[4] It was a mysterious event, defying precise analysis, yet it seems to have been largely the product of a panic-fear engendered by the threat of counter-revolution and invasion. Verdun, a bare 200 miles from the capital, had just fallen to the Prussians, and able-bodied Parisians, responding to the summons of Danton, the new Minister of Justice, were flocking to enrol for service at the front, thus leaving the city more exposed. While the massacres were going on, and for some days after, there were persons in authority who were prepared to applaud them as a necessary act of popular justice, and even to recommend them as an example for other cities to follow. But once the crisis was past, there was no party or faction that would justify or claim credit for them, and the charge of having provoked or condoned them – or even of having failed to stop them – became an accepted weapon in the struggle between parties, in which the two main factions – the Jacobins and the 'Girondins'* – sought to blacken each other, while royalists and moderates hurled the accusation at both parties without discrimination. And yet, whatever their origins and unsavoury as they were, the massacres were an event of some importance: they appeared to complete the destruction of the enemy some weeks before the volunteers at Valmy, on 20 September, routed Brunswick's army and drove it back across the frontier. Thus the Republic, proclaimed that autumn, became established on what seemed a solid enough foundation – by the victory of the Revolution over its enemies at home and abroad.

* For the use and abuse of these terms and the rivalry of the opposing groups see next chapter.

2 *Girondins and Jacobins*

The new Assembly, or National Convention, elected by male adult suffrage[1] – though still in two stages – met on 20 September 1792. Of its 750 members only 96 were former Constituents, while 190 others had sat in the Legislative Assembly. So there were many new faces among them, including that of the youthful Saint-Just, who was to become Robespierre's devoted supporter and lieutenant. Socially, they differed little from the members of the two preceding Parlements: there was a similar preponderance of former officials, lawyers, merchants and businessmen, though appreciably more provincial *avocats*, doctors and teachers. As before, there were no small peasants, and there were only two working men – Noël Pointe, a munitions-worker from St Etienne, and Jean-Baptiste Armonville, woolcomber of Rheims. Politically, the Convention was composed of three main groups, whose political commitments, compared with the more rigidly structured political parties of today, were relatively fluid.[2]

The majority – though by no means a stable one – was generally formed by the great mass of independent deputies, with no permanent commitment to any particular faction or programme, known as the 'Marsh' or 'Plain'. To win their support would, of course, be a vital element in the struggle of the other parties for control of the Assembly. Of the latter, the larger group (in the early stages at least) was that of the 'Girondins' (as the former Brissotins were now termed by their opponents) led by Vergniaud, Brissot, Gensonnet and Guadet, who, though not themselves in a majority, often controlled the balance of voting and supplied most of the ministers. Against them were ranged the Jacobins or Mountain (so called from the upper tiers of seats they occupied in the Assembly). They included all but one of the twenty-four deputies of Paris, headed by Robespierre, the ever-popular Marat and (on occasion) Danton. Among them, too, was the King's cousin, the former Duke of Orleans (now known as Philippe-Egalité).

To pursue the analysis further, can it be seriously maintained, as Mathiez did, that the conflicts that now ensued between the major factions – between the Girondins and Jacobins, in particular – were based on differences in class? According to this argument, the Girondins tended to be wealthier and to draw their main support from prosperous citizens, like the shipbuilders of the south-west (hence the term 'Girondins'). The Jacobins were seen to be poorer, small-town lawyers and the like, and thus naturally drawn towards the *sans-culottes* as their main constituency by their own relatively humble economic situation.[3] Following Mathiez, this view has been often expressed or merely accepted without dispute, but as far as I am aware the attempts so far made to give it a more solid substance by the study of incomes, wills and bequests (by Soboul among others) have yielded only meagre results. So it has seemed preferable in the account that follows to consider the case unproven and to present the conflicts between groups and individuals not in such simplistic terms, but rather in terms of geography, political and social pressures (what Saint-Just called 'la force des choses'), outside events such as war and economic crisis, opportunities offered, and even (though not predominantly) clashes in personality. Differences in ideology certainly played a part, but they applied less to the factions as a whole than to groups or individuals within them.

The first phase of the Convention's history was marked by a prolonged and bitter duel between the Gironde and the Mountain, which only came to an end when, eight months later, the leaders of the former were purged from the Assembly by a popular insurrection in late-May to early-June 1793. In this duel, the Gironde at first had the advantage of numbers, of having at their service the greater part of the Paris press, and of enjoying considerable support in the provinces. On the other hand, their equivocal behaviour in the August uprising had lost them their former following among the Parisian militants. The Mountain, while weak in the provinces, had, as the acknowledged victors of August, the solid backing of the Paris sections and clubs, whose members crowded into the Assembly's galleries to give their continual and vociferous support. Thus the Jacobins now emerged as the consistent champions of Paris and as the main bastion of revolution, while the Girondins – whose policies were not basically different – were driven, partly from choice and partly from the circumstances of their election and from the tactics of their opponents, to advance 'federalist', or national–provincial, policies in deliberate opposition to the pretensions of the capital but, in other respects, not greatly distinguishable from those promoted by the Constituents of 1789–91. Again, while all parties were committed, with varying degrees of enthusiasm, to the prosecution of the war to victory, the Girondins, as firm believers in economic liberalism and spokesmen for business interests, were far more consistent – and doctrinaire – than their opponents in clinging obstinately to *laissez-faire* solutions in all matters relating to the nation's economy, food supplies and the general conduct of the war. The Jacobins, too, were predominantly *bons bourgeois* and showed little inclination for a directed economy, still less for a division of properties. But they were closer to the people, more flexible in their attitudes, and more willing and able to yield to popular pressure, as expressed in the streets and sections and in the galleries of the Assembly, and to adapt their views to meet the needs of the moment. Thus the Girondins, to whom largely fell the task of government, fell foul of the sections and popular movement in Paris (by resisting exceptional measures and controls), and when a further round of treasons and defeats faced the Republic in the spring of 1793 they were held accountable and lost further credit. It was this and their growing tendency to promote the 'federalist' claims of the provinces against Paris and against the Jacobin conception of 'the Republic one and indivisible' that finally provided their opponents with the pretext and the occasion to expel them from the Convention.

Meanwhile, the struggle for power was waged over more immediate issues. In the first round, the Gironde succeeded in persuading the Assembly to disband the 'revolutionary' Commune that had usurped authority in Paris on the eve of the August events and had armed itself with exceptional powers. Once the crisis was over their exercise was bound to be offensive to the nation's elected representatives, so the Jacobins did little to justify the Commune's extra-legal activities and, after a few heated exchanges, gracefully consented to its liquidation. More stubborn and prolonged was the battle over the King's trial and execution. After his surrender to the Legislative Assembly, Louis had been lodged in the Temple prison, lying in the north of the city, to await his fate. Robespierre now proposed on behalf of the Jacobins, that he be brought before the Convention and sentenced to death as a traitor to the nation. There should be no formal trial, he urged in a famous speech, as the King had already been judged by the people under arms: 'The right of punishing the tyrant and the right of dethroning him are the same thing; they do not take different forms.' The people having already passed judgement, the Convention had merely to record a sentence of death. While accepting a part of this argument, the Assembly decided in favour of a trial, but one in which it should itself be both prosecutor and judge. Many of the Girondin deputies wished to spare the King's life, but such was the weight of evidence against Louis (an iron chest containing his secret correspondence had recently been recovered from the Tuileries) that they chose to join in the unanimous verdict of guilty. Following this, they resorted to manoeuvre: having failed to obtain a stay of execution, they demanded a referendum, but again they were outvoted. Finally, the sentence of death was passed by open ballot (*appel nominal*), and Louis was sent to his execution on 21 January 1793.[4]

However, as long as victories could be recorded for French arms – and the troops of the Republic had, following the rout of the Prussians at Valmy and Jemappes, recently annexed Belgium and were preparing to occupy Holland – the Girondins, with greater ministerial support, retained the balance of power within the Assembly. But, in March, Dumouriez was driven back from the Netherlands and, failing to persuade his army to march on the Convention, disperse the Jacobins and restore the Constitution of 1791 with Louis XVII as King, he deserted to the enemy. Mutual recriminations followed in the Convention. The Girondins, as close associates of the General, were the more exposed, but to defend themselves they turned the attack against Danton, who had been sent to parley with Dumouriez on the eve of his desertion. The attempt failed: Danton, hitherto a mediator between the warring factions, was driven into closer partnership with the Mountain, and the Gironde emerged further scathed from the encounter. Another result of this crisis was that the Assembly, under the compelling pressure of events, was persuaded to enact a number of exceptional measures that would prove of the greatest importance to the revolutionary government of the future: they included the creation of a Revolutionary Tribunal, a Committee of Public Safety and 'revolutionary committees' armed with exceptional disciplinary powers in the sections and communes, and agents despatched to the provinces vested with the Convention's authority and soon to be known as 'representatives on mission'.

Meanwhile, the economic situation was also working to the advantage of the Mountain and to the detriment of its adversaries. The *assignat* had fallen to only half of its nominal value in February and the price of food, after remaining comparatively stable in the preceding summer and autumn, had taken another sharp upward turn in the spring. Once more, the prices of colonial products – coffee, sugar, candles, soap – had risen out of all proportion; but, this time, the rise covered a far wider range of consumer goods than in February 1792. The riots that followed were, correspondingly, more intense and widespread than in the year before. On 25 and 26 February, grocers' shops in almost every section in Paris were invaded by *sans-culottes* – both men and women – who refused to pay more than they had paid for such products in 1790, and even (though rarely) helped themselves without paying anything at all. The City Council, the Jacobin Club and all three parties in the

Convention joined in denouncing this infringement of the sacred rights of property: Barère (who was soon to desert the Plain for the Mountain) spoke darkly, though without a shred of supporting evidence, of 'the perfidious incitement of aristocrats in disguise', while Robespierre deplored the fact that 'patriots' should be so far misled as to riot for what he termed '*de chétives marchandises*' ('paltry merchandise'). But, though none of the Assembly's spokesmen was prepared to condone such activities, it was once more the Girondins, as the governing party and that most thoroughly committed to upholding the freedom of the market, which reaped all the disadvantages, while their opponents correspondingly benefited. In March the Paris Commune, led by Jacobin supporters, decided to fix the price of bread with the aid of a subsidy to bakers at 3 sous a pound – a mere 50 per cent above the normal pre-revolutionary level at a time when other prices had more than doubled. Two months later, the Assembly followed by passing its first 'Maximum' law, whereby local authorities all over the country were given authority to control the price and supply of bread and flour.

Meanwhile, a movement had begun in the Paris sections, clubs and streets calling for a popular 'insurrection' to purge the Assembly of the Girondin leaders (and no doubt other deputies were intended as well). Such an uprising was, in fact, attempted on 10 March by the small group of extreme revolutionaries known as the Enragés, whose leaders were Jacques Roux, the 'red' priest of the Gravilliers section, Théophile Leclerc and Jean Varlet. The Enragés stood closer than any other group at this time to the *sans-culottes* in the streets and markets and, alone of the parties, actively supported the demand that a ceiling be placed on the prices of all consumer goods. Jacques Roux had been accused (with what justice is uncertain) of implication in the February riots. Varlet had been drawing large audiences to his open-air rostrum on the Terrasse des Feuillants at the gates of the Assembly, where he demanded the death penalty for hoarders and speculators, the impeachment of Roland, Minister of the Interior, and the removal of Brissot from the Convention. His call and that of his associates for an uprising might well have met with a considerable response had the Paris Commune, the Jacobins and the Faubourg St Antoine been willing to give it their blessing.

But the Mountain and the Jacobin leaders were in no immediate hurry. They had learned wisdom from experience, and while, unlike their Girondin opponents, they were quite willing to use the popular movement to promote their political ends, they had no intention of allowing its direction to pass into other hands – least of all to radical groups like the Enragés or to Hébert, editor of the popular *Père*

Duchesne, whose influence was steadily increasing in the Cordeliers Club and the Paris Commune. Besides, they feared that a premature rising would entail too drastic a purge of the Convention, whose 'Rump' (memories of Cromwell!) would be powerless to resist the economic demands of the *sans-culottes*, that it would be accompanied by a new outbreak of prison massacres, and that it would leave Paris isolated in the face of the combined hostility of the provinces. So they proceeded with caution, but by early April they were ready to formulate a programme of their own to win the support of the sections, and wrest leadership of the popular movement from either group of 'extremists'. Accordingly on 5 April, in the Jacobin Club, Augustin Robespierre publicly invited the sections to present themselves at the bar of the Convention and 'force us to arrest the disloyal deputies'. The response was immediate and, within a week, the sections had 'named' twenty-two deputies of the Gironde, whose removal from the Assembly would both meet the popular demand for a purge and assure the Mountain of a working majority. By mid-April three-quarters of the sections had given their support, many of them further stirred to action by the Girondins' folly in summoning Marat – the most popular of all the people's leaders – before the Revolutionary Tribunal from which, however, he was soon released and carried in triumph through the streets of Paris.

The Commune endorsed the popular demands and, a month later, responding to its invitation, the great majority of the sections formed a Revolutionary Committee at the former Archbishop's Palace, which organized and directed the 'revolution' of 31 May–2 June with almost military precision. The National Guard was enlarged and its command given to Hanriot, son of a domestic servant and a former customs clerk, in succession to Santerre, the wealthy brewer of the Faubourg St Antoine. In addition, it was decided to raise in the sections a revolutionary militia of 20,000 *sans-culottes* who should be compensated for their loss of work by the payment of 40 sous for each day spent under arms. The tocsin was sounded, workshops and points of entry to the city were closed, and after several false starts the Tuileries were surrounded on 2 June by a combined force of National Guards and armed *sans-culottes*. The 'named' deputies, after attempting a dignified sortie from the Assembly and finding every exit barred, surrendered ignominiously to the insurgents' demands. Twenty-nine deputies and two ministers of the defeated party were placed under house arrest. There was nothing said for the moment about the most urgent item on the popular programme — that food prices be controlled – but the Mountain had achieved its immediate aims.

From now on, the Jacobin leaders were assured of a working majority and they proceeded, with remarkable speed, to celebrate and (they hoped) to consolidate their victory by passing through the Convention and primary assemblies a long-prepared and long-debated constitution to replace that of the now irrelevant Constitution of 1791. Discussions on the project went back, long before the Girondins' expulsion, to December 1792. Then a committee of nine, composed of the almost inevitable Abbé Sieyès, six Girondins and two Jacobins, was appointed to prepare a preliminary plan of work. A first draft was debated at length on 15 February, but more urgent matters intervened and debate was adjourned until 15 April and resumed, with the Girondin faction still in attendance, on 24 April and 10 May. But soon after other matters of importance intervened once more and, of course, after the events of 31 May–2 June, the Girondin-inspired text (by now adopted) had also lost its relevance. So it was left to the Mountain, with its newly gained ascendancy both inside and outside the Assembly, to redraft a constitution of its own.

The Jacobin Declaration of Rights was important because it added to that of 1789 the principle of the freedom of worship no longer inhibited by the proviso that it must not 'disturb the social peace'; and the freedoms of trade and of the economy were now more explicitly stated. In addition – and this was a more original departure – the aim of society was declared to be the happiness of all ('le bonheur commun'); work or (if unavailable) financial assistance should be provided for the poorer citizens as 'a sacred obligation'; pensions should be given to soldiers wounded in battle or (if incapacitated or deceased) aid to their nearest of kin; and the government was pledged to provide adequate compensation for damage suffered by its citizens through war or civil war. And, in the last of its thirty-five clauses, the Declaration sternly proclaimed:

> When the government violates the rights of the people, insurrection is for the people, and for any portion thereof, the most sacred of rights and the most indispensable of duties.

The Constitution itself provided for a Legislative Assembly to be elected for the first time by direct male adult suffrage; for an Executive Council to be nominated by the Assembly from candidates previously selected by all enfranchised citizens meeting in their local assemblies; and (adopting a proposal made by Condorcet before the Girondin purge) a popular referendum to ratify the Constitution prior to its final adoption. Yet the Constitution had undoubted shortcomings. Most important of these was its failure to take heed of a number of proposals already put forward by Robespierre in a long speech of 24 April: among them that the rights of property must 'be limited ... by the obligation to respect the property of others', and that the right to work or assistance should be made open to all and not only to '*les citoyens malheureux*' (the poor and needy). And, finally, the Montagnard majority was no more inclined to include four clauses proposed by Robespierre on international brotherhood and the universal Rights of Man than the Girondins had been before them.

Even so, in spite of such shortcomings (and Jacques Roux, the 'red' priest, was able to spell out many more to the Assembly), the Declaration and Constitution of June 1793 marked the highpoint in the liberal phase of the Revolution. Here for the first time in history a nation was given (on paper at least) a system of government, both republican and democratic, under which all male adults (with a few exceptions) had the right to vote and to a considerable measure of control over their representatives and rulers. One class of citizens, in particular, proved to be early beneficiaries of the Constitution and of the Jacobins' assumption of power. These were the peasants who, by a law of 3 June (following hot on the heels of the Girondins' expulsion), were made eligible to purchase in small lots the properties of their *émigré* owners. A second law of 10 June, of especial advantage to the village poor, provided for the division of communal property ('les biens communaux') among the population of the parish, and a third – the all-important law of 17 June 1793 – put the final seal on feudalism in France by cancelling without compensation all that remained of seigneurial dues and obligations.[5]

Yet, as is well known and a melancholy fact to many, the Constitution proved to be short-lived. Within a few months it had been put into cold storage 'for the duration'. Elections were suspended, and a highly centralized and authoritarian government came into being.

3 *Jacobins and* Sans-culottes

But, first, we must look again at the role played in these events by those other contenders for a certain share in government, the Parisian *sans-culottes*. We have already seen something of the part they played in the events of June and August 1792, in the grocery riots of 1793 and in the expulsion of the Girondin deputies and ministers in May–June of the same year. But this presentation has been somewhat piecemeal and, to bring it into sharper focus, we must now attempt to put their acts together in a more structured and formal way. Moreover, the fact that the activities of the Parisian craftsmen and shopkeepers often assumed a social–economic complexion should not blind us to their political significance; and of this the Jacobins, their mentors and sometime partners, were of course well aware.

To begin with, let us go back to the food riots of January–February 1792, briefly mentioned earlier. In that year there were considerable disturbances over the price and supply of food in Paris and in the provinces, the latter occurring in April and November in the *beauceron* plain, lying to the south and west of Chartres. In both cases, the background of the crisis lay in the inflation caused by the depreciation of the *assignat*, which by then had become the sole fiduciary issue and had, by January, slumped to 65 per cent of its former value. The food riots that followed were by no means a faithful replica of those of 1775 and 1789; after nearly three years of revolution, both the cause and the content of such disturbances had undergone an important change. For one thing, the Revolution had given all forms of popular protest a political dimension which they had almost entirely lacked before. We have already noted, through the entries in Hardy's Journal, how this process began in Paris between November 1788 and February 1789. But what had then been only a beginning, and was therefore still sporadic and occasional, had by now become a constant and continuous feature, so that food riots like any other form of popular protest – and this applied as much to the provinces as to Paris – could no longer escape the intrusion of political ideas. In the Beauce, for example, anti-royalist sentiments were expressed that were completely absent from the riots of the past. Itinerant bands paraded to cries of 'Vive la Nation!' and announced themselves to villagers and townsmen as 'brothers and liberators'; and at Amboise in the Touraine, they chanted the slogan: 'Down with moderates, royalists and administrators that are enemies of the People, and up with the *sans-culotte*!' Thus echoes of 1789, and even more of the patriotic war and *sans-culotte* movement of 1792, gave a particular edge to riots whose basic aims were still the same as those of the urban and rural poor of the latter years of the *ancien régime*.[1]

In Paris, there was a new development. Under the impact of war, and above all of the civil war between planters and natives in the French West Indies, the dominant issue was no longer the provision of cheap and plentiful bread. It had extended, as in the Parisian riots of 1792 and 1793, to include the 'chétives marchandises' which Robespierre had scorned – coffee, candles, sugar and other imported colonial goods. In 1792, it was the shortage of sugar that aroused the greatest concern. In January, its price nearly trebled by rising in a few days from 22–25 sous ($1\frac{1}{4}$ livres) to 3 or $3\frac{1}{2}$ livres a pound. Riots followed in the Faubourgs St Antoine, St Marcel and St Denis, and in the central commercial districts adjoining the City Hall. The rioters, believing (with some justice) that the deeper cause of the shortage was the withholding of supplies by speculating merchants and that colonial disturbance was as much a pretext as a cause, broke into the shops and warehouses of some of the larger wholesalers and dealers ('aristocrats' in the current popular parlance) and demanded that sugar be sold at its former price; in some districts they extended their operations to bread, meat, wine and other consumer goods. The disturbance began in the Beaubourg section in the city centre on 20 January with a riot of market women and spread, a few days later, eastwards to the Faubourg St Antoine, where half a dozen grocers were compelled to sell their sugar at a lower price. A further wave of rioting broke out in February. On the 14th, over twenty grocers in the Rue du Faubourg alone were threatened with invasion, and several were forced to sell sugar at 20 sous a pound before order could be restored. The same day, in the Faubourg St Marcel to the south of the river, it was rumoured that large stocks of sugar, long accumulating in a warehouse, were about to be distributed all over the city. Crowds seized the first sacks as they left under military escort and sold them in the street at 25–30 sous a pound. The next day, women – nearly always on such occasions in the forefront – rang the bell in the church of St Marcel, and attempts were made to force the warehouse doors. However, Pétion, Mayor of Paris, arrived on the scene with troops that scattered the rioters and committed fourteen prisoners to the Consciergerie gaol. They commanded considerable sympathy: a petition for their release addressed to the Assembly was signed by 150 local residents, all of them voters and two of them clergy.

It was the first substantial movement of *taxation populaire* (price control by riot) that had convulsed the capital since the grain riots of 1775. It was far surpassed, however, by the disturbances that broke out, for similar reasons, in February 1793. Prices, which had fallen in the summer and autumn, had risen again since the New Year. By mid-February, the price of sugar had once more doubled, while coffee had risen from 34 to 40 sous, the price of soap had risen in proportion and tallow candles had gone from 15 sous to 18½–20. The consequence was a popular outburst, far more extensive and persistent than that of the previous year, in which all, or nearly all, of the forty-eight Parisian sections became involved and which, perhaps more clearly than any other incident in the Revolution, underlined the basic conflict of interest between the urban *menu peuple* and the possessing classes, who included the democrats who applauded in the Jacobin Club or sat with the Mountain on the upper benches of the National Assembly. It is not surprising that, confronted with such spontaneous violence in the streets, even Robespierre should contemptuously denounce the people's concern for the price of 'paltry merchandise', and rather less surprising that Barère (a democrat by recent conversion) should speak darkly of 'the perfidious incitement of aristocrats' and insist that such 'luxuries' as sugar and coffee were unlikely objects of genuine popular concern. Yet, for all the apparent fatuity of such remarks, a further word of explanation needs to be added: such strictures, though clearly falling wide of the mark, seemed sensible enough to men reared in a belief in 'aristocratic plots' and to whom any interference with the free circulation of supplies seemed a negation of one of the most cherished 'liberties' that the Revolution had proclaimed. This basic conflict was further underscored by the events that followed.

There had been two deputations of women to the Convention on 23 February; the first, which included laundresses, complained of the high price of soap. Two days later, the riots broke out. They took the form of a mass invasion of grocers' (and chandlers') shops, in which women once more played a prominent role, and the forcible reduction of prices to a level dictated by the insurgents (the traditional *taxation populaire*): refined sugar was sold at 18–25 sous, unrefined sugar at 10–12, tallow candles at 12 sous, soap at 10–12 sous and coffee at twenty. Starting in the central market at ten o'clock in the morning, the movement spread with remarkable speed to every part of the city. Moving eastwards, it reached the City Hall district soon after ten, the former Place Royale at midday, the

Arsenal (close to the former Bastille) at two, the Driots de l'Homme section at three, the Quinze Vingts (in the Faubourg St Antoine) between three and four, and Montreuil and the Marais at four. Meanwhile, extending northwards, it gained the section of the Amis de la Patrie at two-thirty, the Louvre at four, the Palais Royal at seven, the Tuileries at eight and République at ten. From the Tuileries it appears to have crossed to the other side of the river, for there were disturbances between eight and nine that evening in the Left Bank section of the Fontaine de Grenelle. The next day minor outbreaks followed in a number of sections, in which market women of the city centre and laundresses of the Rue du Bièvre in the Faubourg St Marcel played a part. But Santerre, the commander of the National Guard, absent at Versailles on the 25th, mobilized his forces at an early hour and brought the movement to a close.

Perhaps a word should be added here about the possible part played in these riots by Jacques Roux and his fellow Enragés. It is hardly surprising that contemporaries should have held him largely responsible, though the degree of his responsibility or that of his associates was certainly exaggerated. The Enragés were the only political group in the capital that openly favoured the regulation of prices and supplies of consumer goods. Roux was a member of the Paris City Council and, on the morning of 25 February, he had made a speech defending the rioters' conduct; moreover, the disturbances had actually started in Roux's own section of the Gravilliers. From this it was easily inferred that not only had he instigated the riots but he had played an active part in their direction. Mathiez, the French historian, has been inclined to share this view.[2] But, in practice, it is difficult to establish any direct link between the 'red' priest and the grocery rioters. The most that can perhaps be said is that it appears highly likely that the views that he and his associates had persistently expressed – in the press, the City Council and before the Convention – should have aroused some measure of response among the market workers, craftsmen, small shopkeepers and housewives of the sections in which he lived or worked.

What is perhaps most important is that these movements, unlike similar movements during the *ancien régime*, were remarkably successful and, for all their connections with the past, contributed to something new. This was the law of the General Maximum of 29 September 1793. By imposing a ceiling on the prices of most articles of prime necessity (including wages) it went much further than any of the piecemeal regulations of the *ancien régime* and those that followed in the next four years. The 'Maximum', which in its essentials survived for fifteen months, had a long preparatory history. It was the outcome of the ideas of a handful of pamphleteers, popular pressure and wartime emergency; and of these the last two were incomparably more important than the first. In 1789, several *cahiers de doléances* had suggested that municipal granaries should be constructed and that wages should be geared to the price of bread (as in the later Speenhamland system, adopted as a wartime measure in England in 1795). In 1790, two Parisian pamphleteers published proposals for the state regulation of grain and flour. A Lyons municipal officer, L'Ange, went much further in urging the state to buy up the entire harvest at fixed prices and build 30,000 granaries to house it, while at Orleans Taboureau called for a Maximum and Vergniaud, though a Girondin, favoured a system of public bakeries, a rigorous control of prices based on a sliding scale, and the supervision of all bakers and millers. Something of the kind took place at Lyons when its short-lived radical Commune, in the spring of 1793, municipalized the city's bread supply. Under the impact of the provincial riots of 1792, some local authorities, including those of Orléans and Tours, urged that a ceiling be placed on the price of grain. Most, however, believed, like the National Assembly, that prosperity could only revive by the operation of free-market forces.[3] The Constituent Assembly meanwhile had, by its decrees of August–September 1789, abolished the old stop-gap regulations and restored freedom of trade in grain and flour (even more fully than Turgot had in 1774–75). In September 1792, following the first wave of riots of that year, the Convention had consented to revive the old regulations while refusing a more general control of prices.

Meanwhile, however, the needs of war, as well as the clamour of the small consumer, were gradually compelling the Jacobins, even before they came into office, to modify their views. In early May, as we have seen, the Assembly, following the example set by the Paris Commune, imposed a ceiling on the prices of bread and flour. But this was only a first step; it neither satisfied the small consumers and their spokesmen, nor did it help to solve the increasingly urgent problem of military supplies. The rioters of 1792 and 1793 had already – unlike those of 1775 or 1789 – extended their price-control operations far beyond the primal necessities of wheat, bread and flour: in Paris they had imposed controls on sugar, soap, butter, coffee, candles, meat and wine and, in the provinces, on oats, soap, butter, eggs, and even on clogs, timber, coal and iron, so there were ample precedents to follow. Meanwhile the *assignat*, having slumped to 36 per cent of its value in June, slumped further to a disastrous 22 per cent in August. So food prices rose again in the summer and, although the price of bread had been fixed, there were shortages and queues at bakers' shops in June, August and September while Jacques Roux and his associates, sensitive as ever to popular demands, had for the past eight months been campaigning for the institution of a general Maximum on prices.

Matters were brought to a head by a further intervention of the Parisian *sans-culottes*. Encouraged by their supporters in the Jacobin Club and Convention, they had during July and August poured into the sectional assemblies and purged the remaining strongholds of 'moderation' of their bourgeois and conservative elements (including, interestingly enough, the notorious Marquis de Sade from Robespierre's own section, the Section des Piques). During late August and in the first days of September, resolutions were pouring into the Convention calling for measures to place a ceiling on prices, to curb inflation and restrain speculation and hoarding. Nor was this agitation limited to mere verbal exchanges: these demands of the *sectionnaires* – the small tradesmen and owners of property – were followed up and given a sharper edge by the massive street-demonstrations of the lower order of *sans-culottes* that took place in the city on 4 and 5 September. The 'insurrection' started in the early morning with meetings of building workers and workshop journeymen of the Temple and St Denis districts, north of the City Hall. The Commune's leaders, Hébert and Chaumette, tried at first to fob them off with a display of oratory, but it was agreed, on Hébert's suggestion, that they should reassemble the next morning and march to the Convention and present demands for several measures to be taken against hoarders and political suspects. The Jacobin Club also promised to join in. The same evening the Commune, while giving orders to disperse building workers who were claiming higher wages (so there were those among the *sans-culottes* who had a quite different set of priorities!), instructed workshops to close on the morrow – as had been done for another purpose on 31 May–2 June – so that masters and journeymen might attend the demonstration with the Hébertist leaders' blessing.

In the flood of rhetoric that followed in the Assembly on 5 September, the question of prices and supplies, though they had been the prime movers in the agitation on the 4th, were once more conveniently forgotten. Yet important decisions were made: sections were to meet only twice a week, but needy *sans-culottes* were to be paid 40 sous per attendance; suspects were to be rounded up; and after several months' delay an *armée révolutionnaire*, recruited from city *sans-culottes*, was raised. This was to be an instrument of the Terror, whose purpose was to ensure the adequate provision of supplies to Paris from the neighbouring countryside.[4] At last, having tried or debated every other expedient, the Convention yielded to popular pressure and, on 29 September, passed the law of the General Maximum, which pegged the price not only of bread and flour but of a wide range of essential goods and services at levels prevailing in the departments in June 1790 plus one-third, while raising wages by one-half. The measure was well received by the small shopkeepers, masters and journeymen of the capital who had been its most eager and insistent promoters. 'The people', wrote an agent of the Ministry of the Interior the next day, 'has received with delight the decrees of the National Convention which fix the prices of essential goods.' The measure raised new problems, too, but these were not immediately apparent.

Thus a new and distinctive phase of the Revolution had opened to which the common people or *sans-culottes*, by their constant intervention, had made an essential contribution. But before we go on to consider the political results, let us stop for a moment to ask, more precisely than before, who were the *sans-culottes* and who, in particular, were the Parisians among them? It has become an important question and has met with a variety of answers since Taine, over a century ago, blasted them as a 'criminal element' or a mindless rabble.[5] Such views, expressed with such venom, are no longer fashionable, yet some historians, even today, have in more measured terms given them a degree of credibility. Furet and Richet, for example, deny that the *sans-culottes* played more than a very minor role in the events of June 1793: at best they were called in by the Jacobins as somewhat casual auxiliaries after the real – the bourgeois – revolution 'went on the skids'.[6] More recently, in an altogether different vein, Dr Geoffrey Ellis has questioned the traditional 'orthodox' or 'Marxist' view that the *sans-culottes* were really 'commoners' at all. He has argued, rather, that they belonged to higher social groups, such as prosperous craftsmen and tradesmen, professionals, public servants and the like.[7] Such conclusions are certainly worthy of attention, as the spokesmen for the *sans-culottes* – men like Roux, Varlet, Leclerc and Hébert – were most often of this kind. Yet they are too narrowly focused, they have tended to confuse leaders with followers, and they have failed to take note of the changes that took place as the Revolution advanced.

Who, then, were the *sans-culottes* – not only in 1789, but in 1793 and 1795? Basically (as both police and court records amply testify), they were drawn from the urban *menu peuple* – from the small shopkeepers and craftsmen (both masters and journeymen), servants and day-labourers of the city, but they were not drawn from Taine's social riff-raff or down-and-outs, nor substantially from the vagrants and *gens sans aveu* who flocked into Paris as the Revolution began. But that is not the whole story; for, as the Revolution developed, the *menu peuple*, from both their own and others' experience, acquired a political education and began to form a political movement and a political outlook of their own, often at variance with those of their mentors. So the word *sans-culottes*, used at first as a term of contempt for men and women of an 'inferior' life-style, began to take on a political connotation, from which the poorer elements – unemployed labourers and 'marginals' – became progressively excluded, while – *pari passu* – it became extended (and in this Dr Ellis's case has a certain justice) to include political militants regardless of social *milieu*. Thus the term *sans-culotte*, while social in origin, acquired political overtones which both enriched and obscured it.

So much for the generalities concerning the *sans-culottes* as a sociopolitical group. But how did their composition change – in terms of sex, age and occupation – in the course of their intervention in the greater or lesser *journées* (the days of riot and disturbance) as the Revolution went on? It varied widely, according to both circumstance and the issues at stake, and this again our records show. Young people – apprentices, journeymen and lawyers' clerks – were much in evidence in the early, near-spontaneous riots of the 'pre-Revolution' of 1787 and 1788, while the more structured, organized, 'political' and military occasions, like the assaults on the Bastille and the Tuileries in 1789 and 1792, attracted the master craftsmen and shopkeepers and older men (the average age of the *Vainqueurs de la Bastille* was thirty-four) who tended to be of settled abode and occupation. Wage-earners were in a majority on one occasion only: in the Réveillon riots of April 1789, which raised the question of wages as well as of the price of bread. Women, too, were more prominent on some occasions than on others: in the food riots of 1792 and 1793, in the march to Versailles in October 1789 and, in somewhat similar circumstances, when they marched on the Assembly in March and May 1795. And what these records further illustrate is that Taine's repeated claim of a 'criminal element' – measured in terms of previous convictions of a more or less serious nature – has little or no substance at all.[8]

And now, after this digression, let us return to the events that followed the capture of the National Convention by the new Jacobin rulers. Like their predecessors, the Jacobins owed their ascendancy largely to the active intervention of the people, but unlike them they had quite deliberately courted the *sans-culottes* and accepted them as allies. In return for their support, the *menu peuple* had, by the autumn of 1793, received substantial benefits: they had won the right to vote and their demand for cheap food and the control of supplies had been met. Not only that but, by now, there had also emerged a certain division of authority between the governing party and its popular allies. While the Jacobins controlled the Assembly, the major means of communication and the organs of government from which the junior partners were almost entirely excluded, the popular militants for their part had come to dominate the forty-eight sections, the 'revolutionary' committees and 'popular' societies, and to fill the highest posts and offices in the City Council and the battalions of the National Guard. This partnership, though advantageous to both, was riddled with contradictions and proved to be short-lived; the differences had already become apparent on the morrow of the common victory and would become sharper in the critical months ahead. Its bonds already loosened in October 1793, by the summer of 1794 the alliance would lie in ruins and bring down both partners in its fall.

4 'Revolutionary' Government

The 'revolutionary' government did not begin to emerge until October 1793, yet this new stage of the Revolution really opened when Robespierre and his principal lieutenants joined the Committee of Public Safety, the main organ of government, in early July of that year. Up till then, the Committee had done little more than serve its original purpose of acting as a watchdog over the executive council of ministers. Now it became the core of a strong government, the first that the Revolution had created.

The twelve men who from now on composed the Committee were a remarkable team: 'a stranger set of Cloud-Compellers', Carlyle wrote of them, 'the Earth never saw'. They by no means formed a close-knit party group, and it was only the pressing problems of the moment that forced on them cohesion and unity of purpose. The weakest and shortest-lived was Hérault de Séchelles, former parlementaire and aristocrat, who had achieved temporary distinction for the part he played in expelling the Girondins in June. He fell from the Committee in late December and, three months later, was guillotined with Danton. Two members had, since June, emerged from the Plain: Bertrand Barère, a 'trimming' lawyer, and Robert Lindet, who took charge of food supplies. Four men were to concern themselves mainly with military matters and supplies to the armed forces: Prieur of the Marne, lawyer and emissary to the armies; Prieur of the Côte d'Or, an engineering officer who undertook the supply of munitions; Jeanbon Saint-André, a Protestant ex-pastor and specialist in naval affairs; and the great Lazare Carnot, a military genius whom even Napoleon described as 'the organizer of victories'. There were two strong-arm men of the left recruited from the Cordeliers Club after the September riots: Collot d'Herbois, a former actor, and Billaud-Varenne, lawyer and pamphleteer. They were matched in vigour and eloquence by Robespierre's two intimate associates: Georges Couthon, also a lawyer, confined to a wheelchair; and Louis-Antoine Saint-Just, a law graduate barely twenty-six years of age, a visionary and man of action, proud and courageous and said by an opponent to 'carry his head like the Holy Sacrament'. And, lastly, there was Maximilien Robespierre, who, though holding no particular office, soon became accepted as the Committee's outstanding leader.

Robespierre was born at Arras in 1758, the son and the grandson of lawyers. He acquired a taste for the classics and a love for Rousseau from his Oratorian teachers at the College of Louis-le-Grand in Paris. It was from Rousseau that he drew his belief in the sovereignty of the people and in the social utility of a religion stripped of superstition, and his social ideal of a republic of small and middling property-owners, uncorrupted by either wealth or poverty: this conception lay at the back of much of his talk of 'corruption' and 'virtue'. Already known as a poor man's advocate, he was elected to represent the Third Estate of his native town in the States-General of 1789. At Versailles and in the Constituent Assembly, he soon distinguished himself as a liberal and a democrat and as a consistent champion of the Rights of Man. After September 1791, being debarred, like other Constituents, from sitting in the Legislative Assembly by a 'self-denying ordinance' of his own promotion, he devoted his energies to the Jacobin Club and the administration of the capital. In the winter and spring of 1791–92, his opposition to Brissot on the great issues of the 'revolutionary' war lost him his popularity for a while among the Paris sections and clubs, but by the summer his reputation had been restored and he played a leading part (though behind the scenes) in the overthrow of the monarchy, joined the 'revolutionary' Commune after the event, and became the Mountain's chief spokesman in its duel with the Gironde in the National Convention. He took no direct part in the May–June insurrection that expelled them, but in many ways his was the brain that inspired it. By this time, having long been an ardent defender of the inviolability of the Assembly and of the unrestricted freedom of speech and the press, his cumulative experience of war and revolution had brought him to shed his former liberal beliefs. The Revolution, he now maintained, could only be saved and its external and internal enemies defeated if, with the aid of the armed *sans-culottes*, a strong central government were set up to restrain both the remnants of aristocracy and the 'egoism' of the rich. 'What we need [he wrote at the time] is a *single will*. This rising must continue until the measures necessary for saving the Republic have been taken. The people must ally itself with the Convention, and the Convention must make use of the people.' It was a programme that looked beyond the June 'days' to the tasks facing the Committee of Public Safety in the autumn and winter of 1793.

Meanwhile, the Jacobins had even more pressing problems to attend to. Stirred by 'federalist' agitation, the city of Lyons and parts of the south and south-west had overthrown their local Jacobin authorities and risen in arms against the newly purged Convention. Toulon, the great naval base, was preparing to surrender to the English (at war with France since 1 February 1793). And the revolt of the Vendée peasants – soon to be followed by that of the Breton and Norman *chouans* – had been sapping the country's military strength since March. Danton and his allies, charged with intriguing to make peace with England, were removed from the Committee of Public Safety in July and relaced by men (Robespierre and Saint-Just among them) whose first priority was to conduct a 'revolutionary' war. The west-country rebellion was taken seriously in hand, and a properly equipped force despatched to the Vendée achieved early success. Caen, Bordeaux, Nantes, Marseilles and Lyons were wrested from the rebels and restored to revolutionary authority, and the siege of Toulon was raised, largely through the skill and initiative of a young artillery officer, Napoleon Bonaparte. On 23 August, the Convention agreed in principle to mobilize the nation for war by ordering a *levée en masse* of the whole French population: the young should go to battle and married men forge arms, women stitch tents and uniforms and children make bandages, while even the old men were to 'repair to the public squares, stimulate the courage of the warriors and preach the unity of the Republic and the hatred of Kings'. State workshops were set up to manufacture arms; armies were recruited, trained and equipped by the organizing genius of Carnot; representatives were sent on continuous missions to the front to strengthen the troops' morale and ensure the adequacy of their supplies. Thus the Republic, with nearly a million men under arms, began to clear the soil of the invader: Jourdan defeated Coburg at Wattignies in October; Hoche pursued the enemy across the Vosges; Kellermann freed Savoy; the Spaniards were driven back over the Pyrenees; and, finally, in June 1794, Jourdan's victory over Coburg at Fleurus drove the last enemy soldier across the border.

Meanwhile, the 'economic' Terror had at last brought speculation and inflation under control: the *assignat*, having fallen to 22 per cent of its value in August, rose to 33 per cent in November and to 48 per cent in December. During these months, too, in spite of war, the supply of food to the population of the cities was probably more regularly assured than at any time since the autumn of 1791. The peasants' debt to their landlords was finally written off in the summer of 1793, while some (admittedly half-hearted) efforts were made to encourage small peasants to combine and purchase the lands of *émigrés*, now put up for auction in smaller lots. Possibly more radical in intention, though they came to nothing, were the Convention's later decrees, proposed by Robespierre and Saint-Just, to divide and distribute the confiscated properties of 'suspects' among poor and needy 'patriots' (the laws of Ventôse, February–March 1794). The Committee also looked to the future by laying before the Assembly a succession of drafts relating to education, industry, the civil code and public assistance. Some of them did not survive the fall of their promoters; others became part of the body of laws that eventually emerged from the Revolution. It is little wonder that the great Committee has, on one score or another, won praise even from some of its severest critics.

But, to realize their aims, France's new rulers were compelled, far more by the logic and pressure of events than by the teachings of the *philosophes*, to abandon the haphazard methods of government accepted by their predecessors, and Robespierre's conception of a government of 'a single will', hastily sketched in June, began to take shape in the autumn. Its basis had already been laid by the exceptional measures adopted because of the crisis of March 1793, and others had followed in August and September. But it was one thing to call the nation to arms and to threaten hoarders and speculators with summary justice; to direct the whole operation by what has been commonly called a 'Reign of Terror' was quite another. The matter was urgent as, during the autumn months, administrative anarchy prevailed in a number of departments as local committees, *armées révolutionnaires* (several raised without authority from Paris) and powerful 'pro-consuls' like Fouché, Tallien and Carrier, armed with extraordinary powers to suppress rebellion, tended to interpret and apply the law after their own fashion.[1]

So the needs of war, civil peace and public order – quite apart from any personal considerations – combined to persuade Robespierre and his associates to take further steps to strengthen their control in Paris. Such measures, to be effective, could hardly fail to flout the liberal–democratic provisions of the Constitution of June 1793. On 10 October, the Convention was persuaded to take the first step by declaring that 'the provisional government of France is revolutionary until the peace'. Thus the exceptional measures adopted before were given a greater degree of permanence and the Constitution of 1793 was, for the time being at least, suspended. But to conclude from this, as many critics have done, that this was intended all along and that 'revolutionary' government corresponded to the long-cherished ambitions of the Jacobin leaders is to misrepresent both their principles and the evolution of their policies. We have no means of knowing whether they ever sincerely hoped to restore the Constitution once the war was over; we do know that it was not they but their successors who finally buried it and proscribed its defenders. Marat, it is true, had long since called for a one-man dictatorship on the Roman model; but Marat cared little for 'philosophical' niceties and, anyway, had nothing to do with the new forms of government, having been stabbed to death by Charlotte Corday in July 1793. Robespierre and the other leaders, however, were highly susceptible to the teachings of the *philosophes* and these prescribed not a dictatorship or a Jacobin-style 'revolutionary' government, but a strong legislature, a weak executive and the 'separation of powers'.

Admittedly, Rousseau's writings on the state and on the 'general will' might provide an argument: had he not suggested that it might be necessary to 'force men to be free'? But the system of government that took legislative shape in the law of 4 December 1793 – a system, it should be noted, that was as readily accepted by the Plain as by the Mountain – was the product of neither Rousseau nor Montesquieu. While deriving their authority solely from the Convention, the two Committees of General Security and Public Safety were vested with full executive powers. The first was made responsible for police and internal security: thus the Revolutionary Tribunal and the work of the local vigilance and 'revolutionary' committees were to be its special province. The Committee of Public Safety was given far more extensive powers: to control ministers, appoint generals, conduct foreign policy and to purge and direct local government. In fact, the transfer of authority and the centralization of goverment were effected at the expense not so much of the Convention as of the departments and communes. Only in one respect was the authority of Parlement ostensibly weakened: by curbing the independence of the 'representatives on mission', sent out by the Convention since April, and subjecting them to the rigorous control of the Committee of Public Safety. But the activities of local authorities were far more severely restricted: departments were left with purely routine functions, districts were made responsible for executing 'revolutionary' decrees, and the old *procureurs* (proctors or procurators) of departments and communes were replaced by 'national agents' answerable to the central government. The independence of Paris, long the mainstay of the Jacobins in their struggle for power, was further curbed by depriving the Commune of the right to send commissioners to the provinces, by limiting its control over the National Guard, and by subjecting the 'revolutionary' committees of the sections to the direction of the Committee of General Security. The Terror remained, but it was now institutionalized and directed from the centre. It was the end of anarchy, but it was the beginning of the end of popular initiative as well.

Thus, strong government had emerged, and it is doubtful if the Republic's achievements could have been realized without it. Yet, by its very nature, it could hardly fail to provoke a chorus of protest from former supporters and injured parties. The opposition arose, in the first place, from within the Jacobins' own ranks and from their allies of the Cordeliers Club, but it was by no means united, and it divided early into two main factions. The opposition of the right gathered around Danton and the so-called party of the Indulgents, and that of the left round Hébert and the leaders of the Paris Commune and Cordeliers Club. Danton, dismissed from the Committee of Public Safety in the reshuffle of 10 July, retired at first with a new wife to his country estate at Arcis-sur-Aube and appeared to be nursing his wounds in silence. But encouraged by old friends – among them Camille Desmoulins – he returned to the capital in November and began to lead what was alternately a pressure-group and an organized opposition within the Assembly. In so far as the Dantonists had any precise political programme it was to break the 'revolutionary' government, restore the independence of local authorities, dismantle the Terror, liberate the national economy from controls and negotiate a peace – in the first place by detaching England from the European Coalition. They divided their activities: Danton was their spokesman on matters of higher policy; Desmoulins founded a new journal, *Le Vieux Cordelier*, in which he campaigned for greater 'clemency' and the release of 'suspects'. Others, being perhaps of a more practical disposition, displayed their contempt for economic controls by dabbling in share-deals and engaging in shady financial ventures.

Unlike the Dantonists, the left opposition had little following in the Convention: their main hunting-grounds were the Cordeliers Club, the Commune, the *armées révolutionnaires* and the clubs and sections, among whose militants they enjoyed considerable support. The Jacobin leaders had already destroyed their main rivals for popular favour, the left-wing group of the Enragés, and had arrested their leaders: Jacques Roux had committed suicide in his cell in October. Since then, Hébert had taken over Roux's programme and grafted it on to his own. In his popular and scurrilous organ, *Le Père Duchesne*, he called day in and day out for a more vigorous prosecution of the war and a more frequent use of the guillotine against hoarders and speculators, merchants and shopkeepers, whose activities were undermining the price-controls enacted by the Convention. Hébert and his lieutenant Chaumette also played, with

Fouché, a leading part in stoking up the campaign against the Christian religion in both Paris and the provinces. While the Assembly had generally restricted its coercive measures to the 'non-juring' or 'refractory' clergy, the Constitutional Church now also came under fire; and in the wave of 'de-Christianization' that spread from Paris and the department of the Nièvre (where Chaumette had a following), churches were closed wholesale, priests and bishops were compelled to give up their offices, and the Goddess of Reason was enthroned in the Cathedral of Notre-Dame.

The *sans-culottes*, too, had their reasons for feeling injured: the new government measures were, in fact, partly directed against them. They had, as we have seen, become a force to be reckoned with by those in authority, whether as allies or opponents. Gradually, through a series of purges, the Paris sections and the Commune had been recast in their social image: during this period of the Revolution, nearly three in four of the members of 'revolutionary' committees were small manufacturers, tradesmen and craftsmen; and similar elements accounted for 93 of the 132 general councillors of the Commune.[2] In many provincial centres, the proportion of *sans-culottes* on local governing committees may have been even higher.[3] This created a problem of divided counsels, as it is hardly surprising that the political ideas and social aspirations of such men should differ in important respects from those of the proprietors, lawyers, doctors, teachers and businessmen who sat in the Convention or even from those of the smaller lawyers, tradesmen and civil servants who predominated in the provincial Jacobin clubs and societies.[4] While both Plain and Mountain now favoured strong government to destroy the Revolution's enemies and win the war, the *sans-culottes* clung to the discarded Constitution of 1793. They passionately believed that popular sovereignty was essentially vested in the primary assemblies, and therefore in the Paris sections, and they demanded the frequent recall and constant accountability of deputies to their constituents. Such being their views, they could hardly fail to challenge the Jacobins' claim that, 'for the duration', the Convention and the leading Committees should be the sole custodians and executors of the 'general will'. Again, while the Jacobins and the Convention – even the Robespierrists among them – allowed controls and state-direction of the nation's economy only as exceptional and temporary measures, the *sans-culottes* wanted them to be permanently enforced, as they appeared to ensure security and social justice: in September, a Paris section had even called for a ceiling on incomes and limits to be placed on the size of farms and businesses.[5] And while the Jacobins, as employers and members of parliament and government committees, were concerned to check the steep rise in wages, the wage-earners among the *sans-culottes* (particularly numerous in Paris) had every motive and, owing to the shortage of labour in time of war, every opportunity for pushing up earnings as high as employers would be willing to pay. So, in one way or another, by the end of 1793 the alliance between Jacobins and common people was beginning to wear thin.

At first, it was the Hébertist challenge that faced the Jacobins with the greatest danger. The violent attacks on priests and churches by the 'de-Christianizers' filled the Jacobins with particular concern: they had enough difficulty already with the peasant rebellion in the west, without gratuitously driving great numbers of Frenchmen whose religious beliefs persisted into the arms of counter-revolution. So when, in November, the Commune closed down every place of worship in Paris, Robespierre riposted by denouncing Fouché, Chaumette and their associates as atheists and diversionists, and called for a return to the Convention's agreed policy of the right to worship. Danton, returning from Arcis and seeing an opportunity to drive a wedge between Robespierre and his two former associates of the Cordeliers Club, Collot and Billaud, joined in the fray. So a three-cornered struggle ensued, variously fought out in the Jacobin Club, the Convention and the two Committees, in the course of which the government's spokesmen, led by Robespierre, alternately sought allies in one faction or the other, but more frequently leaned towards Danton and the Indulgents in order to weaken and destroy the left. Thus encouraged, the Indulgents stepped up their own campaign, and the growing violence of their denunciations, particularly those of Desmoulins in *Le Vieux Cordelier*, compelled Robespierre to break with the Dantonists and engage both factions at once.

The outcome was the almost simultaneous destruction of both groups. In early March, Hébert and his Cordeliers Club allies, Vincent and Ronsin, tried to force the pace by threatening another insurrection on the model of that of June or September 1793. But it was a gesture of despair rather than of strength as, by this time, their hold on the Commune and the sections had been weakened. The conspirators were arrested and guillotined on 25 March; Chaumette followed them to execution three weeks later. This equally sealed the fate of Danton and Desmoulins, whose survival, after the destruction of Hébert, would have led to a move to the right and the overthrow of the Committees. Robespierre's personal affection for Desmoulins (dating back to the days of Louis-le-Grand) made him hesitate to sign their death-warrant, but his scruples were overruled by Saint-Just, Collot and Billaud and, after a hurried and embarrassing trial, the Dantonists were executed on 5 April.

Danton's fate, though distasteful to former associates in the Convention, caused not a ripple of protest in the sections or among the *sans-culottes*. Hébert's execution, too, was taken calmly and the prevailing mood was one of apathy rather than anger. But the very silence was ominous: Hébert had been a familiar mouthpiece for popular passions and prejudices and his removal sapped the links that had bound the *sans-culottes* to the Commune, now purged and converted into a Robespierrist stronghold. Besides, Hébert's fall had inevitably been accompanied by an attack on those popular institutions in which his influence had been strongest. The Parisian *armée révolutionnaire* was disbanded, and the committees for tracking down hoarders were dissolved, soon to be followed by those 'popular' societies that lay outside the close scrutiny and control of the Jacobin Club. As the 'revolutionary' committees had already been firmly tied to the Committee of General Security, the sections themselves soon ceased to reflect the independent views and activities of the *sans-culottes* and tended to become mere rubber-stamps for Jacobin direction and government decisions. Saint-Just noted the change and summed it up in a phrase: 'the Revolution has become frozen' ('la Révolution est glacée').

The *sans-culottes*, thus politically silenced, were further estranged by the government's economic measures. The Maximum laws, after rousing early enthusiasm, had proved a disappointment. For a while prices remained stable, but the laws could only be enforced by further measures of coercion and repression, which the government, anxious to retain the support of peasants, merchants and manufacturers, was quite unwilling to take. So producers, large and small, began to resort to wholesale evasions of the law, and shopkeepers, in turn, passed on the higher prices to their customers. The *sans-culottes*, as small consumers, reacted violently, demonstrating against butchers and grocers, and demanding more vigorous measures of control. By January, the authorities were faced with the choice of either intensifying the Terror against the law-breaking merchants and producers or officially relaxing the regulations at the expense of the protesting consumers. Urged by Barère, they decided on the latter course. In late March, an amended Maximum was published providing for higher prices and profit margins, currency speculators were allowed to show their faces again, and the *assignat* had, by July, slipped back to 36 per cent of its nominal value. So the agitation in the markets revived and the Jacobin leaders got their share of the epithets hurled at merchants, speculators and shopkeepers. And more was to come. The Maximum law of September 1793 provided for the control of wages as well as prices. As things stood, this meant that local authorities were required to *reduce* wages to a level no higher than 50 per cent above that prevailing in 1790. This had already been done where workers' resistance was not expected to be strong; but not in Paris, where wages had risen two or three times above their pre-revolutionary level and where the Commune, as long as Hébert and his lieutenants were in control, had little intention for fear of losing popular support of enforcing this part of the law. The government itself, however, was responsible for wages in its own workshops and had introduced new scales (tempered somewhat by expedience) for its arms-workers and others. Meanwhile, to prevent wages in private industry from getting out of hand, it had on more than one occasion invoked the Le Chapelier law against workers' 'coalitions' and had even sent strikers before the Revolutionary Tribunal. Yet the greater problems remained and, even after the fall of Hébert, the Commune hesitated before taking so dangerous a step as to reduce the current earnings of a large part of the Parisian population by one-half, or even more. When they took the plunge and published the new scales on 23 July, it was an ill-chosen moment, and the hostility of the wage-earners no doubt played a part in Robespierre's fall from power a few days later.

5 *Thermidor*

The revolutionary government fell, together with its Robespierrist leaders, in late July 1794 (on 9th–10th Thermidor, according to the Revolutionary Calendar). Its fall may be attributed, in the short term at least, to a combination of factors, including (paradoxically) the successful conduct of the war and the suppression of rebellion in the north, souths and south-west. It was the result of divisions between government and Assembly and between and within the two Committees, as well as the defection of the *sans-culottes*; these were allied to *personal* factors such as the clash of personalities within the great Committee and miscalculations by the Robespierrists – by Maximilien himself, in particular.

Since the early summer, Robespierre and his group had been losing their hold on the Convention and the governing Committees. The Convention had accepted the successive purges of Girondins and Dantonists, but their elimination left fears and resentments that another crisis would bring out into the open. These had been stirred afresh by the law of the 22nd Prairial (10 June 1794) and the speed with which it had been rushed through the Assembly. The law, drafted by Robespierre and Couthon, after an attempt had been made on the lives of Robespierre and Collot, speeded the process of justice within the Revolutionary Tribunal and deprived the prisoner of the aid of defending counsel; but it also appeared to many deputies to threaten their parliamentary immunity. From this law, too, sprang the 'Great Terror' which, in Paris, accounted for nearly 1,300 of the guillotine's 2,600 victims. But more important, perhaps, in weakening the links that had hitherto bound Robespierre and the deputies of the Plain was the victory won at Fleurus on 26 June, as a result of which the Republic was cleared of foreign troops and the road to Belgium once more lay open. So why, the whispering began, continue to support a policy of Terror and tightened belts, a policy reluctantly accepted at a moment of crisis, when that crisis now appeared to be past? Besides, the danger from the left was over: the 'wild' men of the Commune had been silenced and the *sans-culottes* had had their wings clipped and their leaders arrested. So the alliance between Mountain and Plain, having lost its purpose, began to disintegrate and the cordiality of allies to give way to resentment and suspicion – all the more so as it was rumoured by Robespierre's enemies that he and his group, far from preparing to relax the rigours of 'revolutionary' government, were drafting further proscription lists and were aiming at the establishment of a dictatorship, or 'triumvirate'.

Meanwhile, deeper divisions had arisen in the two governing Committees, both within the Committee of Public Safety and in the relations between the two. Since the law of December 1793 that prescribed their respective duties, there had been a certain overlap in their operations: the Committee of General Security was nominally responsible for all matters relating to police and internal security, but the other Committee had its own right of access to the Revolutionary Tribunal. Recently the overlap had become more serious when the Committee of Public Safety in April created its own police department for prosecuting erring and dishonest public officials; this inevitably tended to draw the anger of the rival Committee's members on to the heads of Robespierre and Saint-Just, who had made the new department their special concern. When Robespierre and Couthon hurriedly drafted the law of 22nd Prairial, they omitted to consult those who considered themselves most intimately concerned with its operation. The Security Committee had its revenge: by stacking the tumbrils with victims in June and July (or so it would seem), they contributed to that *nausée de l'échafaud*, or revulsion against the guillotine, that rebounded on the heads of the government's best-known leaders. Again, Robespierre's enthusiasm for a civic religion on a Rousseauesque model had led him to persuade the Assembly to adopt his own creation, the Cult of the Supreme Being (7 May 1794) – a measure calculated to discomfort both 'atheists' and 'fanatics', though it might cater to the beliefs of the great bulk of religiously minded revolutionaries, whether former Roman Catholics or others. Whatever might have been its ultimate reception (the Cult perished with its author two months later), its immediate result was to draw the fire of de-Christianizers and Volitairian deists, who feared a revival of Catholic 'fanaticism' and suspected Robespierre of aspiring to be the 'pontiff' of a new religion. Among those who held such views and did not hesitate to air them were Amar and Vadier, leading members of the Committee of General Security.

Within the Committee of Public Safety a conflict of principles and personalities had been waged since May. Bitter disputes had broken out between Carnot and Saint-Just on the conduct of military operations. Carnot accused Saint-Just, who had been a successful emissary to the armies in Alsace and in the north and had played a distinguished part at Fleurus, of meddling with matters beyond his competence. The 'practical' men, Carnot and Lindet, who tended also to be moderates rather than radicals, clashed increasingly with the 'ideologues', Robespierre, Couthon and Saint-Just, whom they accused of being over-indulgent towards the *sans-culottes*. Lindet, for one, objected on this score to the laws of Ventôse, which he believed would weaken the incentive to work. Robespierre, in turn, found himself increasingly at variance with the views of the 'terrorists', Billaud and Collot, who continued to parade Hébertist sympathies. Collot had been Fouché's partner in the savage pacification of Lyons and was closely associated with a group of other 'terrorists' who had been similarly employed – Barras and Fréron at Toulon, Tallien at Bordeaux, and Carrier at Nantes. As the crisis developed, such men, fearing the hostility of Robespierre, who had had several of them recalled by the Assembly to account for their excesses, tended to rally round Billaud and Collot and stand together in common defence against their accuser.

By the end of June, the atmosphere within the Committee of Public Safety had become so charged with suspicion and mutual recrimination that Robespierre withdrew in disgust from its meetings and confined his activities to his private office in the Rue St Honoré and the forum of the Jacobin Club. In the long run, the gesture had fateful consequences. Suspicion deepened against him when, refusing Barère's offer of mediation, and apparently ignorant of his dwindling support within the Plain, Robespierre decided to appeal to the Convention against his dissentient colleagues. So, in a long speech on 8th Thermidor (26 July 1794), he passionately defended his conduct against his critics and pleaded that the Revolution could once more be saved, and the reign of 'virtue' finally triumph, if only a last surgical operation were performed – the removal of a small group of 'impure' men, men (he charged) who '[were] giving the revolutionary government a bad name in order to destroy it' and at whose identity he hinted but whom he obstinately refused to name. It was a fatal miscalculation – or was it simply prompted by fatigue or a deliberate courting of martyrdom? – of which Saint-Just, who was aiming at a compromise, appears to have heartily disapproved. Robespierre was heard in silence and – a signal indication of disapproval – the Convention refused to allow him the usual courtesy of sending his speech to be printed; while Barère, ever susceptible to changing winds, rallied to the new majority.

That same evening, the identical speech was enthusiastically applauded in the Jacobin Club. But the alliance of moderate Jacobins, Plain and frightened 'terrorists' proved to be the stronger.

During the night, the confederates concerted their plan of action for the Convention's session on the morrow. Saint-Just, who had prepared a speech for the occasion and rose to defend his colleague, was shouted down. Robespierre was greeted with cries of 'Down with the tyrant!' and was refused a hearing. Saint-Just, the two Robespierres and their brother-in-law Lebas were placed under arrest, and sent under close escort to the Committee of General Security.

Yet, even now, the day might not have been lost if the Paris sections and their armed battalions had rallied in support of the Jacobin leaders, as in August 1792 and June 1793. The Commune as well as the Jacobin Club continued to voice support for the arrested men; Hanriot, the Robespierrist commander of the Parisian National Guard, escaped from the squad sent to arrest him; and the turnkey of the prison to which Robespierre and his fellow prisoners were directed refused to acknowledge their escort's mandate, so that they were free to seek refuge among their friends of the Commune. But, despite the dilatoriness of their opponents, the leaders were unable to recover their lost fortunes, partly because they themselves lacked the will or the desire to lead an insurrection (though it seems unlikely from his past career that Robespierre was such a stickler for legal niceties as has sometimes been claimed). But far more important was that the *sans-culottes*, estranged by their recent policies, showed little inclination to take up arms for a cause they no longer believed in. It was certainly not for lack of time or opportunity to make up their minds. All through the afternoon and evening, the two contending parties, based respectively in the Commune and the Convention, sent mutually conflicting orders, threats, pleas and declarations to the sections and the battalions of the National Guard, appealing to their loyalties. At one time, in response to the Commune's summons, over 3,000 armed men, supported by thirty-two pieces of artillery, were drawn up outside the City Hall. But they lacked both leadership and purpose and, as the tide of debate in the sectional assemblies and 'revolutionary' committees turned against the Robespierrists, the whole of this force gradually melted away. Meanwhile, the Convention had declared the 'conspirators' to be outlaws; and Barras, armed with the Convention's mandate, encountered no resistance when, in the early hours of 10th Thermidor (28 July), he appeared at the City Hall with 6,000 men and carried off his prisoners for formal identification by the Revolutionary Tribunal. A few hours later, they were hustled to the Place de la Révolution (the present Place de la Concorde) for execution.

Among twenty-two victims, Maximilien Robespierre, who had

been gravely wounded by a pistol-shot, was the last but one to be guillotined. It was perhaps typical of his austere probity that he should have left an estate of £100 or less. Babeuf, then a critic, wrote a year later that his 'goods and chattels' were sold for a mere 'three hundred francs in coin'.[1] The next day, seventy-one councillors of the Commune, also implicated in the 'Robespierrist conspiracy', followed him to the guillotine. It was the largest, and the last, of the legal holocausts in Paris. With them perished not only a man or a group but a system. The events which followed Thermidor were hardly what the most active of Robespierre's opponents – and still less the passive bystanders, the Parisian *sans-culottes* – had expected or bargained for.

6 *A Republic of 'Proprietors'*

Robespierre's fall led to something of an anti-climax. The Revolution continued, though at a slackened pace, and the Republic – now become a 'republic of proprietors' – lingered on through a series of crises, until Bonaparte's grenadiers swept it away in the *coup d'état* of 18 Brumaire (9–10 November, 1799).*

It was not at all what Barère and his fellow conspirators of Thermidor had planned for. Reporting to the Convention on 28 July 1795, Barère described the recent events as 'a partial commotion that left the government intact'. But he failed completely to grasp the nature of the crisis he had helped to provoke. The Revolution, far from keeping on its course, took a sharp rightward turn (it has even been argued that it stopped altogether). Within a month, the 'revolutionary' government had been abandoned or been recast; within a year, he and his companions, smeared with the Robespierrist taint, had been shipped to Devil's Island. The *sans-culottes* were once more disarmed and disfranchised, and the rulers of 1795 – the men of Thermidor – after a period of hesitation, tried to revive the 'principles of '89' on a new foundation.

It was now the turn of the Plain to take over the direction of affairs. New men came forward: Boissy d'Anglas, consistent advocate of a return to government by men of property; converted 'terrorists' like Barras, Tallien and Fréron; and two lawyers, Merlin of Douai and Merlin of Thionville. Sieyès reappeared after merely 'existing' (as he said) during the months of Jacobin Terror, and for a short while Cambon, financial wizard of the Jacobin Convention, and Robert Lindet carried influence as opponents of the 'Incorruptible'.

* The Revolutionary (or Republican) Calendar was adopted by the newly Jacobin-dominated National Convention in July 1793 and put into operation from 22 September of that year, but it was made retrospective to the year 1792, which thus became 'Year I' on the Calendar. Months were of thirty days each and corresponded broadly to the seasons. Thus Vendémiaire, the opening month, was the harvest month, followed by Brumaire, the misty month; Ventôse, the windy month; Frimaire, the frosty month; Pluviôse, the rainy month; and so on. The remaining five days of the year (six in leap year) were called *jours sans-culottides* in the period of high Jacobin influence, and *jours complémentaires* thereafter, under the Thermidoreans, the Director and Napoleon. The Calendar continued in use until the end of 1805, when the Roman Calendar was reinstated.

But soon, like many others, they became tarnished by their old associations. Later, these groups were reinforced by a return to the Assembly (by election or co-option) of seventy-five former Girondins whom, ironically, Robespierre had saved from execution, and by a handful of royalists: these tended to form a right wing within the Convention. Meanwhile, the Mountain, depleted by the events of Thermidor and desertions to the Plain, formed a dwindling and silent group on the left.

So it was the Plain that emerged as the victors of Thermidor. There were undoubtedly men of high principle among them, but on the whole they were hard-headed men, to whom the Revolution had been a profitable business: it had given them authority and status, and many had been enriched by the purchase of *biens nationaux*, others by lucrative government contracts – a process that would be carried further by the annexation of neighbouring provinces and the spoils of war. As regicides, they were inclined to Republicanism, and were fearful of a restoration – even of a constitutional monarchy. Their complaint against the Robespierrists had been not so much that they had mobilized the nation for war and instituted the Terror as that they had preached social democracy, given too free a rein to the *sans-culottes*, and meddled with private property and the freedom of the market. Robespierre having fallen, their objects were, therefore, to dismantle the machinery of Jacobin dictatorship, end the Terror (now obsolete), put the *sans-culottes* back to work, return to a more liberal economy and carry the war to a successful conclusion. Along with this, they hoped that the new régime might be stabilized with the firm and voluntary support of the 'patriots of '89'.

It was the last of these expectations that proved over-sanguine. This was due both to the divisions among 'patriots' and to the intrusion of a new and embarrassing 'ally' from outside the Assembly. After Thermidor, a triangular political struggle ensued in the Paris sections, now divided between moderates, neo-'Hébertists' and Jacobins. The moderates (the majority) generally reflected the aims of the Plain. The neo-'Hébertists', whose hostility to Robespierre had thrown them into the arms of his opponents, had formed an Electoral Club from which they attacked 'revolutionary' government and called for the application of the Constitution of 1793. At this time, their principal spokesmen included Jean Varlet, the former Enragé, and Gracchus Babeuf, editor of the *Tribun du peuple*. The Jacobins, though renouncing their former devotion to Robespierre, continued to advocate the 'revolutionary' principles and methods of 1793–4. They controlled some eight to ten sections and succeeded, two months after Thermidor, in having Marat's remains transferred to the Panthéon for reburial. But their success was short-lived. Encouraged by the divisions among 'patriots', a new element entered the lists in the form of the *jeunesse dorée*, the 'gilded youth' (or *muscadins*), led by the renegade 'terrorist' Fréron. They were recruited from middle-class youth, bankers' and lawyers' clerks, shop assistants, army deserters and sons of 'suspects' and of guillotine-victims. Organized in bands, they made sallies into the popular districts, beat up Jacobin workmen, shouted anti-'terrorist' slogans, and drowned the strains of the 'Marseillaise' in those of their own song, the 'Réveil du peuple'. Under this impetus, a veritable witch-hunt was provoked in the sections against Jacobins and 'terrorists', both real and alleged. Purges followed, so the moderates regained control of the sections; the Convention, yielding to pressure, closed down the Jacobin Club in November. By this time, the neo-'Hébertists' – and Babeuf in particular – had begun to regret the hopes they had placed in the Thermidorian leaders. But it was too late, and the Electoral Club was closed in its turn and Babeuf arrested soon after.

Meanwhile, the Convention had proceeded with its own reforms. The day after Robespierre's execution, it had been agreed at Tallien's suggestion, to renew the membership of the government Committees a quarter at a time each month. Thus power would no longer be concentrated in the hands of a few. It was only a first step. On 24 August, sixteen committees were set up, twelve of them with executive powers, to carry out the work previously done by the two Committees of Public Safety and General Security. Both these Committees were reduced in powers and independence. The latter, it is true, regained its control over policy and security, though these functions became progressively reduced; while the former, the old mainstay of Robespierrist ascendancy, lost all control over local government and the armed forces, which were now placed under a specially constituted Military Committee responsible to the Convention. Thus, while executive government remained strong, the Assembly resumed some of its old authority. Similar adjustments were made in local government, though here the purge of elements considered undesirable was more in evidence. The old vigilance and 'revolutionary' committees were swept away or brought under central direction. In Paris, the Commune was abolished (it was to have a brief revival in 1848) and the forty-eight 'revolutionary' committees were grouped together in twelve *comités d'arrondissement*, from which all Jacobin militants were excluded and in which the predominant social element ceased to be the small shopkeeper and craftsman who were replaced by the merchant, professional or public servant. Similarly, the civil committees of the sections were purged, put under the direct control of the Convention, and their numbers made up by persons selected by its Committee of Legislation. Here again, the *sans-culottes* and Jacobins of the 'Year II' gave way to 'middling' or substantial property-owners and moderates who had held sway before June 1793. Finally, in the sectional assemblies, now to meet only once every ten days, the influence of the *sans-culottes* was further reduced by withdrawing the 40 sous payment for attendance that had been in force since September 1793.

After the final blood-letting of 28–29 July, the Terror, too, was officially brought to an end. The law of 22nd Prairial was repealed, the prisons were opened and 'suspects' were released: 500 in Paris in a single week. A few public trials were staged – including those of Carrier, held responsible for the mass-drownings at Nantes, and Fouquier-Tinville, notorious as the public prosecutor of the 'Great Terror' of the late spring and summer of 1794 – after which the Revolutionary Tribunal was quietly put aside. Yet an unofficial Terror-in-reverse continued. As 'suspects' were released and some *émigrés* returned, the numbers of those wishing to settle old scores with Jacobins, 'terrorists' and former members of committees proportionately increased. In Paris, the unofficial White Terror was limited to the activities of the *muscadins*: there were beatings, denunciations and intimidation, but there was little bloodshed. In the provinces, however, the Terror assumed a far more violent and vicious form. In the Lyonnais, the Company of Jesus flung the bodies of its victims, men and women, into the Rhône, and prisoners were massacred wholesale in gaol or on their way to prison, while in other cities, bands of the so-called Companies of Jehu and the Sun indiscriminately murdered 'terrorists', 'patriots of '89' and – most eagerly of all – purchasers of former Church properties. Such excesses were deplored in Paris, but the Convention and its Committees were powerless to contain forces that they had themselves done much to unleash.

The economic situation also got out of hand, but here the new rulers, determined to liberate the economy from the controls of their predecessors, bore the direct responsibility. As a first step, in October 1794, the law of the Great Maximum was amended so as to allow prices to rise to a level two-thirds above that of 1790. Soon after, penalties for infringing the law were reduced and controls on imports were abandoned to encourage foreign trade. On 23 December the Maximum laws were virtually abolished and free trade in grain was restored. In Paris alone, the price of rationed bread was still maintained at 3 sous a pound, though bread could now, in addition, be sold on the open market; the basic meat ration was retained at a new price of 21 (formerly 14) sous a pound. Otherwise, prices were free to find their natural level. The consequences were disastrous. Though producers were temporarily appeased, inflation took a rapid upward turn and prices soared beyond the means of all but the prosperous consumer. The *assignat*, which had already fallen to 28 per cent of its old value in October and to 24 per cent in November, fell further to 20 per cent in December, to 17 per cent in January and to 7½ per cent in May 1795. In the provinces, where controls had all but been abandoned, the winter and spring brought near-famine conditions: at Verdun, for example, the workers' daily bread ration was reduced to half a pound and its price rose to 20 sous a pound. In Paris, rationed meat was often unobtainable; and the bread ration, though fixed at 1–1½ pounds per head in March 1795, fell in subsequent months to 8, 6, 4 or even 2 ounces. So small consumers were compelled to supplement their ration by buying in the open market at a price that rose from 25 sous a pound on 25 March to 16 livres (over twelve times as much) seven weeks later. Meanwhile, wages, though freed from the restrictons of the ill-fated Maximum of July 1794, had no chance at all of catching up. So it seems likely that the real wages of Parisian workers in May 1795 were not only far lower than in 1793–94 but had fallen back to the catastrophic level of the early months of 1789.[1]

Such was the background to the great popular insurrections of Germinal and Prairial (March and May 1795), which proved to be the last in the Revolution's history. Political motives also played a part: many of the *sans-culottes* had been won over by revived Hébertist agitation for the restoration of the Constitution of 1793. But it was above all the government's economic measures and their consequences that roused the people from their apathy. In January, when the prices of many goods had already doubled since the repeal of the Maximum laws, the old familiar threats against merchants and shopkeepers were heard again, but threats passed to action only when the bread ration began to fail in the last two weeks of March. On 12th Germinal (1 April) it failed completely in some sections. As in October 1789, women responded by raiding bakers' shops; building workers met to protest against a decree debarring them, as lodgers, from buying rationed bread; and sections on both sides of the river, with women well to the fore, joined forces to march on the Assembly. As Boissy d'Anglas was addressing the Convention, the insurgents burst in with shouts of 'Bread! Bread!'; some wore in their caps the printed slogan 'Bread and the Constitution of 1793'.

But they lacked leaders and, having no settled plans, put conflicting demands before the Assembly. They received little support, and so, when Merlin of Thionville appeared at the head of a mixed body of *jeunesse* and loyal National Guards, they dispersed without offering any resistance.

As the insurrection petered out, the Convention took police measures to restore order, settle old scores and prevent a recurrence. Paris was declared to be in a state of siege and the armed forces were placed under the supreme command of a regular army officer, General Pichegru. More ex-'terrorists' were arrested or disarmed, a dozen deputies of the Mountain (including Robespierre's old enemies, Amar and Cambon) were arrested, and the unfortnate trio, Barère, Billaud and Collot, together with Vadier (of the former Committee of General Security), were sentenced to deportation. But as the Convention did virtually nothing to remove the basic cause of the disorders, both the hardship and the agitation continued. In Normandy, food-convoys were pillaged along the Seine, and Robespierre's name began once more to be invoked with veneration. On 16 May, when the Paris bread ration fell again to two ounces, police agents gave warning of another imminent rising, a prospect that became all the more certain when, three days later, calls to armed insurrection were widely distributed around the city and suburbs – among them a printed manifesto entitled *Insurrection du Peuple pour obtenir du Pain et reconquérir ses Droits*, which precisely outlined the plan to be followed and gave the uprising its central slogan: 'Bread and the Constitution of 1793'.

The popular revolt that followed, one of the most stubbornly fought of the whole Revolution, was essentially a social protest, inspired by hunger and hatred of the new rich, yet it was accompanied by the political demands learned and absorbed since Thermidor: the release of the 'patriot' prisoners, a freely elected Commune and the Constitution of 1793. It lasted four days and opened on 1st Prairial (20 May) with a massive invasion of the Assembly by housewives and women of the markets, followed by the armed battalions of the central districts and Faubourgs. The programme of the insurgents was read to the Assembly which, prompted by the deputies of the Mountain, had little choice but to accept them. But once more, as in Germinal, for lack of leaders and a clear purpose, the intruders, having gained their first objective, spent hours in noisy chatter before being ejected by the loyal battalions of the western sections called in during the evening. But this time the insurrection continued in the Faubourg St Antoine. The City Hall was captured, the gunners of the loyal sections deserted, and the Convention was surrounded, besieged and threatened as in June 1793. Yet the rebels were bought off with promises and, having retired to their homes for the night, left the field to their opponents. The Faubourg was occupied by a force of 20,000 troops under the command of General Menou and, deserted by its allies, it surrendered without a shot.

This time the repression was thorough and ruthless. Fourteen deputies of the Mountain were arrested, of whom six were executed after attempting suicide. A Military Commission tried 149 persons, and sentenced 36 to death and 37 to prison and deportation. In the sections there followed a massive toll of proscriptions, in which the familiar settling of old scores and concern for future security played a far larger part than the tracking down and punishing of the actual culprits of May 1795. In a single week 1,200 were arrested and 1,700 disarmed, and more arrests followed later. It marked an important turning-point. With the proscription and removal of its leaders (both actual and potential), the Parisian *sans-culottes* ceased to exist as a political and military force. While, as we shall see shortly, they had another brief – though more passive – moment of triumph, the 'popular' phase of the Revolution was over. From now on the bourgeoisie, the Notables and *honnêtes gens* could proceed with their work without the embarrassing intervention of their erstwhile allies.[2]

The Thermidorians now faced the task of giving France a constitution that accorded with their own political beliefs and social and economic needs. The democratic Constitution of 1793, with its deceptive promises and calls to 'anarchy' and insurrection, had to be put to rest, and that of 1791, although it was dear to some, could not be restored, because the Republic (it was hoped) had come to stay. The unicameral system had proved defective, and further safeguards would have to be found against royalist and popular pressure. The new constitution – to be known as the Constitution of the Year III – was, suitably enough, introduced by Boissy d'Anglas, the champion of the new rich, who characteristically told the Assembly:

> We must be governed by the best men; those most suited to govern are men of good education and endowed with a great concern for the maintenance of order. You will rarely find such men outside the ranks of the propertied .... *A country governed by men of property belongs to 'the social order'* [the phrase is Rousseau's] *whereas one governed by men of no property reverts to a 'state of nature'*.*

* My italics.

So, not surprisingly, the Declaration of Rights and Duties – the addition is significant in itself – that accompanied the Constitution was conceived, broadly, in the spirit of the 'principles of '89', but with significant departures from it: equality became essentially equality before the law and not in civil rights. The right of insurrection was withdrawn, property rights were more explicitly defined and safeguarded, and a citizen's duties as well as his rights were elaborately spelled out. The male adult suffrage of 1793 was once more abandoned and a return made to something like the restricted franchise and system of indirect election of 1791. Electoral qualifications, however, were more generous: 'active' citizens now included all Frenchmen over twenty-one, of a settled abode and paying taxes (whatever the amount) – that is, all except priests, returned *émigrés* and imprisoned 'patriots'.[3] But, to serve as a brake on legislative experiment, the Assembly was divided into two Chambers: a Council of Five Hundred, aged thirty and above, with powers to initiate legislation by means of resolutions; and a Council of Elders, consisting of 250 members of forty or above and alone empowered to transform such resolutions into laws. Executive authority was vested in five Directors, each holding office for as many years; but the 'separation of powers' was restored and the Directors, though appointed by the Councils, could neither sit in them nor have any part in initiating their laws. (We shall see that such an arrangement boded ill for stable government.) Meanwhile, local government remained a part of its old autonomy, though it held far less than in 1791.[4] Finally, to avert the danger of an anticipated royalist upsurge, the Convention decreed that in the pending elections two-thirds of the incoming deputies must be elected from its own ranks.

The primary assemblies, convened for the dual purpose of approving the 'two-thirds' decree and ratifying the Constitution, met in September 1795. The new constitutional provisions were accepted readily enough, but in Paris the 'two-thirds' decree met with stiff opposition, and before the Convention dispersed in late October it had a royalist rising on its hands that came near to overthrowing it. Royalist and counter-revolutionary agitation had, in one form or another, been a matter of some concern since 1789 but, until war broke out, it had achieved little success. After the King's execution, royalist activity from both within and without had played its part in fostering rebellion in the Vendée and the 'federalist' departments of the south, west and north. Yet as long as the Jacobins remained in power, these dangers had been held in check and had barely affected the capital. The royalists had, however, taken fresh heart from the more liberal policies of their successors. By now, they were divided into two main groups – the 'ultras', who demanded a return to 1787 and the total restoration of the *ancien régime*, and the constitutional monarchists who, broadly speaking, favoured a restoration of the Constitution of 1791. Unfortunately for the 'constitutionalists', the Count of Provence, who 'succeeded' Louis XVI first as Regent for the young Louis XVII and later (following the latter's early death) as Louis XVIII, was a determined 'ultra'. This naturally caused a serious confusion of divided counsels.

It was reflected, most disastrously, in the expedition which, equipped and financed by Britain, landed at Quiberon Bay in July 1795: bungled from the start, it was easily defeated by General Hoche. It was a serious setback for both royalist groups. But, in Paris, soon after, the 'constitutionalists' appeared to be retrieving a part, at least, of their lost fortunes when they exploited with great skill the widespread dissatisfaction caused by the Convention's 'two-thirds' decree. Only one section, in fact – that of Lepeletier, in the financial quarter of the city – was under direct royalist control, but the worthy bourgeois and public servants, who now dominated the great bulk of the sections, were easily persuaded that the Assembly's decree was a dangerous infringement (as indeed it was) of the electors' right of choice. When the Convention, anticipating trouble, brought troops into the capital and allowed former 'terrorists' – or so it was believed – to arm and attend the assemblies, property appeared to be endangered as well. Every section, except that of the Quinze-Vingts in the Faubourg St Antoine, rejected the decrees and, having completed their lawful business, they refused to disperse. Open rebellion broke out on 13th Vendémiaire (5 October) when 25,000 Parisians seized arms and a dozen sections, led by Lepeletier, marched on the Convention. But Barras, who had been given command of the Paris forces, called General Bonaparte and a number of other young generals to his assistance. The advancing sections were met by withering artillery fire (Carlyle called it a 'whiff of grapeshot'), and the rebellion was crushed. Reprisals were strikingly mild: there were only two executions and most of the ringleaders got away. A remarkable feature of the whole affair was the behaviour of the *sans-culottes* who, though starved and oppressed by the Thermidorian Convention, refused to give any support to the royalist rebels.

The Constitution now came into force and the men of 1795, having warded off rebellion from both right and left, appeared to be firmly in the saddle. But this was an illusion, and the period of the Directory, which now began, proved to be one of confusion and intense political instability. In part, this was due to the nature of the Constitution itself. By providing for annual elections (of one-third of the Councils and one in five of the Directors), it offered a constant invitation to ferment and disorder. Moreover, the subdivision of authority (Lefebvre calls it 'l'émiettement des pouvoirs') and the failure to provide adequate machinery for the settlement of disputes between the Directors and the Councils led to continuous appeals to force.[5] More seriously, it soon became evident that the new rulers lacked the support within the country that would assure them of steady majorities and stable government. By their policy of alternative appeasement and repression they had estranged both right and left – both royalists and Jacobins - and their constant manipulation of elections estranged the moderate bourgeois and owners of property as well. From this false start they never recovered, and, compelled to manoeuvre and manipulate in order to maintain themselves in power, they followed a seesaw course of playing off one political faction against another – of alternately encouraging the royalist right against the Jacobin left and leaning on the left to get the better of the right. When this failed, as inevitably it must have done, the only solution was to call upon the army, already installed in Paris before Vendémiaire, to redress the balance. Thus, behind the façade of a liberal constitution, the generals tended more and more to become the ultimate arbiters of political disputes and the ground was prepared, long before the final *coup d'état* of November 1799, for the military dictatorship of Bonaparte.

The uprising of Vendémiaire had swung the pendulum once more to the left, and the new Assembly met to the accompaniment of stirring appeals for Republican unity and concord. There was a revival of Jacobin activity, the clubs reopened, and Babeuf's paper, the *Tribun du peuple*, appeared again on the streets. But the spirit of harmony was short-lived: the onslaught of their 'patriot' critics alarmed the authorities, all the more so because the economic situation was going from bad to worse. By the end of 1795, the *assignat* of 100 livres was worth only 15 sous and, in February, it collapsed altogether. Within six months, its successor, the *mandat territorial*, had suffered the same fate. Prices rocketed further and, in the spring of 1796, bread was selling in the open market for 80 livres a pound and meat for 100. While the new rich displayed their wealth with arrogant unconcern, poverty was (in the words of a police observer) 'at its lowest ebb', and hospitals and almshouses were overcrowded with the sick and destitute. Nor was it only the *sans-culottes* who suffered: small *rentiers* and public servants, their pensions dwindling under the impact of inflation, shared their misfortunes. It was against this background that Babeuf launched his 'Conspiracy of the Equals', the first attempt in history to establish a communist society by political means – and yet a minor episode in the Revolution itself, as it attracted little support at the time and was quickly crushed. Babeuf had, since 1789, been drawn to the 'Agrarian law', or sharing of goods in common, as a means of achieving economic equality. By the time of Robespierre's fall he had abandoned this as an impracticable scheme and was moving towards a more complex plan of collective ownership and production. This, in essence, was still his ultimate aim when, in the winter of 1795–96, he conspired with a group of former Jacobins, club-men and 'terrorists' to overthrow the Directory by force. The movement was organized in a series of concentric circles: there was an inner insurrectionary committee, composed of a small body of intimates who alone were fully informed of the conspiracy's aims; beyond it, a group of sympathizers, ex-Jacobins and others, including Robespierre's old opponents, Amar and Lindet; and finally, on the fringe, the Paris militants who had to be won over, reckoned by Babeuf at some 17,000 men. The plan was original and grievance was rife, but the *sans-culottes*, cowed and silenced since Prairial, failed to respond. The conspirators were betrayed by a police spy to Carnot, now a Director and fast moving towards the right. One hundred and thirty-one were arrested and thirty shot out of hand; Babeuf and some of his principal associates were brought to trial and guillotined a year later.

Once more the pendulum swung to the right, this time supported by a massive influx of royalists into the Assembly. In the partial elections of April 1797, only 11 former deputies to the Convention were returned out of a total of 216; the rest were mainly constitutional monarchists who now gave the Assembly its first royalist majority. Royalists – including Pichegru – were elected to preside over both legislative Councils. To make matters even worse, the near-royalist Carnot was joined as a Director by Barthélemy, a convinced monarchist, and it seemed as if the monarchy might be voted in by constitutional means. While Barras hesitated, the two other Republican Directors – Reubell and La Revellière-Lepeaux – favoured strong action to preserve the Republic. But how? An appeal to the people conjured up all the horrors of 1793, and the Jacobins were too weak to tilt the balance. The generals remained the only choice, both as Republicans and as interested parties in a war that the royalists were anxious to end. Bonaparte, fresh from his victories in Italy,* and Hoche, newly appointed commander of the Army of the Sambre-et-Meuse, promised their support, and soon Bonaparte's lieutenant,

* For the Italian campaign, see Part V, Chapter 2.

Augereau, and a part of Hoche's forces were marching on the capital. Barras now decided to support his more determined colleagues and, on 18th Fructidor (4 September 1797), they struck at the royalist majority. Barthélemy and Pichegru were arrested and imprisoned, while Carnot escaped; the Councils were purged of 214 deputies, and 65 persons were deported to the 'dry guillotine' of Guiana. Returned *émigrés* had, once again, to leave the country, while hundreds of priests were deported and others compelled to take new oaths of loyalty. Following this victory the Directors armed themselves with new powers, but it was too late and the would-be liberal Constitution had already proved to be unworkable.

In any case, by now the fate of the Republic lay less in the hands of the politicians than in those of the generals – particularly of the young and ambitious General Bonaparte, whose part in the *coup d'état* of Fructidor had won him official recognition for his daring, though quite unauthorized, settlement of Italy. He was already determining the foreign policy of the Republic. At Campo Formio, having settled and signed the terms of peace with Austria (October 1797), he boasted of France's imperial mission in the Mediterranean; and, the next spring, he wrecked all chances of an early settlement with England by persuading the Directors to send him to Egypt to open up an empire in the East. He was to return eighteen months later to become master of France.

Yet, once Bonaparte was safely in Egypt, there was no immediate reason for the government to have any fear of this kind. It had emerged from its victory in Fructidor with an enlarged Republican majority in both Councils, royalist activity was temporarily at a low ebb, and the severe measures taken against returned priests and *émigrés* met with little open opposition. Once more, it could turn its attention to the danger from the left. When the Jacobin challenge revived in the elections of 1798, the Assembly passed a law which excluded 106 deputies from sitting in the Councils. So, secure once more, the Directory was able to settle down to some useful – though limited – reforms. Steps were taken to stabilize the currency by withdrawing the discredited paper money from circulation and declaring a moratorium on all outstanding debts – thus paving the way for the financial reforms of the Consulate. The system of taxation was overhauled, brought up to date and put on something like a modern footing. Following good harvests in 1796–8, the price of grain fell – a much-needed relief for the long-suffering consumer. In addition, measures were taken to advance research and higher education: the École de Médecine and École Polytechnique (the prestigious School of Engineering) were decreed and the first steps were taken to found the Institut de France. Yet (such were current priorities) schools for other than upper- or middle-class children were kept short of funds. For government continued to be at the mercy of speculators and financiers and the budget, despite contributions from the annexed territories, remained unbalanced. Industry, too, continued to stagnate, and the maritime war with England – not to mention Bonaparte's Egyptian adventure – played havoc with foreign trade.[6]

A solution to such long-term problems could, of course, only be found through stable government and by one either willing to resort to the draconian measures of the Year II or one having at its command ample resources from satellite or conquered territories. The Directors were naturally drawn to the latter rather than to the former course, but their aggressive ambitions (of which more will be said in a subsequent chapter) brought on their heads a second coalition, this time embracing Britain, Austria, Russia, Turkey and Sweden. The war opened badly: France and her armies, though supported by freshly imposed levies (raised by the *levée en masse*), were defeated by the Austrian Archduke Charles in Germany and Switzerland and driven from Italy by the Russian General Suvorov. Meanwhile, the Belgian provinces were in revolt against the French and the peasant *chouans* were up in arms once more in the west. The Directors repeated their old denunciation of the double-headed hydra, royalism and 'anarchy', but in the elections of 1799 two-thirds of the government candidates were defeated and the Jacobin minority was strengthened. Sieyès, known as a fervent enemy of royalism, took office in the place of Reubell and, with the support of the Assembly, carried through a parliamentary *coup d'état* directed against his more hesitant colleagues. The ministerial reshuffle that followed actually brought a Jacobin – Robert Lindet, Robespierre's one-time associate and later critic on the Committee of Public Safety – to the Ministry of Finance. Once more, the needs of a defensive war compelled the Republic to resort to measures of 'public safety' and to condone a Jacobin revival. The Jacobin press reappeared, the clubs revived – among them the important Club du Manège, directed by Drouet, former postmaster-hero of Varennes and associate of Babeuf. Conscription was universally applied, forced loans were raised, and relatives of *émigrés* and royalist agitators were rounded up as hostages. When the reverses of the spring were followed in the summer by the landing of an Anglo-Russian force in Holland, General Jourdan even invited the Five Hundred to repeat the old declaration, going back to Danton's summons in 1792, of *la patrie en danger*. He was sharply opposed by Lucien Bonaparte, Napoleon's youngest brother, who pleaded that executive powers be extended rather than that they should be 'carried away by a revolutionary tide'. So Jourdan's proposal was quietly buried. It was the old dilemma: should they appeal to the masses or strengthen the authority of a few?

The issue was decided, as it had been after Fleurus, not by the defeat but by the victory of Republican arms. Masséria defeated Suvorov in Italy and drove him back across the Alps, and the Anglo-Russian force came to grief in Holland. The danger of invasion had been removed and 'the great nation' lived again. Meanwhile, General Bonaparte, though victorious against the English in Aboukir Bay, had been thwarted in Syria and decided to return home to seek fresh laurels in Europe. Leaving his army in Egypt and dodging Nelson's patrols, he landed secretly at the southern port of Fréjus on 9 October 1799. His recent failures were ignored and he was greeted by an ecstatic press and public as the great victor of Italy, the peace-maker of Campo Formio, and the one man able to impose on Europe a peace honourable to French arms. But the royalist danger continued. Property-owners, alarmed by the measures of 'public safety' and the Jacobin revival, spoke darkly of 'anarchy' and a return to 1793, and there was further talk of the need to revise the Constitution and to provide stable government by strengthening the executive.

It was in this atmosphere of alarm that Sieyès (that 'mole of the Revolution', as Robespierre had called him) planned a further, more decisive, *coup d'état*. Once more, as in Fructidor, the army must be called in to force the hands of the Assembly – but, this time, an Assembly with a Republican majority. So, having tried Generals Joubert and Moreau in turn (the former died in battle soon after and the latter declined), Sieyès and his fellow conspirators, Fouché and Talleyrand, turned to Napoleon, the man of the hour and one well suited by his popularity, his military record, his ambition and his Jacobin past to play the part assigned to him. By playing on the fears of a 'terrorist' plot, they persuaded the Councils to meet on 10 November (19th Brumaire) outside Paris at Saint-Cloud under the protection of Napoleon's grenadiers. The Elders were soon won over, but the Five Hundred were less easy to persuade and, when Bonaparte entered uninvited to address them, there were shouts of 'Outlaw him! Down with the dictator!' The General lost his nerve, but his brother Lucien, who (conveniently) was in the chair, saved the situation by calling in the guards. The Five Hundred were driven from their Chamber, the Directory was dissolved, and full authority was vested in a provisional Consulate of three – Sieyès, Roger-Ducos and Bonaparte. Though not generally realized at the time, it was the end of the 'bourgeois' Republic, and power passed into the hands of a military dictator.

Three weeks later a new constitution, drafted on Caesarean lines, was offered to the electoral assemblies. It was accompanied by a proclamation from the Consuls that, in somewhat equivocal terms, rang down the curtain on ten years of history: 'The Revolution is established upon the principles which began it; it is ended.'

V Napoleon

1 *Rise to Power*

It has become commonplace among historians to draw a sharp line of distinction between the Revolution (generally seen as ending in 1799) and the Napoleonic era which has most often been presented as a quite separate phenomenon. This appeared sensible enough when scholars were inclined, as in the greater part of the nineteenth century, to see the Revolution almost exclusively in ideological and political terms, while leaving its longer-term economic and social aspects largely neglected. But since the advent at the turn of the century of a new school of historians, concerned with prices, wages, social conflicts and popular movements, such a rigorous distinction has ceased to make much sense. If, as M. Furet has rightly insisted, the social and economic factors in revolution must be treated as part of a longer-term projection in contrast to the comparatively brief time-span of the political 'event', the era of the revolution in France must be prolonged until the fall of Napoleon in 1815 at least, and even until the completion of France's own 'bourgeois' revolution in 1848 – and beyond this, too, if we are also concerned with the Revolution's repercussions in Italy, Germany and other parts of Europe. This applies in particular to the wider European scene, where the French Revolution made its greatest impact not in the 'high' revolutionary period itself but under the influence of Napoleon's conquests and armies of occupation. Even in France, the changes made by the Revolution were not firmly absorbed and established until the period of authoritarian and stable government imposed by Napoleon had run its course.[1]

In summoning Napoleon Bonaparte to their aid in Brumaire, Sieyès and his associates had hoped, like Barère in Thermidor, to keep the political controls firmly in their hands. Their purpose had been to install a short-term military dictator who would, on their own terms, defend the threatened 'natural frontiers' of France and stabilize the government by keeping the royalist, Jacobin and *sans-culotte* factions at bay. The resort to authoritarian government was not entirely new: the Plain had, in the emergency of 1793–94, given its blessing to the near-dictatorship of the Committee of Public Safety; the 'liberal' Contention of 1795 had deprived the electors of their constitutional rights by their decree of 'two-thirds'; and their successors under the Directory had, on more than one occasion, brushed their own Constitution aside to cope with the alternating challenges of royalism and Jacobinism. But this time the man selected for the task in hand was of a different stamp and temperament from any called upon to play a similar role before. Far from retaining control of the situation, the Brumairians were soon to find that their intended auxiliary was fully determined to impose his own pattern on events. He would, in fact, by a rare combination of will, intellect and physical vigour, leave his mark on France for years to come.

Yet, in so far as it is possible to separate reality from myth in so rare a phenomenon, he was a man of strange paradoxes and contradictions: a modern romantic cast in the mould of a Caesar or Alexander; a man of action and rapid decision, yet a poet and dreamer of world conquest; a supreme political realist, yet a vulgar adventurer who gambled for high stakes; the enemy of privilege who boasted of his Imperial connections and of his desire to found a new dynasty of kings; an organizer and statesman of genius, yet as much concerned to feather the nest of the Bonaparte clan as to promote the glory of France; a product of the Enlightenment who distrusted ideas and despised intellectuals and 'systems'; a lucid intellect with a great thirst and capacity for knowledge, yet strangely impervious to forces he had himself helped to unleash. And the greatest paradox of all: the upstart 'soldier of the Revolution' who carried the 'Principles of '89' into half the countries of Europe, and yet was driven by personal ambition and contempt for his fellow men to build a new despotism and a new aristocracy from the ashes of the old. The picture is obscured by the 'legend' created during his island-exile on St Helena, when he was anxious to portray himself as a man of peace eager to unite Europe in a confederation of self-governing states.[2] This hardly corresponds to fact, yet in a sense myth and reality have become blended in history. His intentions were certainly never as pure as he claimed, yet the 'legend', if judged by the results, has not proved entirely false, for the image of the 'soldier of the revolution' has as great a claim to reality – and a far greater claim to survival – as that of the despot and conqueror.

And there can certainly be no doubt about Napoleon's debt to the Revolution, for no career illustrates better than his own the justice of the revolutionaries' claim to have opened careers to talents. He was born at Ajaccio in Corsica in 1769, the son of a minor nobleman who, though Genovese by birth, had become a Frenchman by the French conquest of the island a year before. Between 1779 and 1785, young Napoleon attended a succession of military colleges in France and learned his lessons well. Like many young officers of the day he welcomed the Revolution. He eagerly read Rousseau and flung himself into the 'patriot' politics of Corsica as an ally of Paoli, the 'Liberator'. Even before his final breach with Paoli and his expulsion from Corsica, he came back to Paris and, in June 1792, witnessed the humiliation of Louis XVI in the Tuileries at the hands of the Paris 'mob'; the experience was one he would not easily forget. Yet, in the struggle of the parties, he declared for the Mountain against the Gironde and distinguished himself, as a captain in charge of the artillery, at the relief of Toulon in September 1793. He was promoted to brigadier and won the friendship of Augustin Robespierre, then on mission to the Army of Italy. The alliance nearly cost him his career for, in Thermidor, he was held in the Fort Carré at Antibes for a month as a suspected Robespierrist and, on his release, found himself without a job. A year later he refused the post of commander of the Army of the West. But, coming to Paris in September 1795, he caught Barras' eye and, having crushed the royalist rising in Vendémiaire, was rewarded with the rank of general. Moreover, through Barras he met Joséphine de Beauharnais, widow of a revolutionary general, and they married in October 1796. A week before, he had been given the prestigious command of the Army of Italy, and was now launched on his long and successful military and political career.

It was Bonaparte's remarkable success in Italy, his popularity with the public and the aura of fame that clung to him – in both victory and defeat – throughout his Egyptian campaign, that marked him out for the part he played in Brumaire. Yet, in retrospect, it seems surprising that Sieyès and his allies should have expected a man of his record and temperament to submit so tamely to their direction. At all events, they were soon disabused and, before a year was out, he had created a political system of his own and, thereafter, proceeded to consolidate his personal authority as the opportunity offered. His first brush with Sieyès came over the new Constitution that followed Brumaire. As the past-master of constitutional manipulation, Sieyès proposed an elaborate system of checks and balances based, as he put it, on 'authority from above' and 'confidence from below'. Male adult suffrage was to be restored, but voters in the primary assemblies would only be empowered to elect one-tenth of their number to compose a 'national list'. From this list a centrally co-opted Senate would select a Tribunate to propose laws and a Legislature to adopt them. Central and local government officials would be chosen by the Consuls from the national and departmental lists. The Executive would be composed of a Grand Elector, appointed and subject to recall by the Senate, and two

Consuls, one for external and one for internal affairs, to be nominated by him. Thus effective political authority would remain in the hands of the Notables who, by their control of the Senate, could terminate at will the rule of their appointed dictator.

The General accepted without demur the plans to restrict the rights of voters (his earlier experience had soured him on popular democracy), but he had quite other views about the role he should play himself. Aiming at sole executive authority, he adroitly played off one faction against another and ended up with a system that looked like a compromise but which, in practice, accorded with his own ambitions. Sieyès' list of Notables, his Senate and Tribunate were retained (the last with its legislative powers reduced), but, above all, there emerged a First Consul elected for ten years, with powers overriding those of his colleagues, answerable to no one and solely responsible for the appointment of ministers and officials, and with the authority to initiate legislation after consulting a Council of State appointed by himself. The Constitution, put to a plebiscite in February 1800, was adopted by 3 million votes to 1,500.

The Senate, however, and the Tribunate and Legislature that it appointed retained considerable authority, and Sieyès and his colleagues believed that, by their control of these, they could at least compel the First Consul to take them into partnership. But Napoleon had no such intentions. The Constitution allowed him to supplement the work of the Legislature by issuing decrees known as *senatus-consulta*: these he used freely and to good effect. Moreover, quite illegally, he permitted the Council of State to interpret the decrees passed on to it by the Assembly before they became law. It was the Council, in fact, which co-operated with him in framing several of the most enlightened enactments of the Consulate. Much of this legislation was of course intended to centralize administration and strengthen the authority of government. An early priority was the police. The Ministry of Police, created by the Directory, was enlarged and given extended powers. It was entrusted to Fouché, considered to be well qualified for the post by his 'terrorist' past and his supportive role in Brumaire. Under Fouché served Dubois, prefect of police in Paris, and similar prefects in every department. This was but one instance of Bonaparte's reversal of the principle of local election and the retransfer of control from region to centre: in this he followed the practice of the *ancien régime* and the Committee of Public Safety far more than that of the Constituent Assembly and Directory. Thus, while the communes and departments created in 1790 were retained, a law of February 1800 placed the departments in the charge of prefects, responsible to the Ministry of the Interior and modelled on the Intendants and 'representatives on mission' of the past; and now even mayors were to be nominated by the government. In finance and justice, too, the First Consul abandoned the more liberal practices of 1790 and reverted to the methods of the *ancien régime*. The collection of taxes was removed from the local authorities and entrusted to a central body; this completed a process already begun by the Directory. Again, criminal courts were set up in the departments, with judges appointed by the First Consul himself, to try common law offences. Further exceptional courts were created to deal with royalist subversion. For additional security of state juries were suspended in several departments, and recourse was even had – though in a disguised form – to the notorious *lettres de cachet* of the Bourbon monarchy.

Such exceptional measures were sternly opposed by the liberal opposition in the Tribunate and Legislature and led to Napoleon's final breach with his allies of Brumaire. By this time he had further scores to settle as Paris, when he set out on his second Italian campaign in May 1800, became a hive of intrigue of disgruntled rivals and frustrated aspirants to office, and the new reigme appeared briefly to hang in the balance. However, his victory at Marengo in June, followed by Moreau's at Hohenlinden six months later, restored confidence at home and persuaded the Austrians to negotiate. Having prepared the ground for the Peace of Campo Formio, Bonaparte returned once more in triumph to the capital. He lost no time in reasserting his authority. The Tribunate was purged of its more fractious members; a military plot, implicating Moreau and Bernadotte, was nipped in the bud; Madame de Staël, whose salon had become a centre of opposition, was banished from Paris; and the timely discovery of an 'infernal machine', designed by royalist terrorists to blow up the First Consul on his way to the Opera, was made a pretext for deporting, shooting or guillotining several of his Jacobin critics. So order was once more restored, but more drastic constitutional measures were required to silence the opposition in the Senate and Legislature. The Peace of Amiens, ending the nine-year war with England, afforded the opportunity. Amidst the general jubilation, the Senate proposed at first that the Consulate should be extended for a further ten years, but Napoleon insisted on a plebiscite which, by $3\frac{1}{2}$ million to 8,000 votes, conferred on him the Consulate for life. In addition, a *senatus-consultum* of May 1802 so amended the Constitution as to give him virtually complete dictatorial powers: the Senate, over which he now presided and whose numbers he filled by co-option, was given authority to revise the Constitution at will by means of *senatus-consulta*, to dissolve the Legislature and Tribunate and nominate the subordinate Consuls. Sieyès' national list of Notables was finally abandoned and replaced by a network of electoral colleges, where his nomination was once more the controlling influence. Finally, he was empowered to negotiate treaties without submitting them for approval and was invited to nominate his own successor.

By these means, Napoleon had taken the first step towards restoring the hereditary monarchy. All that was needed was to add the trappings of an imperial Crown and Court and a new imperial aristocracy. External events again provided the opportunity. War with England broke out again in 1803 and the royalist leader, Georges Cadoudal, won English support for a plan to kidnap Napoleon and take him to London. The plot was betrayed to the police by a former Jacobin turned informer. Moreau and Pichegru, long hovering on the royalist bandwagon, were implicated: the first was exiled and the second strangled in his cell; while the Duc d'Enghien, Condé's grandson, was seized on German territory, spirited across the French border and shot as an English agent. All this pointed to the need for a hereditary succession, and, in May 1804, the Senate proclaimed that 'the government of the Republic is entrusted to a hereditary Emperor'. For the moment, as Napoleon had no son, the heir-designate was to be his brother Joseph and, after him, his brother Louis (Lucien, the youngest, naturally came last on the list). The police were further reinforced; Fouché, whose intrigues had lost him his office after Marengo, was reinstated and from now until his final disgrace in 1810 he supplied the Emperor with daily bulletins from his vast network of agents. Otherwise, the administration remained much as before, but the Court, already emerging at the Tuileries in the latter days of the Consulate, was given greater formality, substance and decorum. A new imperial nobility was founded by conferring the rank of prince on the Bonaparte brothers, hereditary Italian dukedoms on Bernadotte, Talleyrand and Fouché (all now restored to favour), while even Sieyès was soon to appear in the full regalia of a baron of the Empire. And, to endow the proceedings with further solemnity, Pope Pius himself, ignoring the protests of *émigrés* and royalist dissenters, hurried to Paris in December 1804 to witness the Emperor's coronation at Notre-Dame Cathedral, now restored to its ancient splendour.

So the First Republic, after teetering on the brink for the past five years, was finally buried, and Napoleon, having achieved his ambitions at home, was able to devote his attention to other, more far-ranging, problems. These would involve him in a further ten-year war, a long succession of victories and eventual defeat. But before he embarked on this new European adventure, he would have four years of almost untroubled peace in Paris. So, not surprisingly, these were the years which spawned most of the great reforms that the Emperor (then still as First Consul) carried out in France – reforms that, in many respects, complement and consolidate the work of the revolutionary Assemblies.

2 *Reforms in France*

The major reforms of the Consulate were carried out between February 1800 and May 1803. For most of this time Napoleon was in Paris, attended by a small group of ministers and Councillors of State, mainly moderate Republicans or former royalists: among them Cambacérès, Lebrun, Talleyrand and Portalis. Their role was an important one yet strictly subordinate to their leader, who attended most of their meetings, gave them unity and direction, and stamped them with the brand of his own devotion to authority, realism, contempt for privilege and abstract rights, scrupulous attention to detail and respect for an orderly hierarchy.

The revolutionary period in France had been bedevilled by weak and haphazard financial and banking policies. Under Feuillants, Girondins and Thermidorians inflation ran riot, metal coinage had disappeared, and a succession of governments had been held to ransom by speculators, financiers and contractors. For a short period, the Committee of Public Safety had, by means of political and economic Terror, driven speculation underground, arrested the fall of the *assignat* and given temporary stability to the nation's finances. The Directory too had belatedly, after some years of chaotic inflation, taken steps to restore the currency and centralize taxation, but their measures remained uncompleted. The *coup d'état* of Brumaire and Bonaparte's promise of strong government had restored the confidence of the bankers and it was with their co-operation that the Bank of France was founded in February 1800. Its original share capital of 30 million francs had increased to 45 million by 1803, when the Bank was given the monopoly of issuing notes. But paper issues were kept under strict control, and metal once more became the general currency. It was a measure of this new financial policy – and of Napoleon's own distrust of paper money – that between 1799 and 1814 some 75 million francs in gold and silver came back into circulation.

Most renowned of all the measures enacted by the First Consul and his Council of State was the Civil Code, completed in 1804 and renamed the Code Napoleon in 1807. It was by no means an innovation, though Napoleon was to take greater pride in this achievement than in all his forty battles. The work of codifying the numerous laws and decrees of the Revolution had been begun by the Convention in 1792: a draft code of 779 clauses appeared a year later and these had expanded to 1,104 under the Directory in 1795. Five drafts had, in fact, been discussed before Napoleon and his collaborators began their work in 1800. It was a vast undertaking, and one long overdue. Before the Revolution, the monarchy had achieved little in the way of legal unity: some 360 local codes were in force and the country had been broadly divided between the Roman law prevailing in the south and the customary law of the north. While the Revolution had eased the problem by sweeping away feudal privilege and inheritance and withdrawing property relations from the operation of the canon law, the great questions still remained – should the new Code be firmly based on abstract natural law, ignoring the traditions of the past, or should it aim, while taking full account of all changes effected in the relations of properties and persons since 1789, at striking an agreed balance between the rival claims of Roman and customary law?

The Convention had been strongly influenced by the rational arguments of the Enlightenment and recognized such absolute rights as the equality of persons, civil marriage, divorce, adoption, the inheritance of illegitimate children, and the equal division of property among heirs. It had been hostile to the authoritarian spirit of Roman law and favoured the greater liberalism of customary law. The Code of 1804 strikes a balance between the two: it preserves the legal egalitarian principles of 1789, but they are tempered by a new and sharper insistence on the rights of property and on the authority of parent and husband. For, unlike his predecessors, Napoleon saw much to admire in Roman law. It appealed to his own authoritarian nature, and besides its operation might help to overcome much of the moral laxity of post-Thermidorian society. Had he not had his own experience of this in the case of his wife Josephine? Accordingly, those clauses of the new Civil Code dealing with marriage, paternity, divorce and adoption are both those most strongly influenced by Roman law and those in which Napoleon intervened most vigorously. So divorce becomes severely restricted; property, up to a quarter of the whole, may be bequeathed outside the family; illegitimate children may only exceptionally be given recognition; the paternal authority over children, as practised under the *ancien régime*, is restored. In the clause dealing with 'the Respective Rights and Duties of Husband and Wife', we find such gems as the following: 'A husband owes protection to his wife, a wife obedience to her husband', 'Married women are incapable of making contracts', and 'a wife may sue for divorce only in the case in which the husband introduces a permanent mistress into the family household'. But this is, of course, only a part of the picture. While rejecting the liberal-democratic principles of 1793, the Code adopted in their entirety the new property rights and rights of citizenship enacted by the revolutionaries of 1789: the destruction of feudalism and feudal privilege are endorsed as are liberty of conscience and employment, while perhaps the most important of all the articles of the Code is that which insists (contrary to traditional usage) on the equal division of estates between sons. Provisions such as these have profoundly influenced the social development not only of France but of some thirty countries in all continents outside Australasia.

The Legion of Honour, founded in May 1802, reflects a similar inclination to blend authority with equal opportunity. Unlike his Civil Code, it was Napoleon's personal invention, and it met with spirited disapproval in both Tribunate and Legislature and even within the Council of State. The Convention had abolished the old royal insignia, like that of the Order of St Louis, both for its religious associations and as a relic of privilege; yet 'civic crowns' had, on occasion, continued to be bestowed for meritorious service to the nation. It was with both types of distinction in mind that Napoleon devised his Legion. Its fifteen 'cohorts', each composed of 250 members of varying rank, were selected by a Grand Council over which the First Consul would preside. His intention was two-fold: to create a new order open to all who qualified by personal service to the state and one that would be strictly under his personal control. His critics, suspicious of this further attempt to extend his authority, were quick to raise objections, but it was to no avail and the Legion still survives as yet another monument to authoritarian rule.

Napoleon's educational reforms spread over both Consulate and Empire. They reflect similar social and political attitudes, including his contempt for women. The purpose of education, as he saw it, was to equip young people for service to the state – the boys as doctors, teachers, public servants and officers, or simply as craftsmen, labourers and common soldiers; and the girls as dutiful and obedient housewives and mothers. The Consulate had inherited from the Convention and Directory about a hundred public secondary schools. These they reorganized and placed under the control of a Director of Public Instruction, but with the Church providing a large part of the teachers. In education, however, Napoleon's particular innovation and source of pride was the *lycée*, a selective secondary school for the training of leaders and administrators. It had a strictly secular curriculum whose direction was reserved for the state alone. There were to be forty-five *lycées* at first with 6,400 places financed by state scholarships, of which about a third were reserved for the sons of officers and civil servants and the rest for the most able pupils of the public secondary schools. They got off to a slow start, however, as some middle-class parents resented the imposed military discipline, yet by 1813 the education they provided had acquired the reputation of being the finest in Europe and 6,000 *lycée*-trained students were in universities. But the education of girls was not considered a matter of primary importance, and could be safely left to the religious orders. Writing to his Minister of the Interior from his campaign headquarters in 1807, the Emperor urged that high-school girls should receive a solid grounding in religion. 'What we ask [he wrote] is not that girls should think but that they should believe,' and he added (and it was not a tongue-in-cheek observation) that 'care must be taken not to let them see any Latin, or other foreign languages'.

As both Consul and Emperor, Napoleon took an active and continuous interest in the direction of the nation's economy. His authoritarian views naturally led him to favour state direction over the free-trade theories of Adam Smith or the French 'economists' of the eighteenth century. But his conception of state intervention was far closer to the mercantilism of the seventeenth-century Colbert than it was to the controlled economy practised by the Committee of Public Safety in 1794. The Jacobins were naturally anxious to harness the economy to the needs of war, to equip their armies and feed the civilian population, but they were also concerned with the status and dignity of human beings. Napoleon's aims were more conservative and pedestrian: the state must intervene to protect agriculture and to ensure a favourable trade balance and an adequate supply of weapons and soldiers for his wars. The material conditions of the people, provided they did not lead to public disorder or interfere with recruitment, were a relatively minor concern. His passion for regulation actually led him, in defiance of the whole trend of revolutionary legislation, to toy with the idea of resurrecting the trade guilds of the *ancien régime*. Meanwhile, as was to be expected, workers continued to be denied the right to organize. Moreover, a new law was passed in 1803 which compelled them to carry a passbook stamped by their employer and, in industrial disputes, the employer's word alone could be taken as evidence.

Yet, in these matters as in others, Napoleon's political realism did not desert him. Haunted by memories of the food riots of the Revolution (the danger of a recurrence was particularly great in 1801), he recognized that public order and stability, and therefore the supply of recruits, would depend in no small degree on an adequate provision of food. Doctrine must therefore, in this respect as in others, yield to the pressing needs of the state. Except in years of abundance, strict limits were placed on the export of grain, and in 1812 the Emperor actually followed the example of the Convention in imposing a ceiling on the price of bread and flour. It was for such reasons as these that Napoleon retained the support and confidence of the peasants and *menu peuple*, even in moments of crisis when many of his former bourgeois allies were ready to desert him. This served as a powerful social base for resisting the frequent attempts made by his critics to unseat him, and the loyalty of the common people, for whom the brand of political liberalism offered by the opposition had little meaning or attraction, remained remarkably constant and only broke under the weight of the excessive depletion of resources and manpower – as well as their heartfelt desire for peace – in the dark days of the 'battle of France' in November 1813.[1]

It was considerations of state again that prompted Napoleon to re-establish the Catholic Church in France by signing a Concordat with the Pope in 1801. After its chequered history in the early years of revolution, the Church had been disestablished in September 1795. The policy of the Directory was alternately one of toleration and indifference or of bitter persecution, particularly of priests who refused to take the oath and were often accused or convicted of treasonable activities. During this period a variety of cults had sprung up and, at the time of the Brumaire *coup d'état*, religious practices were variously observed, and with relative immunity from persecution, by Catholics (both juring and non-juring), Protestants, Decadists and Theophilanthropists. This had produced what Aulard has called 'a rich and varied flowering of religious life', but it was not a state of affairs that could commend itself either to Roman Catholics or *émigrés* or to a ruler of Napoleon's orderly disposition. He himself was a Voltairian sceptic, little inclined to mystical experience or belief of any kind; it is certainly unthinkable, for example, that he could have shared Robespierre's belief in the immortality of the soul. But, like many freethinkers and deists of the time, he was convinced that organized religion might be good for others if not for himself – and particularly so for women. Besides, religion would help to keep the social peace. 'In religion,' he once wrote, 'I do not see the mystery of the Incarnation, but the mystery of the social order.' It might also be a valuable political weapon. His experiences in Italy and Egypt had warned him of the danger of allowing 'philosophical' preoccupations to dictate policies that might ruffle the religious susceptibilities of those he was called upon to govern. In Egypt, he had strictly forbidden his army to offend Moslem religious practices, and in his dealings with the Papacy in 1797 he had refused to follow the anti-clerical instructions of the Directors. He destroyed the ghettos in Rome and Venice not only to gain Jewish support but also to give expression to his own 'enlightened' views, and he said on one occasion (with all sincerity it seems): 'If I were governing Jews, I would restore the Temple of Solomon.'

Nevertheless, before consenting to re-establish the Catholic Church in France, he carefully weighed the political consequences. On the one hand, a decade and more of 'enlightenment' and revolution had eradicated from men's minds and actions much of the former influence of the Church.[2] The Republican bourgeoisie, for example, had generally discarded religion and did not consider it a necessary concomitant of civic virtue, and for those who did, such new cults as Theophilanthropism might serve the purpose equally well. Anti-clericalism, too, was strongly entrenched in the army, as became only too evident when the Concordat was finally endorsed. On the other hand, the mass of the French population, the peasants, had never become fully reconciled to the abandonment of their old forms of worship, and it was a reasonable calculation that their restoration would remove the main grievances that still kept the civil war smouldering in the Vendée and Brittany. Moreover, even in intellectual circles, the old scepticism had lost much of its former attraction and had given way to a romantic religious revival. Again, France had since 1795 expanded far beyond her pre-revolutionary borders and latent rebellion might be nipped in the bud and Catholic opinion appeased among the subject populations of Belgium, Switzerland, the Rhineland and Italy. Not only that, but an accommodation with the Pope might help to bring about a general peace on France's terms and remove the apprehensions of many *émigrés*, more Catholic than royalist, whom the First Consul was anxious to bring back and reconcile with his regime. But, of course, before any settlement could be reached, the Pope must accept two important conditions: 'This religion [to quote Napoleon's own words] must be in the hands of the government'; and there could be no question of restoring the Church's confiscated properties to their old owners.

A new pope, Pius VII, had been elected shortly before Marengo, and on the eve of leaving Italy in June 1800 Napoleon had already made overtures at Rome. Agreement was reached only after a full year of bargaining, and after ten separate drafts had been exchanged between the principals. The main points at issue were the appointment and payment of bishops, the future of the Catholic Church among the community at large, and the relations between Church and state. Pius at first insisted that all non-juring bishops should be restored to their sees and that no recognition should be given to those who had usurped their functions since the Civil Constitution of 1790. He also refused to recognize the rights of the purchasers of Church properties, he wanted the clergy to be paid from endowments, and he demanded that Roman Catholicism should be defined as the sole *religion d'état* (established Church) and that there should be the minimum of interference by the state in the affairs of the Church. For his part, Napoleon argued that all bishops, both 'refractory' and 'constitutional', should relinquish their sees and contend for reappointment, that purchasers of Church properties must be guaranteed possession, that the clergy should be paid as state servants and that the Catholic faith should be defined not as 'dominant' – which implied a restriction on the rights of other believers – but as the 'religion of the great majority of the citizens'. This was, in fact, the final form agreed upon. It was also agreed that the government should remove all obstacles to the free exercise of the Catholic religion. The method of reappointment of bishops was settled to Napoleon's satisfaction while saving the Pope the indignity of an abject surrender: they should, in fact, resign *en bloc* and be reinstated by the Pope (who issued two separate Bulls – one for jurors and one for non-jurors – for the purpose) after nomination by the First Consul. Moreover, Napoleon won his point that bishops and clergy (the latter to be appointed by the bishops) should be paid salaries by the state, while all clergy should take an oath of allegiance to the government – but not to the Constitution of the Clergy as in 1790. Finally, an elegant formula was found to make it easier for the Pope to accept the surrender by the Church of its former estates. This was crucial as even Napoleon could not have persuaded the numerous purchasers of Church properties, enriched by the Revolution, to accept the settlement on any other terms.

The Concordat appeared, then, to be a compromise, yet on all major issues the First Consul had won his point. Even so, he needed all his prestige, reinforced by the Treaty of Amiens recently signed with England, to overcome the stiff opposition within the Tribunate and Council of State and among the generals. The most serious objection was that Roman Catholicism, in spite of the agreed formula, had once more become the sole and official state religion. To meet this criticism it was decided, without any papal sanction whatever, to tack on to the Concordat two sets of Organic Laws, of which one was a charter of Protestant liberties while the other placed the Gallican Church more firmly than ever under the control of the secular power.

The partnership of Pope and Emperor did not prove an easy one, and the arrangements reached were fraught with constant disputes over temporal matters which were never satisfactorily resolved. But the Concordat was not revoked as, basically, it served both parties well. It outlived a long succession of governments and constitutions, and Church and state in France remained reunited according to the Napoleonic formula for the next hundred years.

VI The Revolution and Europe

1 *From Constituents to Directory*

So far, we have mainly considered the Revolution's impact on France herself. But now the time has come to extend the scene to the world outside – in the first place, to the rest of Europe. Was the French Revolution a unique event arising from quite particular causes, or was it part of a far wider movement that developed not only in France but, at least, in Europe and America if not elsewhere? Such questions are prompted by a number of considerations. One is that, even before the Revolution broke out in France a number of European countries had political movements which challenged, in one form or another, the accepted traditions, institutions and values of the society – the largely 'aristocratic' society – of the *ancien régime*. Movements took place in Belgium and Poland, in the United Provinces (present-day Holland) and in Rousseau's home-town, the small city-state of Geneva.[1] These movements were comparatively short-lived and ended in failure at the time, but it is perhaps not surprising that the dramatic events in France during the next ten years should have given a fresh edge and stimulus to these earlier movements and, in some cases, given them a new revolutionary content. This happened sometimes through the contagious propagation of French revolutionary ideas, sometimes by the impact or occupation of France's crusading armies, and, to a greater or lesser degree, by the action taken against their own rulers by the people, or the 'patriots', of the countries concerned. The eventual outcome was so to transform the old Europe of the *ancien régime* that, at the close of the revolutionary and Napoleonic eras, there was hardly a country west of Turkey and Russia and north of the Pyrenees that had not been profoundly affected. As a result, some historians have set the Revolution in France in quite a new perspective: for (they have argued) it now no longer appears as a unique and particular phenomenon in its own right, but rather as a single phase of a far wider convulsion, spread over the European and American continents, which they have variously termed a 'Western', an 'Atlantic' or a 'Democratic' revolution.[2]

One early result of the French Revolution was to divide European society into two distinct and opposing camps – its supporters, or 'patriots', on the one side and its opponents, or 'counter-revolutionaries', on the other. Yet this was not immediately apparent, as such early episodes as the fall of the Bastille were generally well received. There were, of course, exceptions: the Empress Catherine of Russia, the Kings of Spain and Sweden and Edmund Burke in England were resolutely hostile, though for the moment they held their fire. But the prevailing reaction in Europe was one of enthusiasm, relief, benevolent neutrality or (as in the case of France's old enemy, England) a sort of malicious glee; even the 'liberal' emperors, Joseph II and his successor Leopold, though brothers of the Queen of France, were not unduly concerned at first and were disposed to let sleeping dogs lie. In general, the overthrow of 'despotism' evoked a chorus of approval, and so the Revolution got off to a good start. It had time to promote and consolidate its gains before, a year or two later, the privileged and propertied classes became aware of its wider implications and the spread of revolutionary ideas. Many were alarmed at the influx into France of democrats and dissenters from other countries; while many, returning to or corresponding with their homelands, began to concern themselves increasingly with the problems of their fellow 'patriots' abroad. Such developments filled the Revolution's opponents with growing alarm.

The alarm was first loudly sounded by Edmund Burke when he published his *Reflections on the Revolution in France* in November 1790. He found a ready audience that bought up 30,000 copies and eleven editions of his book in a little over a year. Burke's message, unlike that of the 'liberal' emperors, was one of total condemnation. The French, he argued, in sharp contrast to the English of a hundred years before, were embarking on a headlong course of destruction that threatened to tear down the whole social fabric, not only in France but elsewhere, and to rush blindly along an uncharted path of renovation. 'It is with infinite caution', he proclaimed, 'that any man should venture upon pulling down an edifice, which has answered in any tolerable degree for ages the common purposes of society, or on building it up again without having models and patterns of approved utility before his eyes.' So the past was being invoked to instruct the future: a dangerous precedent, as the American constitutionalist Thomas Paine rebuked him, for 'man has no property in man; neither has any generation a property in the generations that have to follow'.[3] But Burke found many followers, the nucleus of a counter-revolutionary force that would draw further strength from the many *émigrés* and exiles who streamed across the French border in search of arms and a haven more congenial to their taste.

So now new battle-lines were beginning to be drawn, but for the moment the future promoters of an armed counter-revolution against the French had other, more pressing, problems to engage them: Russia, Sweden and Prussia were preoccupied with Poland; Austria with Turkey and her own Belgian and Hungarian subjects; while England was ready to pursue her waiting game until her own island security appeared to be threatened. So the guns remained silent and would continue to be so until April 1792, thus giving the French a further breathing-spell and allowing them to pursue their Revolution at home and project its ideas abroad by peaceful means. In some countries that impact was startling, while in others it was not; nor is it surprising that it should have varied widely depending on a subtle combination of factors from one country to the next. Some countries, like Russia and Turkey, were far removed from France's borders, and their traditions and social development made them almost completely immune to the penetration of revolutionary ideas. Others, like Bavaria and parts of Belgium, were protected against contagion by a pious peasantry and clerical domination. Spain, though sharing a common frontier with France, had similar problems and had, moreover, a small educated middle class unfit to serve as a suitable channel for the new ideas. Italy was divided between a receptive north – Piedmont, Savoy and Lombardy are obvious examples – and a south that was on the whole hostile to the ideas coming out of France (Neapolitan *lazzaroni* rioted, as of old, for Church and King, and a French ambassador was murdered in Rome). England's evolution had been different again, but she was made the more resistant to French ideas (though this was by no means universal) by her relatively high standard of living, her island position and her traditional enmity for France. Moreover, as Burke reminded his readers, she had had her own, in some ways similar, revolution in the century before – though he omitted to add that she had also, as France would later, cut off the head of her anointed King! There were countries, on the other hand, whose proximity to France, cultural traditions and social development made them highly susceptible to French revolutionary ideas – and, when it came to the point, to the penetration of French armies as well. These countries were Holland, Belgium, the Rhineland, the Swiss cantons (there was no 'Switzerland' as yet) and Italy, and although all countries in Europe, to a greater or a lesser degree, felt the impact of the events in France, it was in these alone that revolutions closely modelled on the French developed. Yet, even here, no revolutionary government survived once French military protection had been withdrawn.

So much for the largely peaceful penetration of French ideas in the early years of the Revolution. And it must be remembered that the Constituent Assembly, which inaugurated this three-year period of peace, had (with few exceptions) no intention of waging war on Europe either to extend its territories or to implant in its neighbours the new revolutionary ideas. In fact, the Constituents, in their first declaration on war and peace made in May 1790, solemnly proclaimed: 'The French nation renounces the undertaking of any war with a view to making conquests, and it will never use its forces against the liberty of the people.' This famous 'no-conquests' formula found its place in the Constitution of 1791 and was repeated by the Legislative Assembly in a statement of foreign policy on 14 April 1792, a few days before war was declared on Austria – admittedly, therefore, under conditions somewhat dissimilar from the peaceful days of May 1790. However, it has been suggested that the deputies – even those of 1790 – spoke tongue-in-cheek and never had any intention of abiding by these pious intentions. But this is to be wise after the event. The truth is rather that to members of all parties it was almost an article of faith that conquest and territorial expansion, while inseparable from the dynastic wars of the past (and those still waged by their opponents), were incompatible with the new ideas of Fraternity and the Rights of Man. When war broke out in 1792, the majority of the Legislative Assembly, persuaded by Brissot, believed that the Belgian, Dutch and Rhenish 'patriots' were waiting to receive them with open arms and that their 'liberation' – far from involving conquest – would be swift and painless. At this stage, apart from those working secretly for the Court, it was only Robespierre and the small group of his supporters who raised two pertinent objections: first, that the French army was not yet ready for the task to which it was being assigned; and, secondly, that 'armed missionaries' (as proposed by Brissot) were liable, even among would-be 'patriots', to be resisted rather than welcomed.

The first of these propositions was put to the test two months after war began, and Robespierre was proven correct; but the second could only be tested when the French armies, having won their first victories at Valmy and Jemappes, were ready to march into Belgium and Holland and when the Assembly was faced with requests by the 'patriots' of Savoy, Nice and the Rhineland to annex their territories to France. That the Assembly would consent to do so was no more a foregone conclusion than it had been in September 1791, when after a long delay it consented, in response to the wishes of the local population, to take over the papal enclave of Avignon. But Avignon lay a hundred miles within French national territory and it hardly seemed compatible with 'popular sovereignty' to leave the Avignonnais, against their own expressed wishes, under alien rule. But Nice and Savoy lay beyond the existing frontiers of France and belonged to the Kingdom of Sardinia; even so, the precedent of Avignon was quoted in support of the Savoyard request for union with France. The question was hotly debated in the National Convention in September 1792, when so ardent an internationalist as Camille Desmoulins argued that to annex Savoy, even in response to popular request, would be to embark on a policy of conquest such as the Assembly had expressly abjured. So the request was at first rejected but, soon after, the combined efforts of Danton, a number of Girondin deputies and internally minded foreign 'patriots' like the Prussian Anacharsis Cloots persuaded the Convention to find a new formula to justify such procedures. This led to the famous doctrine of France's 'natural frontiers' which, as first defined by Carnot, lay along the Rhine, the Alps and the Pyrenees. Such arguments prevailed and, on 27 November 1792, the Convention consented, with only two dissentients, to annex Savoy.

So the road now lay open – by logical development rather than by any preconceived intent – to engage in further experiments. The occasion arose, even more acutely than before, over the Low Countries and the Rhineland. France had, for the moment, been cleared of her enemies; the Austrians had been driven out of Belgium, the German princes from the Rhineland and the Sardinians from Nice; and the Convention issued a declaration on 19 November that it would 'grant fraternity and aid to all peoples who wish to recover their liberty'. It was a fateful step and was, of course, a direct and deliberate provocation to the rulers of Europe, including the English. But it also raised other questions: who should speak for 'the peoples', who should define 'liberty', and what would be the fate of those who rejected it? In the case of Nice, there was no great problem as the Niçois, like the Savoyards, were eager for union with France, and this was accepted. But the Convention had also decreed on 15 December that the new revolutionary authorities and assemblies to be formed in the occupied territories should be elected only by citizens taking an oath 'to be faithful to liberty and equality and renounce privilege'. So 'patriots' alone had the vote. But the 'patriots' of Belgium and the Rhineland, who welcomed 'liberation' and voted for annexation, proved to be a minority. Thus the Convention, far from acceding to the spontaneous and enthusiastic wishes of the 'liberated' peoples, had been led by the persuasive oratory of Dantonists and Girondins, the lobbying of foreign 'patriots', the logic of France's 'natural frontiers' and the exigencies of war to take the first steps along the road to conquest and annexation.

The Gironde and the 'patriot' groups in Paris had other expansionist aims as well – in particular, to set up 'sister republics' in those countries beyond France's 'natural frontiers' where she might be assured of a reasonable measure of support. Besides, such republics might, like the annexed territories, be expected to put the *assignat* into circulation, place their gold and silver at France's disposal and contribute, by subsidies and taxes, to her war expenses. Such plans were already well advanced in January 1793 when the occupation of Holland was on the order of the day. But the Dutch and English joined the war against France in February; by April, the French had been compelled to withdraw from the Low Countries and the Rhineland, and the Girondins fell soon after. Thus a new situation had arisen and new men came into power. Robespierre, their leader, had been opposed from the start to the war of 'liberation', to the conquest of France's 'natural frontiers' and the formation of 'sister republics'. Against such notions he urged the need to respect existing treaties and the rights of small nations and neutrals: the most that France should promise would be to assist a revolution that was already under way. Accordingly, foreign 'patriots' in Paris came under suspicion and Cloots, their most vociferous exponent, implicated in a 'foreign plot', went to the guillotine. Yet, though rejecting a proposal to annex Catalonia (which French armies entered in April 1794), the Committee of Public Safety compromised by simply placing her under French 'protection'.[4] But, in general, not only principles but circumstances had changed: from April 1793 to June 1794 the Republic, far from being in a position to expand or to impose its solutions on others, once more faced foreign invasion and was fighting for survival. Robespierre, as we know, fell from power a month after the victory of Fleurus; and it was only after Fleurus, when new opportunities arose, that the policies advocated by Robespierre could have been put more fully to the test.

The Thermidorians, however, did not share his views and reverted to the expansionist aims of the Girondin Convention; nor did they have to wait long to put them into practice. By the autumn of 1794 Belgium and the Rhenish provinces were once more under French military occupation. Republican troops entered Amsterdam, and the Stadholder fled to England. What should be done with the occupied territories? Some former 'expansionists' had by this time had a change of heart: Carnot, for one, had abandoned his belief in France's 'natural frontiers' and, with the support of a number of generals – Joubert and Kléber among them – argued that a policy of annexation would lead to endless war, and the royalists, now advocates of peace at any price, added their voices. However, other, more influential, voices prevailed: they included Sieyès and Merlin of Douai, champions of a network of 'sister republics'; Reubell of Alsace, who favoured outright annexation; and a medley of Dutch 'patriots', generals, army contractors and industrialists for whom expansion and annexation in their various forms appeared to offer a solid, material advantage. So Belgium was annexed as a province of France in October 1795; the Rhineland, pending annexation, was placed under military government; and, beyond France's 'natural frontiers', Holland was declared a Batavian Republic closely allied with France in 1795, and the Swiss cantons, after a long delay, were united in a Helvetic Republic in 1798.

Meanwhile, Bonaparte's victorious Italian campaign, which had begun in late 1796, had opened up far wider vistas of expansion beyond the Alps. Indeed, they form an impressive list. After the early victories, the Sardinians had been forced to accept the accomplished fact of the cession of Nice and Savoy. Later, by the peace of Campo Formio, Austria agreed to cede Belgium (another accomplished fact), to recognize the German princes' surrender of their Rhineland provinces, and to acknowledge France's title to the Ionian Islands in the Adriatic. In return (and in defiance of every revolutionary precedent) Venice, liberated from its local aristocracy by the French, was handed to the Emperor. The disposal of the rest of Italy was also necessary. The Directors, whose eyes were on Germany rather than Italy, preferred to exact a substantial tribute while leaving the direction of Italian affairs to the present rulers. But Bonaparte had plans of his own and was in a strong position to enforce them. Piedmont, in spite of local 'Jacobin' protest, was formally annexed by France; Genoa, pending similar treatment, earned a temporary respite as a nominally independent republic. Italian 'patriots' also hoped for a republican status for the liberated northern cities of Parma, Modena, Ferrara and Bologna, but Bonaparte nipped such aspirations in the bud and merged the cities with Lombardy and bits of former Venetian and papal territory into a sprawling Cisalpine Republic. A Ligurian Republic, based on Genoa, was organized along the north-west coast. With Napoleon's return to France and his departure for Egypt, these republics became models for his successors to follow. In 1798, the Pope was removed to Siena and a Roman Republic, under French military protection, was proclaimed in the centre of the peninsula. Early in 1799, General Championnet occupied Naples, whose King had joined Austria in an assault on Rome, and proclaimed a Parthenopean Republic in the south. These 'sister republics' (or at least the ones that survived) were to assume new forms under the Consulate and Empire. For the present, they accorded well enough with the revolutionary–

expansionist aims of the Directors and flattered the ambitions of their generals.

For one thing, as the Directors had hoped, these 'sister republics' and other annexed territories proved to be a profitable source of income. During the first occupation of Belgium, the Convention's decree of 15 December had already provided that the 'liberated' peoples must raise taxes to contribute to the upkeep of France's armies, and this policy was pursued with even greater vigour when France's expansion resumed in 1795. For example, on becoming a Batavian Republic, Holland agreed to support an occupation army of 25,000 men and to pay an indemnity of 100 million florins in silver or in bills of exchange drawn on foreign banks. These exactions increased as the war continued and as the Directors were faced with multiplying financial obligations. The procedure worked to Bonaparte's advantage, as he found that the surest way to persuade the Directors to condone his Caesarean methods in Italy was to replenish the Republic's coffers with loot and treasure drawn from the occupied regions. So the tax collector followed close on the heels of the conquering army and, in July 1797, Salicetti, commissar to the Army of Italy, reported that the first three months' campaigning had already yielded a tribute of 60 million francs. But Napoleon went even further. In a message sent to the Directors in November, he presented a remarkable balance sheet of successful operations in terms of prisoners, captured field-guns, treaties and 'liberated' peoples. To this account he appended the boast:

> Sent to Paris all the masterpieces of Michelangelo, Guercini, Titian, Paolo Veronese, Correggio, Albano, the Caracci, Raphael and Leonardo da Vinci.

However, it was not simply a one-sided business. The French Republic, in projecting its revolution into Europe, did not confine itself to exacting tribute or exporting treasure; it gave back something in return. Napoleon's 'victory-banner' (from which we have just quoted) also bore a list of a score of provinces and cities on whom he claimed 'liberty' had been bestowed. And this was no empty boast or rhetorical flourish, nor did it simply mean that France's enemies had been defeated in battle and that the local rulers had been driven from office or estate. The Republic's armies in Italy, as earlier in Belgium, Holland, the Swiss cantons, the Rhineland and Savoy, did not confine their activities to military operations, to plunder and to raising subsidies, even under the Directory. With the support, wherever possible, of local 'Jacobins' (the term was widely used), they introduced new laws and political institutions modelled on the French, and even transformed the old social system. Princes, Stadholders (as in Holland) and foreign governors were deposed; new revolutionary authorities were installed; national armies were levied; and French laws and constitutions were imposed. Of course, the nature of these measures, and the degree to which they were strictly 'bourgeois' or 'democratic', tended to reflect what was going on in France herself. The French liberal–democratic constitution of 1793, though widely acclaimed by 'Jacobins' abroad, had found few imitators, but this was because France was at that time in no position to impose her institutions on others and the foreign 'patriots' who admired them were, in most cases, powerless to do so without French support. There was, however, one exception: in the small city-state of Geneva the democrats, having won a majority in their newly formed National Assembly in February 1794, devised a constitution that, in many respects, was similar to that adopted, half a year before, by the Jacobin Convention. But it only survived for two years, for with Robespierre's fall the ideas and institutions of the Jacobin era ceased to be fashionable either in France or among her neighbours. So a new Genevan constitution, more closely modelled on the French of 1795, took its place.

This, by now, had become the general rule, and it was the same 'bourgeois' constitution of the Year III, which had brought the Directors into power in France, that became the model for the succession of constitutions – ten in all – that were introduced in the 'sister republics', whether in Italy or elsewhere, between 1796 and 1799.[5] They varied considerably in detail and some were more freely discussed, and less peremptorily imposed by France's agents, than others. In the Batavian Republic, for example, the constitution that emerged in 1798 had been hotly debated for three years: the Dutch democrats had long sought male adult suffrage and a single-chamber Assembly and only agreed to a compromise on the insistence of the French agent at The Hague. Elsewhere constitutions were imposed or adopted, with the minimum of local debate, from blueprints brought from Paris or issued by Napoleon's staff headquarters. But, whatever the method of consultation, the final results were nearly always the same: a more or less restricted suffrage (though sometimes more liberal than the French), elections in two stages, a bicameral Assembly, civil rights for Jews, and religious toleration. Moreover, the ghettos in Rome and Venice were closed down, as had previously occurred in Bonn; feudal dues, tithe and the surviving remnants of serfdom were abolished, as in the Rhineland, some Swiss cantons and Sardinia; privileged orders or 'corporations' were dissolved; and the lands of the Church were sequestered and put up for public sale.

In short, the general pattern was a 'liberal' settlement, broadly similar to that adopted in France by the Constituent Assembly in 1791 and to whose principles the Directors returned, after the interim of the Convention, in 1795.

But, not surprisingly, the changes did not satisfy everyone. The south of Italy, for example, was a region of small and landless peasants, impoverished but not enserfed; they gained little or nothing from the new regime and had little hope of doing better. In the Swiss cantons, tithe and seigneurial obligations were only redeemed at a heavy price, while in Belgium and parts of Italy the new measures of public assistance failed to compensate the poor for the loss of Church charities. So the French 'liberators', instead of meeting with universal gratitude, often encountered the hostile demonstrations of peasants and small urban consumers. These occurred as in Belgium, the Swiss cantons and much of Italy from the mid- to late 1790s – sometimes with the evident connivance of the Church. The most remarkable outbreak of all was that which occurred in Piedmont, in the north, after its annexation by the French in 1799. For there, far from clamouring for Church and King (as so often happened elsewhere), the insurgents, composed of peasant bands led by local 'Jacobins', protested against the French violation of the proclaimed rights of 'popular sovereignty'. They carried portraits of the revolutionary 'martyrs', Marat and Lepeletier, and demanded the formation of a united Italian Republic. The incident is significant because it was the first – and at the time unique – example of the revolutionary concept of 'popular sovereignty' being hurled back in the teeth of the 'liberating' French. It showed also that the Piedmontese, alone of the Italians of the 1790s, were ready to follow the French along the path of a broader popular revolution than France's present rulers were willing to tolerate. In so doing they also anticipated that revival of Italian radicalism – drawing its inspiration from Babeuf – which attended the collapse of Napoleon's Empire a dozen years later.

2 *Under Consulate and Empire*

The years of the Consulate, as we have seen, were largely devoted to Napoleon's reforms in France. But it was also during this period that the First Consul defeated the Austrians at Marengo (1801) and imposed on them the Treaty of Lunéville; and this incursion into Europe was soon followed by the annexation of Piedmont, Parma and Elba, the further occupation of Holland and Napoleon's election as President of the newly constituted Republic of Italy. So the 'revolutionizing' of Europe beyond France's own borders continued, though at a slackened pace. In fact, it was only after war broke out again with England in 1803 – and, notably, after England was joined by her three eastern allies two years later – that this became a continuous process, attended by a long series of French victories on land which would only end with the Emperor's final defeat and surrender after Waterloo in 1815.

Yet first, after the resumption of war, there was Napoleon's ill-fated attempt to invade England, and the loss of the combined French and Spanish fleets at Trafalgar in October 1805. But, anticipating this disaster, Napoleon had already abandoned the battle for the English coast and marched his newly formed Grand Army into Bavaria, where he routed the Austrian General Mack at Ulm and forced him to surrender with 50,000 men. There followed, in rapid succession, the French occupation of Vienna and the crushing defeat of a joint Austro-Russian force, commanded by the Tsar Alexander, at Austerlitz in Moravia on 2 December 1805 (to become a day and a month of annual commemoration in the Napoleonic saga). Francis II, the Austrian Emperor, was now induced to sign the Peace of Pressburg, by which he lost the Veneto and the Tyrol and, by recognizing Bavaria, Baden and Würtemberg as independent Kingdoms, surrendered his last foothold in Germany.

Meanwhile Napoleon, with little time to lose in negotiations, defeated the Prussians, the last of the eastern allies to join the war, at Jena and Auerstädt, and occupied Berlin. A further defeat of the Russians followed at Friedland in June 1807, and this, in turn, was quickly followed by the peace and alliance signed in July by Tsar and Emperor at Tilsit, where in terms of spheres of influence they virtually divided the whole of continental Europe between them.

England, now declared the enemy of both, would be brought to heel and made to acknowledge the long-disputed freedom of the seas.

So the campaign of 1805–07 had brought Napoleon dazzling successes, and though he did not yet know it he stood at the pinnacle of his fame and fortune. But it had also brought him new problems: how should he assimilate his conquests and how should he deal with the old enemy, 'perfidious Albion'? The answer to the first would lie in his organization of the 'Grand Empire', by now extending beyond the *French* Empire itself over a considerable part of Europe, and to the second in the economic blockade of England which was soon known as the Continental System.

The System, which was to cause its author far more headaches than its intended victim,[1] need not delay us here, as it added nothing to the 'revolutionizing' process which is our main concern. However, the Grand Empire that, with its network of annexed territories, satellites and principalities, had already begun to take shape, is strictly relevant. Since 1802 Europe's frontiers had, under the impact of French arms and diplomacy, undergone frequent and drastic revision. These changes were variously reflected in the transition from Republic to Empire, Napoleon's dynastic ambitions and the constant needs of war. In so far as they followed any master-plan, they were inspired by memories of the universal monarchy of Rome or Charlemagne rather than by any recent precedent. Least of all did they betray, despite his protestations at St Helena, any deep-felt desire by the Emperor to satisfy the national aspirations of the European peoples. Yet he was not averse to exploiting such feelings when it seemed opportune, as in his dealings with Italy and Poland. In Italy, the creation of the Cisalpine Republic based on Lombardy had roused the hopes of the 'patriots' of 1796, even though Venice was ceded temporarily to Austria and Piedmont was annexed to France. National hopes revived again when the Cisalpine was given the name of Italian Republic in 1802, but all this changed with the coronation of the Emperor in France. In 1805 there emerged a Kingdom of Italy, ruled in Napoleon's name by his stepson, Eugène de Beauharnais. By 1810 its territories had been extended along the Adriatic to enclose Venetia, the Marches, Ancons and Trentino. Meanwhile, the French Empire had absorbed Genoa in 1805; Parma, Piacenza and Tuscany (the short-lived Kingdom of Etruria) in 1808; and, in 1809, the Papal States and the Illyrian provinces across the Adriatic. In 1806, the Kingdom of Naples (the one-time Parthenopean Republic) had been given to Joseph Bonaparte and, in 1808, when Joseph was translated to Spain, it passed to Murat, husband of the Emperor's sister Caroline. All of these territories appeared to be destined for eventual absorption by the French Empire when, in 1811, the Emperor's son by his second wife, Marie Louise of Austria, was given the title of King of Rome. At that time, apart from tiny vassal enclaves like Lucca and Piombino, Italy was divided into four parts – the long stretch of French imperial territory reaching along the Mediterranean coast beyond Rome; the satellite Kingdoms of Italy in the north-east and of Naples in the south; and the remaining anti-French bastions, Sicily and Sardinia, held by the British fleet.

To the north of Italy, the Helvetic Republic had, as fashions changed, become the Swiss Confederation. Flanked by Berthier's principality of Neufchâtel and the annexed cantons of Valais and Geneva, its nineteen cantons, though not absorbed by France, were under French protection. To their north lay the Rhineland and Belgium (both enclosed within France's 'natural frontiers') and Holland. But Holland had undergone further changes in status: the Batavian Republic of 1795 had become the Kingdom of Holland in 1804 and had been absorbed within the French Empire in 1810.

Unlike Italy and the Low Countries, the frontiers and political system of Germany beyond the Rhine had not been touched by France's earlier conquests. The campaign of 1805–07, however, led to drastic changes. An early step was the creation in July 1806 of the Confederation of the Rhine, formed by sixteen (later eighteen) German princes, most of them nominally independent but to a greater or a lesser degree owing allegiance to the Emperor. Among them were Baden, Bavaria and Würtemberg (now freed from their Austrian connection), the Grand Duchy of Berg (recently ceded by Prussia), and the Kingdoms of Saxony and Westphalia. Westphalia was a new creation, pieced together, between 1807 and 1810, from parts of Hanover, Brunswick and Rhineland territory surrendered by Prussia at Tilsit; it was ruled by Jerome, the youngest surviving, as well as the ablest, of Napoleon's brothers, and became the object of his frequent attention.

While the new Confederation served as a counter to Prussia in the north and Austria in the south and east, Prussian Poland, renamed the Grand Duchy of Warsaw, was joined to Saxony and served as a buffer against Russia. Thus, on the eve of the Russian campaign of 1812, the Grand Empire and its satellites formed a network of interlocking states. The French Empire itself, its centre, stretched from Hamburg in the north to Rome in the south; divided into 130 departments, it covered nearly half a million square miles and enclosed a population of 44 million. Beyond it, to the east and south, lay a complex of satellite and vassal states, some ruled by the

Bonaparte clan, others by client princes nominally independent but incapable, even had they wished, of asserting their independence. Two states fitted into this pattern in theory rather than in practice – Sweden, where Bernadotte, elected Crown Prince through French influence in 1810, was planning a betrayal; and Spain, where Joseph, sent to fill a vacant throne in 1808, soon found himself to be a ruler without a kingdom. And outside this system, though on its fringe, lay a group of Continental powers – Austria, Prussia and Denmark – who in name were equal and self-governing but whose alliance, owing to French military preponderance, might as occasion demanded be bought, cajoled or imposed. (Prussia, in fact, in 1812 lost her *de jure* independence and became another vassal state.)

In time, Napoleon dreamed of imposing a greater measure of political uniformity on his conquests, but as they were the outcome of wars they were subject to continuous expedients and shifts of policy. Yet with all their variations they bore the mark both of their creator's orderly mind and of the changing constitutional pattern of France herself. For it was hardly conceivable that Napoleon, having assumed dictatorial powers in France, should leave the earlier representative institutions of the 'sister republics' unchanged. From 1800 onwards there had been a growing tendency for electors' rights to be circumscribed, for democrats to be pushed aside, for Notables and aristocrats to take over the main positions of authority, for the executive to be strengthened and the administration to become more fully centralized. In the Italian Republic of 1802 the popular vote was eclipsed in a system of hand-picked electoral colleges, and when the Republic became a Kingdom in 1805 the Legislature was scrapped altogether. In imperial France the Tribunate was abolished in 1807, the Legislature was rarely summoned and the Council of State, once it had completed its work on the Civil Code, was confined to judicial functions. This set the tone for the new constitutions of the Grand Empire, and in those drafted in 1807 and 1808 for the Kingdoms of Westphalia and Naples the Emperor first revealed his ultimate intent of dispensing with the elective principle altogether. Whatever freedoms the Emperor might accept – religious toleration and internal free trade were among them – they certainly did not include the freedom of political expression and the effective right to vote. 'It is ridiculous', he wrote to Jerome, 'to quote against me the opinions of the people of Westphalia. If you listen to popular opinion, you will achieve nothing.'

But, though denying the rights of democracy and popular election, Napoleon was nonetheless concerned to carry through drastic political and social reforms wherever his dominion extended. He found this both expedient and desirable: it was expedient to woo the peasants and middle classes and it suited him, as the heir of the Revolution, to transport to Europe such of the principles of 1789 as were not incompatible with his autocracy and military needs. Here the Civil Code was to be the cornerstone. As he further instructed Jerome in 1807: 'The benefits of the Code Napoleon, public trial, and the introduction of juries will be the leading features of your government.... What people will want to return under the arbitrary Prussian rule, once it has tasted the benefits of a wise and liberal administration?' Westphalia was intended as a model for the German Confederation, not least because of the effect it might have on its neighbours, but the recipe prescribed for Jerome was, with modifications, that applied in each of the annexed or vassal states. Like any 'enlightened despot', Napoleon was concerned to centralize and modernize his government, to strengthen his authority against any 'intermediate body' between the sovereign and his people. We therefore find high on the list of his reforms in each of his dominions the building of roads and canals, single customs areas, unified systems of justice and weights and measures, economy in government spending, the institution of national armies, written constitutions, the secularization of Church property and dissolution of monasteries. We also find such social reforms, reminiscent of the Emperor Joseph II, as religious toleration, civil rights for Jews and – almost universally – the abolition of serfdom where it still persisted. Reforms of a different order included the Concordat, which did good service in winning supporters or neutralizing opponents in Catholic Belgium, Naples and southern and western Germany. But, far more drastically than any 'enlightened despot' before him, Napoleon tore up the institutions of the *ancien régime* by the roots in parts of Europe where they were most deeply embedded, and introduced equality before the law, civil marriage and secular education. He abolished privileges, corporate bodies, tithe and feudal dues, and applied the new rights of inheritance and property (with the limitations we have noted) as enshrined in the universal panacea, the Civil Code. For the Code, as he wrote to Joseph at Naples, 'will fortify your power, since all entails are cancelled, and there will be no longer any great estates apart from those you create yourself'. Thus, as the ruler determined, a transfer of both property and status should take place: from the old exclusive owners of inherited estates and privileges to new social groups, enriched by trade or the purchase of land and entitled to their full share of honours, according to their service or social standing, in the new Napoleonic state. But there was to be no question of reviving the old practices of 1793. Neither small peasants nor urban *sans-culottes* would have more than meagre pickings from the redistribution of property and wealth.

While this was the general pattern, the changes made tended to be more far-reaching in those areas already incorporated under the Directory and Consulate, or where the emergence of an educated middle class favoured their development. Such was the case with Belgium, the Rhineland, Geneva and the Piedmontese and Ligurian provinces of Italy. Here the Napoleonic system had been almost uniformly applied, and there had been time for new classes to develop which, though suffering from his taxes, the lack of political freedom and restrictions imposed by the blockade, had benefited nevertheless from economic development, greater opportunities for advancement and the abolition of tithe and feudal obligations on the land. Whatever their secret grievances, such people, in fact, showed little inclination to shake off the Napoleonic yoke. In the Kingdom of Italy the regime also had time to become solidly established: the old landed aristocracy proved difficult to win over, but the Milanese bourgeoisie and officials, many of whom were masons, were among the Empire's most loyal supporters. In the rest of Italy – in Rome and the south – the case was different. In Rome, trade had suffered and, strangely enough, the French found most favour with the liberal aristocracy. In Naples, the nobility refused to cooperate and the small peasants and *menu peuple*, having little to gain from Napoleonic reform, remained sullen or, when stirred up by the priests, actively hostile. Even middle-class 'patriots', after 1806, joined disgruntled nobles in secret anti-French societies like the *Carbonari* and *Federati*. Yet Murat's administration was enlightened – and remarkably independent – and reform, though it began late, took firm root: so much so that when the Bourbon King Ferdinand returned to Naples in 1815 he did not think it advisable either to restore feudalism or to repeal the Napoleonic Code.

Like Italy, Holland had gone through a number of constitutional changes since its occupation in 1795, but unlike much of Italy it had a powerfully entrenched middle class, it had no serfdom and few feudal relics, its people were mainly Protestant, and as the Batavian Republic it had been forged into a unified state. Consequently, fewer changes had to be made there than elsewhere. Even so the guilds, though nominally abolished in 1796, still survived in Amsterdam a decade later; it was not until 1809 that the fiscal discrimination against Jews was finally removed; and the Civil Code was fully applied only after Holland's incorporation within the French Empire in 1810. Remnants of the *ancien régime* still survived: to appease the landowners, land-reform was never completed as in France and

Italy; the tithe remained as a secular rent and manorial dues were not redeemed.

The German and Polish provinces were brought into the Napoleonic system only after 1805. In consequence, reforms here were more hurried or more piecemeal and, on the whole, they tended to make concessions to the old ruling groups and interests. In the tiny Grand Duchy of Berg, for instance, after two years of enlightened rule by Murat hand-picked Notables took over, delayed the application of the Civil Code for several years, left the estates of the Church much as they had been before, and made the peasants pay for the remission of their old feudal obligations. In contrast, Jerome's Kingdom of Westphalia, intended as a model for others to follow, was submitted from the start to the clean sweep of Napoleonic reform. Here a constitution was proclaimed in 1807, quickly followed by a unified administration; the Civil Code and the French judicial system were introduced; Church lands were put up for auction; serfdom, privilege and guilds were abolished; but again (and this was the general European experience), feudal rents and *corvée* were made redeemable or enforced against peasant resistance. Yet assimilation was rapid and on the whole successful and in Westphalia as in northern Italy, the Napoleonic regime found ready support among the liberal aristocracy and professional bourgeoisie.

The Grand Duchy of Warsaw, formed from Prussian Poland after Tilsit, presented its own problems. On the one hand the Poles, unlike the Germans, had acquired a taste for national independence. On the other, the middle class was weak. Political and social life was dominated by the nobility, among them an active liberal group that had studied Rousseau and French ideas and had carried through the liberal Constitution of 1791. To them, the French appeared as liberators from Russian or Prussian tyranny and aggression. This gave Napoleon a decided advantage as long as he could appear as the champion of Polish nationalism and did not vitally injure the interests of the aristocracy. This was done by creating a unified state, while maintaining 'liberties' (read 'privileges') denied or abolished elsewhere, and leaving the social system substantially untouched. Under the brief rule of the King of Saxony, Napoleon's nominee, the Grand Duchy was given a strong central government and a judicial system and administration – with departments, communes and prefects – strictly modelled on the French. The Church was made subject to the state and its bishops were appointed by the Grand Duke; a new constitution guaranteed equality before the law and freedom of conscience to all citizens; conscription was introduced and the Civil Code applied in 1810. For the first time in its history, Poland was given a strong government and a centralized administration and was beginning to build up a corps of professional public servants. Though the government was authoritarian, the political aspirations of the nobility were appeased by maintaining a Diet composed mainly of noble deputies. Serfdom was abolished, but the peasants gained little as the old land-system with its feudal dues, rents and *corvée* continued, and tithe and the estates of the Church were left intact. Moreover, to allay clerical anxiety, the Jews were deprived of a part of their constitutional liberties by suspending their political rights and their right to purchase land. From this piecemeal operation the main beneficiaries were the lesser nobility, and it was their loyalty, rather than that of the landed magnates, that assured Napoleon of a Polish contingent when he went to war again with Russia in 1812.

Most of the princes of the Confederation of the Rhine, which by this time sprawled over the greater part of Germany, were nominally independent and were Napoleon's allies rather than his vassals. Supposedly he allowed them a considerable degree of independence within the Empire, as long as their pursuit of private interests did not conflict with their military obligations. Thus, in Mecklenburg and Thuringia, improved methods were found for raising troops, but the old aristocratic society and the old balance between monarchy and aristocracy remained undisturbed; and the King of Saxony, though a reformer by necessity in Poland, was not one in his own hereditary dominions. Yet several of the princes, particularly those in the south, had an interest in consolidating their recent acquisitions, both lay and ecclesiastical, and this led them, if not to imitate Napoleon, at least to emulate the methods of the more enlightened kings of Prussia or Sweden. King Frederick of Würtemberg, for instance, was an autocrat who denied his people any representation or civil liberties, and created an all-pervading police state. Yet he abolished serfdom, stripped the nobility of the right of private justice, granted religious freedom to Jews and secularized the lands of the Church, while leaving guilds, feudal obligations, aristocratic privilege and the old social order virtually untouched. The neighbouring rulers of Bavaria and Baden were more enlightened, adopting Napoleon's Civil Code and introduced constitutions guaranteeing civil liberties and equality before the law. Yet, with one tiny exception (the state of Anhalt-Köthen with its 29,000 subjects), the French system was not completely followed anywhere and the privileges of the old aristocratic society, its system of land tenure and its freedom to dispose at will of peasant labour were, in substance, left intact. Even the most 'enlightened' of the German princes had learned from the sorry experience of Joseph II that to disturb the old compact between monarchy and aristocracy was fraught with peril.[2]

Yet the Revolution, with its new experiences, had of course taught otherwise; and, within the Grand Empire, riddled as it was with contradictions and with the seeds of its own decline, Napoleon's conquering armies had shaken the structure of the social order and laid the foundations of the modern bourgeois state. For all his despotism, his arrogant unconcern for popular sovereignty, his dynastic ambitions and his devotion to a hierarchic order, the Emperor in his dealings with Europe still saw himself as the heir and soldier of the Revolution. And, hesitantly and imperfectly, Europe continued to be 'revolutionized' under the Empire as it had been, at a slower pace, under the Directory and Consulate.[3]

But, before we continue with the 'revolutionizing' of Europe after Napoleon's fall, we must return to the question posed at the beginning of the last chapter. Have we been discussing an essentially *French* revolution with its offshoots in other western countries; or are Messrs Palmer and Godechot right to maintain that all these revolutions, the French and American included, are merely 'phases' of a more general 'democratic' or 'Atlantic' revolution of the West? There might, in my view, be some point in attaching a general label to all the revolutions taking place in Europe and America from, say, 1550 to 1850 – this would encompass not only the American and the French Revolutions, but also those of the Dutch in the sixteenth century, the English in the seventeenth, and various South American and European revolutions in the early nineteenth century. All of these raise, in one form or another, common problems relating to feudalism, capitalism, democracy and national sovereignty. In this wider context, the American Revolution of the 1770s and 1780s and its preliminary skirmishes of the 1760s, appear to be as closely linked with the English Revolution of 120 years before as with the French of a dozen years later; and the German and Italian revolutions may be seen in full flood, rather than just at their earliest beginnings. But if one chooses to limit one's focus to the revolutions or near-revolutions of the eighteenth century, one is struck more by differences than by similarities and by the small number that can claim to be revolutions in their own right. In Europe, the only 'democratic' (or, more accurately, 'liberal') revolutions of the century in any way independent of the French were those at Liège, Brussels and Geneva; the first two had been defeated by 1790 and revived only as the result of French military occupation. Revolutionary movements were also germinating, inspired by the French example, in the Rhineland,

Piedmont and parts of Switzerland, but, again, they only came to a head on the approach of France's armies. Elsewhere in Western Europe revolutions, though owing something to local 'patriots' and local conditions, were largely imposed by the French. In fact, of twenty-nine constitutions adopted in European countries between 1791 and 1802, all except three (two Genevan and one Polish) were the outcome of French intervention.[4] So, strictly speaking, outside America and perhaps the tiny state of Geneva, the only internally-generated revolution was that of France.

Even more important perhaps is the fact that the Revolution in France went much further than any other – not only because it was more violent, more radical, more democratic and more protracted, but because it posed problems and aroused classes that other European revolutions (and the American too for that matter) left largely untouched. This was of course partly due to the differences in historical development in these countries, and also because the French after July 1794 (when they began to impose their ideas on their neighbours) were no longer interested in promoting the democratic ideals of 1793 – and ruthlessly crushed the Piedmontese when they attempted to do so. If we are only concerned with the spread of the ideas of the Enlightenment, the long-term legislation of the revolutionary Assemblies and the liberal 'Principles of '89', then the similarities between the revolutions in France and in these other countries are strikingly close: all went, with greater or lesser thoroughness, through a common bourgeois revolution which did away with the old feudal institutions and impositions, expropriated the estates of the Church, abolished serfdom, legal inequalities and the privileged orders, and declared careers 'open to talent'. This process continued, though in a muted form, in Germany and Poland under the Empire. Yet, important as this is, it omits an essential and quite distinctive element of the French Revolution: the active participation of the common people from 1789 onwards and all the consequences that flowed from it. John Adams, who witnessed the events of 1787 in Holland, charged the Dutch Patriots with having been 'too inattentive to the sense of the common people', and they continued to be so. This was by no means a feature peculiar to the Dutch: Belgian, Hungarian, Roman and Neapolitan 'Jacobins' were equally divorced from the people and made little serious effort to bridge the gap. In some of these countries, it is true, there were temporary movements in which both 'patriots' and peasants or urban poor took part, in which the latter classes voiced the slogans and ideas of their bourgeois allies; but these were exceptional and short-lived. In France alone, owing to the particular circumstances in which the Revolution developed and broke out (and certainly not to any innate Gallic quality), the 'Fourth Estate' became the indispensable ally of the Third, exacted its reward and even, for a time, built up a distinctive political movement of its own.

So in France, and not elsewhere, there were such phenomena as the peasant 'revolution', the *sans-culotte* movement of 1793, the Jacobin Dictatorship, the *levée en masse* and *armées révolutionnaires*, and the social experiments and Republic of the Year II. These factors reappeared, sometimes in more advanced forms, in the European revolutions of the nineteenth century; but, with minor exceptions, they did not appear in those of the 1790s – and still less so under the Consulate and Empire. In this sense, the revolution in France, though casting its shadow all over Europe, remained unique.

3 *Balance Sheet of Revolution, 1815–1848*

Of course, the victory of the Congress Powers[1] (the Russians, Prussians, Austrians and British) did not leave France and her neighbours as we described them in the last chapter. For to leave things as they were would hardly have accorded with the victors' new aims as they gathered to settle accounts with the defeated French – first in Paris in 1814 after Napoleon's first abdication and exile and, later, at Vienna in 1815 after his final surrender. From these prolonged, and interrupted, deliberations emerged the resettlement of Europe, with France's boundaries pushed back to those of 1790 (she nearly lost Alsace and Lorraine as well) and the rescrambling of the boundaries of the old European states to something broadly resembling those of the *ancien régime*.

But not entirely, for the victors had other aims in mind as well. Their aim was not only to punish the defeated aggressor and reduce her to her former size. They also wished to reward the victors by satisfying claims, some of which went back to a decade before the Revolution started whereas others had been voiced only after the war began. Thus – to cite a few examples – a new Kingdom of the Netherlands was formed with Holland as the senior partner and with Luxembourg and Belgium assigned junior roles. Prussia was given the Rhineland and a part of Saxony; Austria was given the Veneto (following Napoleon's example at Campo Formio) and the overlordship of Parma, Modena and Tuscany. The Spanish Bourbons returned to Naples and Sicily and the Pope to Rome and his Papal States. The Grand Duchy of Warsaw was entrusted to Russia; Norway was transferred to Sweden from Denmark (which had remained an ally of the French too long) and Finland from Sweden to Russia. England enlarged her colonial possessions by gaining Cape Colony and Ceylon from Holland; Mauritius, Tobago and St Lucia from France; and Malta from the Knights of St John. And, of course, in all this scrambling, in spite of the loud denunciations of Napoleon's contempt for national rights, little consideration was given to the national aspirations of the European – let alone the colonial – peoples. The Poles were redivided as readily among the Prussians, Austrians and Russians as Norwegians were handed over to Swedes, Belgians to Dutch and Venetians to Austrians, while

Italy resumed its old chessboard pattern of foreign-dominated states. Haunted by their fears of revolution, the powers pledged themselves to a twenty-year agreement (the 'Concert of Europe') whose purpose was both to settle disputes without recourse to war (in itself an admirable innovation) and to maintain by force their political settlement against all efforts by Bonapartist pretenders, liberal democrats or nationalists to upset it. While all five major powers bound themselves to this agreement, the absolute monarchs of Russia, Prussia and Austria, prompted by the Tsar, wanted to go further. Eighteenth-century rulers, reared on the teachings of the Enlightenment, had eschewed the old crusading slogans and ideological battle-cries, but the fear of revolution and the revival of religion had changed all this and provided new opportunities. So the Tsar and his associates formed a Christian union or 'Holy Alliance', whose object was to wage an ideological crusade against the rationalist and sceptical ideas of the Enlightenment and Revolution. Eventually, all European rulers signed this undertaking except an oddly assorted trio: the Prince Regent of England (advised by his Prime Minister Castlereagh that it was 'a piece of sublime mysticism and nonsense'), Pope Pius VII and the infidel Sultan of Turkey.

So, ostensibly, the victor powers appeared determined to restore the old order and restrain, by violence if need be, the political forces released in Europe by the Revolution. This was not their whole intention, and a great part of their settlement was sensible, just and not vindictive. But in so far as they attempted to obliterate the memory of the last quarter-century of history, their work was doomed to failure. This, as in all their previous efforts to hold back the Revolution, arose partly from their old dissensions. From the start, Castlereagh had made it clear that Britain, while pledged to maintain the frontiers agreed at Paris and Vienna and to prevent a Bonapartist restoration, would not support armed intervention in any state's internal affairs. His successor, Canning, carried the discrimination further; and, after 1822, Britain not only refused to suppress national and liberal movements but actively encouraged them in Greece, Spain, Belgium and Latin America. Even Russia was not averse to doing the same where it suited her imperial interests, as in Greece and Serbia, and by 1830 the Congress System lay in ruins, with Metternich, the Austrian Chancellor, its only consistent upholder. But even more decisive than these political divisions in obstructing the restoration of old Europe were the new forces released and the changes brought about by twenty-five years of war and revolution. These changes, as we have seen, were by no means confined to France and her satellites of the Napoleonic era.

It was a process of change that, far from being reversed by the victory of France's enemies, would continue to disrupt the old order and to shape the future.

Society itself had, in the first place, been thoroughly uprooted: the old aristocratic society had been either disrupted or transformed (or would become so shortly) beyond the point of no return. This was, of course, particularly true of France herself, where from 1789 onwards the old aristocracy had been stripped of what remained of its old rights of jurisdiction, its virtual monopoly of high office in army, Church and state, its feudal dues and services (eventually without compensation), its titles and privileges and its rights to dispose freely of common lands and to bequeath its estates undivided to elder sons. Part of the aristocracy had lost much more: the *noblesse de robe* had forfeited its old hereditary offices, and the properties of *émigré* nobles as of all dignitaries of the Church – bishops, canons and cathedral chapters – had been confiscated and were only exceptionally restored. Admittedly, the aristocracy had not disappeared. The majority, though shorn of their titles and privileges, had retained their lands even at the height of the Jacobin Terror. Napoleon had used undistributed 'national properties' (*biens nationaux*) to endow his new imperial nobility, partly composed of the Notables of the Revolution and partly of old aristocrats reconciled to his regime. These titles and bequests were recognized by Louis XVIII, his immediate successor, in 1814; and since then the Restoration monarchs, while generally respecting the rights of the purchasers of Church and noble lands, had created new titles and found new estates to reward their followers returned from emigration. Thus the aristocracy had been enlarged, owned substantial properties and, moreover, wielded considerable power in the Chambers and the ministries. But it was a new aristocracy, more closely associated with trade and finance and with the bourgeois owners of large estates, and sharply separated from the old *noblesse* – particularly from the former *moyenne noblesse* – by the land settlement of 1789 and the operation of the Code Napoleon.

The status of the peasantry, too, had been radically changed: although in France there had been relatively few serfs in the first place. Far more important than the abolition of serfdom was the removal from the soil of the burden of tithe and seigneurial obligations, and some peasants (though a minority) had been able to benefit from the sale of *biens nationaux*, particularly after the law of June 1793 had made it possible for a short while for villagers to combine their resources to bid for smaller lots. The poor and landless peasants had also succeeded, by their resistance to enclosure and the appropriation of common lands, in retaining some of the collective rights and protection of the old rural community: remnants of these survive to the present day.[2] Yet the transfer of land between classes had been on a relatively modest scale, and it was the bourgeoisie rather than the peasants that had reaped the main reward. The losers were the Church rather than the nobility, and those least favoured (other than the poorer *sans-culottes*) were the landless peasants. Yet the peasants as a whole had gained a new status and a measure of economic security that may possibly account for the persistent conservatism of much of rural France during the early decades of the nineteenth century.

A similar process, though more recent and less complete, had followed beyond France's own traditional borders. France's new laws and institutions, and the consequent social changes, were most immediate and most thorough in the territories that she directly absorbed within her Empire or those that lay closest to her frontiers. Thus the overthrow of feudal survivals and aristocratic privilege was almost as complete in Belgium, the Rhenish provinces, parts of Switzerland, Savoy, Lombardy and Piedmont as it was in France herself. In Venice, even before its absorption into Napoleon's Kingdom of Italy, the destruction of the old civic oligarchy had been the work of Austria, just as the first blows to aristocratic, patrician and ecclesiastical immunities in Tuscany and Lombardy had been dealt before 1789 by 'enlightened' Austrian reformers like Joseph II and Leopold. But this, as in Naples (where the reforms of the Bourbon Charles III had also preceded the Revolution), had been only a beginning; it was Napoleon's viceroys and vassals that finally uprooted feudal tenures (and serfdom where it still persisted) throughout most of the Italian peninsula. Sicily, under the English, saw similar reforms, and even the reactionary Ferdinand I, though he withdrew the liberal constitution and restored the Holy Office at Palermo, slowed down but did not reverse the process. But, although the old immunities and privileges of aristocracy were thus diminished or withdrawn, the effects on the peasantry were rarely the same as in France. For one thing, the redistribution of property that followed the sequestration of Church estates was less widespread. Though middle-class and even aristocratic purchasers prospered, little or nothing was done to help the poorer peasants to acquire land; they might even be the losers through forfeiture of common rights. In Lombardy and Piedmont, it is true, the abolition of feudal dues and tithe benefited all rural proprietors and made for a degree of general peasant prosperity, but in the south – in Calabria, Naples and Sicily – the problem was one of large estates and impoverished and landless peasantry rather than of feudal tenures, tithe and servile obligations, and for these conditions the revolution exported from France after 1795 offered no solution. Consequently, the basic land-problems remained and, through the shattered hopes of the Risorgimento, have survived to be solved, or left unsolved, today.

Patrician and aristocratic society had been undermined in Holland and parts of Germany in much the same way as in the north of Italy. King William of the United Netherlands was persuaded to retain the substance of French reforms in order to appease his new Belgian subjects; and Prussia's newly restored, or acquired, provinces in the west (the Rhineland, Berg and parts of Westphalia) similarly inherited the social results of the Civil Code and the abolition of feudal dues, tithe and serfdom. Metternich had higher hopes for the southern German states, now restored to Austria's sphere of influence; but, here again, such reforms as their rulers had carried out as Napoleon's allies were largely left untouched. Even traditionalist Prussia, in her eagerness to shake off the Napoleonic yoke, had found it expedient to borrow from the French – to abolish personal servitude on the land and to profit from the Jena defeat by abandoning the great Frederick's 'thin red line' (suited to an aristocratic society) in favour of Napoleon's appeal to the nation-at-arms. Meanwhile the Habsburg Empire, though resolutely opposed to experiment, had inherited what remained of Joseph's land reforms in Austria, Bohemia and Hungary, and more of Napoleon's in northern Italy and Illyria, yet the hard core of unpaid labour service survived till 1848. In Sweden Bernadotte, the sole usurper allowed to keep his throne, had helped to weaken aristocratic privilege by opening public office to men of humble birth. In Spain, the pro-French liberals of Madrid and Catalonia and the anti-French liberals of Cadiz had competed for middle-class favour by abolishing tithe and breaking up the *señorios*, but this was one of the few countries in Europe in which the clock had been firmly set back by the monarchy restored in 1814. In Poland, alone of the countries occupied by Napoleon's armies, though serfdom had been abolished the land system and relations between landlords and peasants had otherwise been left untouched, and Tsar Alexander, for all his liberal talk, refrained from doing more.

The uprooting of feudal survivals, the removal of impediments to trade and industry and the freeing of the soil from seigneurial dues, tolls and jurisdiction of course helped to promote and stimulate the growth of bourgeois society. In France, as we have seen, it was the middle classes (including the wealthier peasants) that reaped the greatest benefits from the Revolution. Napoleon, though denying them political liberty and spreading the rewards less widely, did nothing to change this pattern. Essentially the same can be said of the French-occupied countries other than Poland: the sale of sequestered properties, the sweeping away of old feudal enclaves and immunities, the opening of careers to men of talent, the creation of a new class of civil servants, the liberation of the internal market from restrictive tolls and guilds – not to mention the restraints on workers' associations – could hardly fail to raise the social status of the bourgeoisie. In such ways, too, particularly where labour had been released from the land and become a freely saleable commodity in manufacture, the ground would be cleared for the development of industrial capitalism. Yet it was not Revolutionary or Napoleonic France but England, her most inveterate and implacable opponent, who reaped the lion's share of industrial and commercial expansion and emerged from the twenty-year contest with the balance tipped even more firmly in her favour than before. The war imposed a heavy tax-burden on the English: between 1793 and 1815 they paid £52 million in subsidies to their allies alone; and England's industrial expansion was slowed down by the Continental System. But she found new markets, gained new colonies and, once the war and the painful post-war readjustments were over, she managed in a remarkably short time to lord it over all comers as the unchallenged 'workshop of the world'.

War and civil war had wrought havoc among France's manufacturers. Even under Napoleon her production in many fields stagnated, she lost further colonies to England, and the commerce of her great Atlantic ports sank to a trickle of their former volume. And this occurred although she was able, under Napoleon's Empire, to exploit the resources and dominate the markets of a large part of the Continent, to compel her vassals and allies to pay the greater share of the cost of her wars, and to use the Continental System to promote her own national advantage at the expense of her neighbours – even those she had enclosed within her own borders. The explanation of this phenomenon lies partly in the dislocation caused by revolution (though not after 1799) and in more immediate effects caused by the British blockade of her coastline. But even more important, England alone had in the 1780s been involved in an industrial revolution that not only 'revolutionized' her technical processes but had begun to transform society by calling whole new productive classes – industrial manufacturers and factory workers – into being. For France and her neighbours, the clean sweep of revolutionary and Napoleonic reform had cleared the way for a similar social transformation, and technical innovation had made progress, after 1800, in the textiles of Lyons and Normandy and in the mines of Belgium and the Sarre. But this was only a beginning; and, to create the new industrial society, in which *sans-culottes* would give way to proletarians and workshop masters to industrial manufacturers, it needed an industrial as well as a political revolution. The Revolution of 1789 had hastened this process in some ways while delaying it in others. The remedies would be found in the years of peace that followed – mainly after 1830.[3]

Other institutions, too, had been profoundly affected. Wherever Napoleon's armies had passed, the French Civil Code had been implanted, the administration had been overhauled, pockets of ecclesiastical and seigneurial justice had been uprooted and a nationwide system of law courts and juries had been introduced. Cheap and efficient government had replaced or amalgamated the myriad competing and overlapping authorities and jurisdictions surviving from a feudal, or near-feudal, past. In Germany, from 1803 onwards, Napoleon had abolished the outworn Holy Roman Empire, hacked through the network of petty principalities and Free Cities and reduced their number from 396 to 40. Of the surviving German states, eighteen had eventually been grouped together in the Confederation of the Rhine and had begun to be welded into a common customs union. Here again, there was no going back to the prerevolutionary past. Old dynasties were re-enthroned, liberal constitutions were withdrawn, and most of Europe's rulers were incapable of understanding the new forces that were at work. But there was remarkably little reshuffling of the Grand Empire's geographical boundaries and many of its institutions were left substantially unchanged. The Civil Code remained in a score of European countries from Belgium to Naples and from the Rhineland to the new Kingdom of Poland, carved out of Napoleon's Grand Duchy of Warsaw. The Vienna confederates dissolved Napoleon's Confederation of the Rhine and put in its place a larger Confederation of thirty-nine German states, presided over by Austria and not intended to foster German national aims. But, whatever the authors' intentions, it created the framework for a closer political union and soon began to serve as a single tariff area.

Relations between Church and state had also been profoundly and permanently affected by revolution and Napoleonic reform. Admittedly, the settlement of 1815 had been attended by a notable religious revival: the Pope was re-enthroned at St Peter's amidst general jubilation; the Index, the Inquisition and the Jesuit Order were reinstated; the Catholic Church recovered its control over education and, in Spain, Bavaria, Sardinia and Naples, most of its old authority; and rulers of all denominations professed to base their policies on Christian principles. But a great deal of this was short-lived, as the temporal power of the Church had been undermined and the rule of episcopal princes (as at Salzburg, Mainz and Cologne) had become all but a thing of the past. In fact, of all the princely prelates of the pre-revolutionary era, the Pope alone retained his temporal dominion, although not for long. Twenty-five years later, he, too, would have to surrender his power as part of the price to be paid for a united Italy under a Catholic king.

Nationalism, also, survived as a legacy of the Revolution. Napoleon, though his views on the nationalist spirit were, to say the least, ambivalent, had unwittingly fostered it. At St Helena, of course, he was indulging in propaganda at the Congress powers' expense when he claimed deliberately to have sought to unite 15 million Italians and 30 million Germans, as well as 30 million French and 15 million Spaniards, 'each into one nation'. Thus (he claimed) 'the European System would have been laid and my only remaining task would have been its organization'.[4] Yet, though the boast was quite misleading, the reforms that he had brought to Europe had given it a certain credibility, for such reforms could hardly fail to have something of the same unifying effects on the occupied countries as the reforms of the Constituent Assembly and Convention had had on France herself. Not only this, but he had deliberately exploited the national spirit in his dealings with Poles and Italians: the Kingdom of Italy, for example, though by no means satisfying the wider aspirations of Italian patriots, had been created partly with the intention of whetting their appetites for more. Inevitably, the dashing of these hopes had alienated many, whose sympathy for the French had turned, in the course of time, to resentment and hostility and even to the organization of anti-French secret societies. In Germany this resentment, while it never burst into open rebellion, had become more sharply focused by identifying itself with the national policies of Prussia and Austria. The reorganization achieved in 1815, instead of finding solutions, exacerbated the problem and drove the German, Italian and Polish nationalists (not to mention the Belgian, Greek and Latin American) to seek more desperate remedies in the coming decades.

Another result of the 1815 settlement was to bring nationalism and liberalism together. Though both stemmed, in large measure, from the years of revolution, their partnership had not generally been a close one in Napoleon's Europe. Patriots – if we include nationalism of the Spanish as well as of the German and Italian type – were inclined, after 1808, to be hostile rather than sympathetic to the French. Liberals, on the other hand, being composed of middle-class Notables rather than of petty craftsmen, nobles or peasants, were more often the allies than the opponents of France. In France herself, liberal political ideals had been proclaimed and fostered by Constituents, Girondins and Thermidorians, whereas, for differing reasons, they had been discouraged or proscribed by the Jacobin Convention and Napoleon. But, though muzzled or held in check under the Consulate and Empire, European liberals had naturally gravitated towards the French who brought reforms, rather than towards their own rulers who obstructed them. There were, of course, notable exceptions: the Italian Jacobins who, after 1805, formed secret societies to oppose the French, included liberals as well as revolutionary democrats; in Spain, anti-French liberals predominated in the Cortès at Cadiz that adopted the Constitution of 1812; and in Germany there were liberals among the patriots who looked to Prussia to lead a German crusade against the French and to reform their own feudal institutions. Yet it is probably true that in Italy and Germany, no less than in Holland, Switzerland and Poland, liberals tended to pin their hopes on the survival rather than on the collapse of Napoleon's Empire. The 1815 settlement, by its very nature, tended to end this divorce between patriots and liberals. In Spain peasant anti-liberal nationalism died a natural death with the ending of the French occupation and the restoration of Church and dynasty; and, in 1820, the liberals of both the Napoleonic and anti-Napoleonic camps, reunited by the departure of the French, combined to proclaim the Constitution of 1812. In Germany and Italy, the Congress settlement offered no greater comfort for liberals than for nationalists: both met with equal condemnation from the three central and eastern powers. Austria, in particular, remained the target of liberal and 'patriot' animosities until 1848, for Austria now occupied the northern Italian states, dominated the German Confederation, and invoked more persistently than her partners the provisions of the European 'Concert' restraining the activities of German, Italian, Spanish and Belgian patriots and liberals.

Democracy, another product of the Revolution, had a somewhat different history. Though inherent in Rousseau's 'popular sovereignty', it was not, like liberalism, an inevitable outcome of the victory of the Third Estate. Like their fellows in other countries, the French middle classes of 1789 had wished to end royal 'despotism', destroy aristocratic privilege and extend the franchise to all men of property; but, although proclaiming the common Rights of Man, they had no intention of sharing authority with the 'lower orders' or 'Fourth Estate'. This partnership and the common right to vote came about through circumstances outside their control. It had proved impossible to deal adequately with privilege and despotism without the co-operation of the *menu peuple*. Yet this stage of the Revolution had been short lived: the Constitution of 1793, after being put into temporary cold storage by the Jacobins, was repealed by their successors; male adult suffrage was withdrawn and the popular movement that promoted it was destroyed. After that there was no further serious suggestion, under either the Directory or Napoleon, of restoring democracy in France, and in Europe, although there were popular–democratic movements in northern Italy and Geneva in the mid-1790s, they were by now no more tolerated by authority than they were in France herself. After Napoleon's defeat, they were more systematically repressed by the Congress powers than they had been before. Yet democracy survived and took firm root: not in any country within France's own political orbit, but in England, where radicalism, after a fifteen-year proscription during the wars with France, revived around 1807 and began to feed democratic ideas back to the reform movements springing up in early-nineteenth-century Europe. Here again, the industrial revolution played a part, as it created in England, earlier than elsewhere, a politically literate working class, which eagerly read the writings of Thomas Paine and assured the radical movement of a major base in factory, mine and mill. In other countries, after its setback in the mid-1790s, democracy was slower to recover; but, with the collapse of the Congress System, it revived in France, though in a new guise, in the Revolution of 1830 and, accompanied by new slogans and ideas, in that of 1848.

Here again, it was the industrial revolution, with its new challenges and perspectives, that proved a decisive factor. Thus, in France, the workers that thronged the streets of the capital to overthrow the Bourbon Charles X in the 'July days' of 1830 were no longer the old social medley, or *sans-culottes*, of 1789 but, with the development of manufacture, were becoming moulded into a new industrial workforce which, barely a dozen years later, would call themselves *prolétaires*. To them the events of 1830 meant not only – as they did to the liberal bourgeoisie – the completion of the unfinished business of 1789 and a return to the neglected 'Principles of '89', but something new as well: the right to work and, through association, to earn a living wage. This led, as it had shortly before in England, to the emergence in France of a national working-class movement: first at Lyons and later in Paris and elsewhere. This produced in turn a new ideology of popular protest, of which a central feature was the demand for a 'social and democratic republic' – that is, one no longer fashioned in the image of the liberal bourgeoisie (as in 1789 and 1830), but one that corresponded more closely to the new needs of the basic producers.[5] It was first voiced in the streets and the clubs of Paris in the spring of 1848, but was repeated in other revolutions, such as in Hungary, Greece and Romania, later that year.[6]

So 1848 was a culmination in that it brought to a head, or completed, some of the developments of the 'revolutionizing' process emanating from France from the days of the Directory onwards. But in other respects it was a defeat and proved to be a turning-point of quite a different kind. Even in France, where the February Revolution appeared so full of promise, the hopes for a 'social and democratic republic' proved short-lived and went down to bloody defeat in June. In Italy the revolution of 1848, while a stepping-stone to later national unification, affected no social change; and in Germany (though, as in Austria, serfdom was abolished or undermined) the revolution was a failure far more than a success, for the liberals, who had made their revolution under an all-German national banner and had convened a national parliament to mark their victory, abjectly surrendered when the voice of the masses began to be heard, dissolving their parliament and handing back power to Austria and the princes as the Congress System provided. Moreover, in both countries liberals and nationalists took a sharp turn to the right and, to unite their nations, swung behind the conservative, or near-conservative, policies of Bismarck and Cavour. So it is not altogether inappropriate that for Paris, too, 1848 marked a turning-point. Having served for sixty years as the almost indispensable launching-pad for revolution, it now began to take a back seat.

VII The Revolution and the Wider World

1 *As a World-historical Event*

But the projection of the Revolution beyond France's borders did not stop at Europe. From the Consulate onwards, the ideas and institutions of the Revolution and the Napoleonic era were carried across the oceans. In the course of the next 200 years, though its effects were spread unevenly, it became something like a world event. The degree to which it elicited a response depended, as it had in Europe, on a number of factors including accessibility to its common source, the changing governments in France and, inevitably, the social climate and past history of the countries in which it sought a haven. The process began under the Consulate, though even by then France's relatively poor overseas communications hampered its penetration.

Yet, paradoxically enough, in the late eighteenth and early nineteenth century, it was England rather than France – and not only because of her more developed communications – that evoked the first significant response (though, admittedly, a negative one) to the recent events in France. For England, after the French wars started in the spring of 1793, had an interest in combating rather than promoting the revolutionary cause. To some extent, indeed, this process began – as France and England were already at war over North America – several years before the revolution in France broke out. Having conquered Canada in 1759, Protestant England found herself faced with the problem of the future status of the Roman Catholic Church in Lower Canada (Quebec). The solution she found – much to the indignation of the ultra-Protestant faction in her Parliament and in the City of London – was, under the Quebec Act of 1774, to confer on the Lower Canadian Church a remarkably high degree of independence to control its own affairs.[1] Thus the Church was firmly established as a bulwark against the twin dangers of irreligion and social disorder, whether emanating from the United States (whose revolution had just begun) or from Europe. So when, nearly twenty years later, a steady stream of 'refractory' priests and nuns sought refuge from persecution in France, many were able, with British protection, to find a haven from revolution in the Catholic Church of Quebec. Moreover, in 1798–9, serious consideration was given to establishing a militarized colony of *chouans* (French peasant anti-Jacobin guerrillas) at York in Upper Canada; but the plan fell through because an agreement could not be reached.[2] And England did more: as a further bulwark against disorder, she maintained the French seigneurial system for close on a century after her occupation began; she only consented to abandon it (in 1854) after the French peasant settlers themselves, long its enthusiastic upholders, had been calling for its removal for twenty years.[3]

More positive, no doubt, has been the impact of France and her Revolution on the history of the United States. It began with the comradeship formed under arms in the American War with England and led to close ties between old allies during the early years of the French Revolution. This was followed, under Napoleon, by the Louisiana Purchase in 1803, whereby France sold an old overseas possession to the new American nation. Through Louisiana, both before and after the Purchase, the Code Napoleon was able to gain a foothold on the American continent. It seems, in particular, that the French notion of 'liberty', as first proclaimed in the 'Principles of '89', has made a lasting impression on the people of the United States. We may perhaps ascribe to this influence (though here motives may have become mixed) the frequent sallies made by Americans in the 1820s and 1830s across the Canadian border in order to 'liberate' (or so it was claimed by the Invaders) the provinces of Upper and Lower Canada from British colonial rule.[4] The love-match continued for a century or more; witness, in the 1880s, the enthusiasm with which New Yorkers greeted the erection of the Statue of Liberty on the Hudson river, based on a French design. And it is remarkable how many Americans of the 1920s and 1930s made an almost annual pilgrimage to France – and, notably, to Paris – as the birthplace of 'freedom' and the Rights of Man.* It was also perhaps reflected in American literature of the time, as in the sentimental nostalgia for Paris and its bistros expressed in some of Hemingway's novels and – on a somewhat lower literary plane – by Elliot Paul in his book *The Narrow Street*, written in the 1920s. Of greater substance, however, has been the conscious attempt of the French, in the post-Napoleonic era, to spread the message of the Revolution and transplant its institutions to its colonies or spheres of influence overseas, as in Algeria after 1829, Latin America in the 1820s to the 1840s, or Black Africa and Indo-China in the years of the New Imperialism that preceded the First World War. And, as on these occasions the flag followed trade, the best indication of the

* This, admittedly, was not the only attraction, and it has probably become a dwindling asset.

French ability to bring their institutions to other continents – to Africa in particular – is perhaps to examine the influence of France's own tricolour flag.

To do so we must turn to Africa after France's liberal revival during her long second period of imperial rule; both were features of the 1870s and the years that followed. According to a useful compendium by Whitney Smith (writing in 1980) of 174 national flags, 45 were tricolours apparently modelled on the French, and were then being flown, or had previously been flown, in four of the world's five continents (Australasia was the exception).[5] The process began in Europe during the sixty 'revolutionary' years that ended in 1848. First came Napoleon's Republic of Italy in 1802; then followed the Czechs in 1818, Belgium in 1831, Poland and Greece in 1839, and Romania, Germany and the Croat Republic in 1848. And there were two late starters not directly connected to the French: the Irish Easter Republic of 1916 adopted it (and it still survives), as did Bulgaria (on the centenary of its independence from Turkey) in 1971. Meanwhile, during the revolutions in Latin America, Mexico had adopted the French tricolour in 1821, Nicaragua in 1823 and Venezuela in 1830, followed by Paraguay in 1842, Colombia in 1861 and Bolivia in 1868. But it was almost a century later that France began to leave behind her a growing trail of former African colonies that celebrated their independence and their long French connection by adopting the tricolour flag as their national emblem. It began with Egypt and Syria in 1952 and Niger in 1954. These were followed by French Guinea in 1958, the Ivory Coast, Upper Volta, Chad and Senegal in 1959, East Gabon in 1960, Mali in 1961, Sudan (recently linked in an Anglo-French Condominium with Egypt) in 1969. Syria (across the Suez Canal in Asia), the Cameroons and Equatorial Guinea followed suit between 1972 and 1978.

But, before closing this chapter, two words of caution need to be added. One is that not all the tricolour flags recorded by Whitney Smith derive, even indirectly, from French influence or occupation – perhaps only thirty of the 45. The remainder have had different histories. The Dutch tricolour, for example, which reappears in South Africa, had its origins in the 1600s – a full century before revolution broke out in France. There is also the 'Pan-African' tricolour which, though it may owe something to 1789, is more a symbol of African solidarity than a token of any particular regard or affection for France.[6] Again, there is, or has been, in India and the Middle East a French-style tricolour that derives from a Moslem tradition: such flags have been flown (as fashions change) in Iran, Jordan, Yemen and Iraq. Lebanon's flag is a special case owing to its one-time connection with France: it began to fly the tricolour under French rule in 1929, but abandoned it (unlike several of its African neighbours) on attaining independence in 1943.[7]

The other word of caution is that, after 1917 in particular, the great revolution in France – although the most richly documented of any – was not the only major revolution exporting its institutions and ideas to other lands. Before 1789, the Dutch and Americans had done so in a more muted form; and the influence of the English Revolution, though considerable in the United States, was never on a scale comparable to the French. Besides, these revolutions, whether of the seventeenth or eighteenth century, had shared broadly similar political and social aims and had in common the setting of a pre-industrial society. The Russian Revolution – not to mention the Chinese or the Cuban – was something else again. On the scale of the wider world – even more than in the context of western or southern Europe – it was from this later revolution rather than any preceding it that there developed an industrial working class and the new dominant conflict between capital and labour which had been almost unknown outside England in 1789. With these came the widespread dissemination of the new socialist and collectivist ideas (of modern industrial society), first formulated systematically by Marx. So it is hardly surprising that, in subsequent generations, the old watchwords of Liberty, Fraternity and Equality should have become overlaid with other ideologies and with demands for new solutions. It might appear that the old liberal ideas of 1789, stemming from the earlier revolution in France, have become absorbed or even lost their relevance, yet this would be a profound mistake. For, as Gramsci wrote half a century ago, the needs of the present feed on 'the cultural past': Renaissance and Reformation, German philosophy and the French Revolution with its 'secular liberalism', all 'lie at the root of the whole conception of life'.[8] The battle for the Rights of Man continues and, in spite of new slogans and new leaders and faces, it is still as relevant today as it was 200 years ago.

2 *Legacy and Tradition in France*

There is a further word to be added. The Revolution not only left tangible bequests such as flags, institutions, the Civil Code and new modes of social organization. It also left, more allusively, its traditions and myths. These too (as Georges Lefebvre has reminded us) may exercise a powerful influence on the historical record. Nor did the legends and myths all derive from social classes such as the bourgeoisie or prosperous peasants, who gained more than their share from the balance sheet of revolution. The *sans-culottes* and small cultivators, as we have seen, gained little in the way of material benefits, but they left memories that were not forgotten to the generations that followed. In the first place, the tradition of popular revolution itself: the violence, heroism and passionate idealism of the 'days' of 1789, 1792 and 1793 were re-enacted by similar crowds – though stirred by new objectives – throughout Europe in 1848 and in Paris as late as 1871. Indeed, their echoes were heard in the student 'events' of a century later. Again, on a different political plane, we have noted how the Spanish liberals of 1820 and 1836, like the French, German, Belgian, Swiss, Polish and Italian liberals of the 1830s and 1840s, drew at least some of their inspiration from the Declaration of the Rights of Man and the Constitution of 1791. And even in England in 1830, it seemed reasonable to attribute the ferment over labourers' wages in the southern counties in part to the events of the July Revolution in France.

Moreover, such traditions and lessons were repeated far beyond France's national borders and persisted, or revived, long after the 'high' revolutionary period of the 1830s and 1840s had passed. The Russian revolutionaries of 1917, far from scorning the experiences of their Jacobin forerunners of 1793–4 (as M. Furet and others sometimes appear to think they should), eagerly debated the lessons of Thermidor, while Lenin considered the 'democratic dictatorship' of the Year II to be a suitable model for the Bolsheviks to follow. So Jacobinism, briefly at least, became the ally of Bolshevism and, to cement the union, Robespierre was given a niche under the walls of the Kremlin and a quay was named after him along the Neva in Lenin's new capital city.[1]

However, as the two revolutions had quite different ultimate goals, the model could only serve a temporary purpose. Fifty years before, Marx had warned the French workers not to follow too slavishly the precepts of 1792, and in the Second Address of the Council of the First International (September 1870) he charged them 'not to let themselves be carried away by the national memories of 1792, as the French peasants had been duped by memories of the First Empire; for their task should not be to relive the past but to build the future'.[2] Yet when, six months later, the Parisians challenged Thiers' government at Versailles and set up their Commune, Marx saw that useful lessons could be learned and praised them for 'storming the heavens'.

The need for discretion in such matters remains, though it does not preclude the value of seeking out the revolutionary traditions in a country's history and drawing conclusions from them. In the case of the Revolution in France we may, broadly, divide these traditions into four. First, there was the liberal tradition centred on the Rights of Man and the 'Principles of '89' which, though it denied the vote to 'passive' citizens, championed freedom of speech, worship and assembly and civil rights for Protestants and Jews (and, later, for men of colour in the colonies). There followed the popular democratic tradition of 1792–4, according votes to all adult males and promoting popular participation at street and municipal levels. Thirdly, there was the Bonapartist tradition which, though authoritarian and distrustful of 'liberty' and popular democracy, was – with some important modifications – the consistent upholder of equality before the law and careers being 'open to men of talent'. And lastly, as the Revolution had its counter-revolution, each of these traditions had its antithesis among those who, fearful for property, religion or privilege, have felt threatened by the Revolution and all its consequences and implications. This tradition, too, though negative and disapproving, is as much as any other a part of the legacy of revolution.

Sometimes two or three of these traditions may be found together, rubbing shoulders uneasily within the same community. An example can be found in Gabriel Chevalier's account of the village of Clochmerle in Beaujolais (1934), where the *baronne*, nostalgic for the vanished past, and her confessor, the village priest, are in conflict with the mayor, the lawyer and the schoolmaster, all champions of the 'Principles of '89', over the official opening of a public urinal, bedecked with the tricolour, in front of the village hall![3] At other times and in other places a transition may take place, from rejection of the Revolution to acceptance, or vice versa. Thus we have the example of the peasants and rural craftsmen of the Var who, though conservatives during the 1830s and 1840s, became militants by 1849 and took up arms to resist Louis-Napoleon's *coup d'état* of December 1851.[4] On the other hand, we have seen how Frenchmen like the historian Taine, liberal–democrats in 1848, switched sides to blast the Revolution and all its works after the experience of the Paris Commune.[5] And to continue the saga, we have the case of the French colonels in Algeria who, in May 1958, staged a Bonapartist *coup d'état* to bring de Gaulle to power; when de Gaulle tempered repression with conciliation, they resorted to counter-revolution and attempted murder instead.

Another way to consider the problem is to see how the traditions stemming from 1789 have impinged on certain events in France's history and shaped the reactions and behaviour of certain groups. Starting with the fall of Napoleon, we have seen how an important body of liberal-minded historians bred on the 'Principles of '89' chose to promote liberal reform in the 1820s by extolling its virtues under the Constituent Assembly.[6] We saw, too, in the generation that followed, how historians like Michelet returned to the democratic–Republican tradition in 1793 to prepare the way for the Revolution of 1848. This phase ended in 1849 when, with massive peasant support, Louis-Napoleon, the great Emperor's nephew, was carried to power – first as President, later as Emperor – for a twenty-year term. When this ended in defeat and humiliation, three of the Revolution's traditions blended or, for a short while, existed side by side. On the one hand, the popular–democratic tradition, hostile to both liberalism and Bonapartism, was re-enacted in the Paris Commune. On the other, there was the liberal–conservative National Government at Versailles, which crushed the Commune with the aid of the liberal Gambetta. Ten years later, while France was still smarting from her Prussian defeat, there was an attempted resurgence of Bonapartism, when General Boulanger, assuming the role of the nation's saviour and Man of Destiny, rode into Paris on a white horse. Yet it proved to be a five-days' wonder that left few memories or regrets.

But, meanwhile, the high hopes raised by the new 'socialist–radical' Republic of the 1870s had begun to turn sour with economic and financial crises, unemployment and the beginnings of a substantial immigration from the North African colonies. It was against this background that a new right began to form, drawing support from the 'middling' classes and the poor of the big towns. It found its first national expression, reinforced by the counter-revolutionary triad of Church, army and Establishment, in the hysteria of the Dreyfus affair which in the 1890s divided France into two opposing camps, ranging a broadly based right against liberals, socialists and other traditional upholders of the principles of '89 and '93. The *Dreyfusard* agitation inevitably died down as Dreyfus himself, the victim of the hysteria, returned vindicated from his temporary exile on Devil's Island. But the new right lived on under the changing guise of *Cagoulards* (Hooded Men), *Croix de feu* and National Front, to plague French politics with its provocative assaults on liberal employers, labour militants, immigrant Arabs, aliens and Jews.

This brings us to the element of mystery surrounding events in France after her military disaster of 1940. Briefly, France was once more divided into two main factions – with those determined to fight on for another day rallying to de Gaulle in exile or joining the Resistance in France, and, with the new right and others eager to settle accounts with 'the enemy within' actively supporting the Nazi Occupation or, behind closed doors, denouncing Jews and other 'undesirables' as suitable objects for prison, deportation, torture, execution or forced labour. When the Occupation ended and some degree of normality returned, the experience was hard to forget, to forgive or to live down. Who had been a traitor, who a patriot; who had signed on with the Resistance at the last moment to cover his tracks? Such questions continued to be asked and even now, after forty-odd years have passed, they have not been finally answered. And this may explain why – for fear of the lid being lifted in open court – there was so much speculation on whether Klaus Barbie, the reputed 'Butcher of Lyons', though a prisoner in France for the past four years, would really be brought to trial.[7]

Moreover, have such doubts and suspicions any relevance to the continuing debate dividing historians on the origins and meaning of the French Revolution? Some of the arguments now being used by the Revolution's critics suggest that they have; and it seems a fair bet that, as the Bicentenary approaches, the debate will become more bitter and unyielding. It appears likely, too, that the Revolution will continue to divide Frenchmen along ideological lines. But how many Frenchmen will, in fact, be drawn into the debate; how many will really feel 'divided' today as they appear to have felt over Dreyfus ninety years ago? There will certainly be among them militant upholders of the Republic of the 'Year II' and champions of that 'greater' France conceived by Napoleon. Who can doubt that the 'counter-revolutionaries' of today will be less vocal and less inclined than their forbears to damn the Revolution and all its works? Yet there is some doubt whether Frenchmen in Paris or elsewhere still feel the same degree of involvement, and it is likely that the experience of the past fifty years blunted the image of the Revolution as a continuing vital force. Has it not rather become a page from a history book, or a museum piece to be safely locked away or forgotten until the next National Day?

Index of Main Characters

BABEUF, Gracchus (François). Journalist and communist. In Electoral Club. Plotted to destroy Directory.

BAILLY, Jean Sylvain. Mayor of Paris during 1789 Revolution.

BARÈRE, Bertrand. Lawyer, originally a monarchist. Became a supporter of Robespierre.

BARRAS, Paul François. Jacobin. Conducted siege of Toulon. A 'Terrorist' hated by Robespierre. Brought about the downfall of Robespierre. Member of Directory with Bonaparte.

BOISSY D'ANGLAS, François. Advocate of men of property. Member of States-General. Member of conspiracy against Robespierre.

BRISSOT, Jacques Pierre. Lawyer and author. Leader of Girondins, opposed Robespierre.

BURKE, Edmund. Stimulated counter-revolutionary attitudes in Europe.

CARNOT, Lazare. Military genius, 'organizer of victories' and *armées revolutionnaires*. In Directory, but a near-royalist.

COLLOT D'HERBOIS, Jean Marie. Member of National Convention and Committee of Public Safety. Responsible for Lyons Terror. Deported because of his plot against Robespierre.

DANTON, Georges Jacques. Lawyer and orator, leading member of Cordeliers Club. Patriot and member of Committee of Public Safety, but sought to modify extremists. Minister of Justice. Sent to the guillotine by Robespierre.

DESMOULINS, Camille. Journalist and orator. Member of Cordeliers Club. Friend of Danton.

FOUCHÉ, Joseph. Responsible for Terror, especially in Lyons. Became Minister of Police.

HEBERT, Jacques René. Called 'Père Duchesne' after his journal of that name. Jacobin leader of Paris Commune. Orchestrated the de-Christianization campaign. Executed by Robespierre.

LAFAYETTE, Marquis de. In National Assembly of 1789. Brought American influence to bear on Declaration of Rights. Moderate liberal hated by Jacobins. Commander of the National Guard.

LOUIS XVI. Attempted reforms in administration and taxation. Accepted Constitution of 1791 but overcome by events of Revolution. Executed.

MARAT, Jean Paul. Darling of the populace. Journalist. Member of Cordeliers Club and 'Terrorist'. Stabbed by Charlotte Corday.

MIRABEAU, Honoré Gabriel. Orator of 'Patriot' party. In National Assembly of 1789. Member of Jacobin Club.

NAPOLEON BONAPARTE. Military commander of genius. Administrative reformer. First Consul, then Emperor.

NECKER, Jacques. Minister of Finance during *ancien régime*. popular figure whose dismissal triggered '89 Revolution.
ORLÉANS, Duke of (Philippe Egalité). Hero of 1789. Supported pamphleteers and the Abbé Sièyes.
PÉTION, Jérôme. Jacobin ally of Robespierre. Later became a Girondist. Mayor of Paris.
ROBESPIERRE. Maximilien. Democrat, leader of revolutionary government. Jacobin, leader of Committee of Public Safety. Instigator of Terror.
ROUX, Jacques. Leader of Enragés. The 'red' priest. Blamed for grocery riots (1793), spokesman for *sans-culottes*.
SAINT-JUST, Louis-Antoine. Proud lawyer and military leader. Ally of Robespierre.
SIÈYES, Abbé. Pamphleteer, supporter of Third Estate. The 'man of '89'. Member of Directory and Consulate with Bonaparte. 'Mole' of the Revolution.
TALLEYRAND, Charles (Bishop of Autun). In States-General and Committee of Thirty. An *émigré*. Later member of Directory as Foreign Minister, and supporter of Bonaparte.

Chronicle of Main Events, 1775–1851

1775 American War of Independence.
May: Grain riots in northern France.
1776 Fall of Turgot.
American Declaration of Independence.
Adam Smith's *Wealth of Nations*.
Watt's steam engine.
1778 France enters American War.
1780s–1820s Industrial revolution in Britain.
1781–2 Attempted 'democratic' revolution by 'Natives' at Geneva; crushed with the aid of France.
1783 Treaty of Versailles ends American War.
1781 Joseph IIs peasant reform in Habsburg Empire.
1786 French 'free trade' treaty with England.
Peasant revolt in Norway, led by C. Lofthuus.
1787 Assembly of Notables convened in France; beginning of 'aristocratic revolt'.
1788 September: Victory for 'aristocracy' in France and return of Parlement to Paris, followed by popular riots.
December: food riots in France soon turning into peasant revolt against 'feudalism'.
1789 January–May: Preparation of *cahiers de doléances* and elections to States-General.
May–July: States-General at Versailles.
June: National Assembly formed by Third Estate and allies at Versailles.
July: Revolution in Paris; fall of Bastille.
King accepts Revolution at City Hall.
July–August: Peasant revolt against 'feudalism'. The 'Great Fear'.
August: Assembly responds with 'August Decrees'. Beginning of end of 'Feudalism' in France.
Declaration of Rights of Man and Citizen.
October 'days': Women's march to Vesailles; return of King to Paris, followed by National Assembly.
December: Sale of Church lands; issue of *assignats*.
Property qualifications decreed for voters and deputies.
1790 June: Abolition of nobility and titles by Constituent Assembly.
July: Civil Constitution of the Clergy.

Feast of the Federation.
Counter-revolutionary riots at Lyons.
November: Publication of Burke's *Reflections on the Revolution in France*.

1791 March: Pope condemns Civil Constitution of the Clergy; beginning of counter-revolution by 'non-juring' clergy.
April: Death of Mirabeau.
Spring–summer: Counter-revolution continues in south.
King's flight to Varennes.
Feuillants secede from Jacobin Club.
July: Massacre of Champ de Mars.
August: Declaration of Pillnitz.
September: Adoption of Constitution of 1791.
Opening of Legislative Assembly.
November: Pétion elected Mayor of Paris.

1792 January–February: Food riots in Paris.
Spring: Counter-revolutionary riots in the west of France.
April: France declares war against Austria.
June: Dismissal of Girondin ministers.
Popular invasion of Tuileries.
July: Brunswick Manifesto.
August: Overthrow of monarchy.
Failure of Lafayette's attempted *coup* against Paris.
September: Prison massacres in Paris.
Meeting of National Convention.
French victory at Jemappes and first occupation of Belgium.

1793 January: Execution of King.
February: France declares war on England and Holland.
Levée en masse (300,000 men) provokes revolt in west of France.
March: Beginning of revolt in Vendée.
Revolutionary Tribunal set up.
April: Treason of Dumouriez.
Committee of Public Safety (including Danton).
May: Anti-Jacobin agitation at Marseilles, Lyons, Rennes, etc.
May–June: Girondin leaders driven from Convention.
June: Adoption of 'Jacobin' Constitution of 1793.
July: Assassination of Marat.
Abolition of 'feudalism' by Convention.
Robespierre, St Just and Couthon appointed to Committee of Public Safety.
August: Royalist surrender of Toulon to British.
September: Popular insurrection in Paris.
Law of 'suspects' and beginning of Terror.
Law of General Maximum setting ceilings on food

prices and wages.
Relief of siege of Toulon by Bonaparte.
October: Constitution suspended 'for the duration'.
Lyons revolt suppressed.
De-Christianization campaign opens.
Execution of Marie Antoinette and of Girondin leaders.
December: 'Revolutionary' government installed.
Vendéan revolt crushed by Republican armies.

1794 February–March: Laws of Ventôse.
March: Arrest and execution of Hébertists.
March–April: Arrest and execution of Dantonists.
April: Revolt of *chouans* in west.
June: Festival of Supreme Being.
Law of 22nd Prairial.
French victory at Fleurus.
June–July: The 'Great Terror'.
July: Conspiracy and crisis of Thermidor. Fall and execution of Robespierre and allies.
November: Jacobin Club closed.
December: Repeal of Maximum laws.

1795 Year of near-famine in France.
April–May: Insurrections of Germinal and Prairial in Paris.
May–June: 'White Terror' in south.
June: Royalist landing in Quiberon Bay.
August: Adoption of Constitution of Year III.
October: Failed royalist rising in Paris (13th Vendémiaire).
Directory installed.

1796–7 Bonaparte's Italian campaign.

1797 March: Royalists gaining majority on the two legislative Councils in Paris.
September: Anti-royalist *coup* of Fructidor by Directors with military support.

1798 February: Roman Republic set up.
September: Jourdan's conscription law in France.
October: 'Peasant war' declared against French in Belgium.

1799 January–June: Revolts against French in Italy.
Rising in support of democracy in Piedmont.
Bonaparte in Egypt.
October: Bonaparte's *coup d'état* of 18th Brumaire.

1800 February: New Constitution with Bonaparte as First Consul.
Revolt of *chouans* crushed in west.
June: Battle of Marengo.

1800–3 Bonaparte's major reforms in France.

1801 July: Concordat signed with Pope.

1802 Peace of Amiens with England.

1803–8 Major 'revolutionary' reforms in Europe.

1803 Sale of Louisiana to Americans.
1804 Napoleon crowned Emperor of the French.
1805–7 Major Napoleonic victories over Austrians, Prussians and Russians in Central Europe.
1806–12 Economic blockade of England – the Continental System.
1808 Treaty of Tilsit with Russia; zenith of Napoleon's fortunes.
1809 Napoleon's decline and fall starting with 'Spanish ulcer'.
1812 Russian campaign.
1814 First abdication and exile to Elba.
1815 The 'Hundred days': Waterloo and final defeat, surrender and exile to St Helena.
Congress of Vienna.
1821 Death of Napoleon at St Helena.
1820–36 Period of revolutions (major and minor) in Europe and Latin America: Spain, Belgium, France, Germany, Argentina, Mexico, Brazil, etc.
1835–48 Chartism in England.
1848 'Year of revolutions' in Europe: beginning in southern Italy in January; in France in February; in Germany and Austria in March; followed by offshoots in Hungary, Poland, Ireland, Romania, Croatia, etc.
1849–51 Counter-revolution sets in.

Glossary

Accapareur. A real or alleged hoarder of food.

Ancien régime. France before the Revolution. Sometimes seen as the immediate pre-Revolutionary era and sometimes extended to include the latter half of the reign of Louis XIV (1660–1715).

Anobli. A recently ennobled commoner of the *ancien régime*.

Armée révolutionnaire. A citizen army of *sans-culottes* (q.v.), raised in various centres in the autumn of 1793 and primarily intended to ensure the grain-supply of Paris and other cities.

Assignat. Revolutionary paper money, at first issued to finance the sale of Church lands, but in general use after the summer of 1791.

Ateliers de charité. Public workshops set up in 1789 to give work to the unemployed.

Autel de la patrie. A civic altar, dedicated to the nation, erected in the centre of the Champ de Mars in the west of Paris in July 1790.

Babouvism. Political (socialist) ideas based on those of Gracchus Babeuf in France during the Directory and those subsequently voiced by Italian 'patriots' or secret societies (e.g. the *Carbonari*) against the French after 1808.

Bailliage, sénéchaussee. A local centre of royal jurisdiction, presided over by a *bailli* or a *sénéchal*, of which the first operated in the northern and the second in the southern part of France.

Banalités. A feudal monopoly entitling the local *seigneur* (lord of the manor) to compel his tenants to bring their corn, flour and grapes to his mill, bakehouse and wine-press.

Barrières. The customs posts surrounding the City of Paris, erected by the Farmers-General shortly before the Revolution.

Biens nationaux. Confiscated properties of Church, aristocracy or 'suspects', nationalized and sold by auction during the Revolution.

Bourgeois, Bourgeoisie. A generic term more or less synonymous with the urban middle classes – bankers, stockbrokers, merchants, large manufacturers and professional men of every kind.

Brissotins. Followers of Jacques-Pierre Brissot during the Legislative Assembly; later called *Girondins* (q.v.).

Brumaire. The 'foggy' month (23 October to 20 November) of the Revolutionary Calendar. The term is applied, in particular, to Bonaparte's *coup d'état* of the 18th–19th Brumaire of the Year VII (9–10 November 1799).

Cahiers de doléances. The lists of grievances drawn up separately by the three 'orders' in towns, villages and guilds in preparation for the Estates-General of 1789.

Capitation. A tax levied on individual incomes, originally paid by all classes; but, during the eighteenth century, the clergy were legally exempted and the nobility were often so in practice.

Champart. A feudal rent in kind.

Chouans. Counter-revolutionary peasant guerrillas operating in Brittany and Normandy after 1793.

Comité des Trente. The Committee of Thirty, attended by Duport, Talleyrand, Mirabeau, Sieyés and others, and often credited with an exaggerated responsibility for the events of 1789.

Comités révolutionnaires, or 'revolutionary committees'. The local committees attached to the sections (q.v.) and responsible for police and internal security.

Committee of General Security. One of the two main government committees of the Year II, specifically charged with responsibility for police and internal security.

Committee of Public Safety. The more important of the two leading government committees of the Year II. Generally responsible for the conduct of both internal and external affairs, its powers overlapped with those of the Committee of General Security in police and judicial matters.

Commune. Name given to the Paris local government that emerged at the City Hall after the fall of the Bastille. The so-called 'Revolutionary Commune' temporarily usurped its powers, with Jacobin support, in the crisis of August–September 1792. The Commune was abolished soon after Thermidor (q.v.) but reappeared briefly in 1848 and in the Paris Commune of March–May 1871.

Complot de l'étranger. The 'foreign plot' which Pitt and his agents in France were alleged, and widely believed, to be hatching against the Republic in 1793–4.

Continental System. Name given to the economic blockade of Britain by Napoleon and his allies after his defeat of Austria, Prussia and Russia in 1805–7.

Coqs de village. Term applied to prosperous or 'improving' peasants, whether tenants or proprietors.

Cordeliers Club. The more 'plebeian', and generally the more radical, of the two major Clubs of the Revolution in Paris. The best known of its leaders were (at various times) Marat, Danton, Hébert and Ronsin.

Corvée. The peasant's obligation to do unpaid labour on the roads, or to make payment in lieu.

Décade. The ten-day periods into which the thirty-day month was divided in the Revolutionary Calendar (q.v.). Hence *décadi* for the periodic rest-day.

Districts. Name given to the sixty electoral units into which Paris was divided in April 1789. After May–June 1790, they were superseded by the sections (q.v.).

Don gratuit. The 'voluntary gift' made by the Assembly of the French clergy to the Crown in lieu of paying the usual taxes.

Émigrés. Nobles and others who emigrated from France, from July 1789 onwards, during the Revolution.

Enragés. The extreme revolutionary party, led by Jacques Roux, Jean Varlet and Théophile Leclerc, who, while condemned by the Jacobins and Cordeliers alike, yet had considerable influence on the Paris *sans-culottes* (q.v.) in 1793.

Faubourgs. Literally 'suburbs', originally lying outside the Paris city walls but, since 1785, enclosed within them. More particularly, the term is applied to the great popular 'faubourgs' of St Antoine and St Marcel.

Fédérés. Militia units from the provinces brought to Paris to attend the Federation on 14 July 1792. Here applied in particular to the men of Marseilles and Brest who helped overthrow the monarchy.

Feuillants. The large group of deputies from the centre of the Constituent Assembly that seceded from the Jacobins to form their own Club in protest against the campaign to suspend or depose Louis XVI after his flight to Varennes in June 1791.

Gabelle. The salt-tax, most unpopular and vexatious of the indirect taxes of the *ancien régime* in France.

Garde nationale (or *milice bourgeoise*). Citizens' militia, first raised by the Paris Districts in July 1789.

Généralités. Areas roughly corresponding to the old provinces into which France was divided, from Richelieu's time onwards, for taxation purposes. There were twenty-three *généralités*, each in the charge of an *Intendant*, in 1789.

Gens sans aveu. Vagrants or persons without fixed abode.

Girondins. Name given to the main body of opposition to the Jacobins within the National Convention. See also Brissotins (q.v.) and pp. 80–81.

'*Guerre des farines*' (or 'flour war'). Popular name for the grain riots of May 1775.

Hébertists. The followers (real or reputed) of Jacques-René Hébert, editor of *Le Pére Duchesne.* The label applies equally to Hébert's associates on the Paris Commune and the Ministry of War (Chaumette Vincent), the 'de-Christianizers' en bloc, the proponents of 'universal war' (Cloots) and leaders of the *armée révolutionnaire* (q.v.) and Cordeliers Club (Ronsin).

Intendants. See Généralités.

Jacobins, Jacobin Club. Name assumed by the Breton Club (formed in the first National Assembly) when it moved to the Couvent des Jacobins in Paris in October 1789. The Club went through a series of transformations – such as the secession of the Feuillants in June 1791 and the successive purges of Girondins, Dantonists and Hébertists; and ended up in the summer of 1794 as the group remaining loyal to Robespierre. The Club was dissolved by the Thermidorians in November 1794. See also Mountain.

Jacquerie. Peasant revolt, traditionally (as in the fifteenth to seventeenth centuries) attended by violence to both property and persons.

Jeunesse dorée (or 'gilded youth'). See Muscadins.
Journée (or *journée révolutionnaire*). A day of revolutionary struggle in which crowds (generally made up of *sans-culottes*) participated.
Laboureur. The typical large, or 'middling', French peasant proprietor.
Lazzaroni. The poorer classes of the city of Naples.
Lettres de cachet. 'Sealed letters' issued in the name of the King committing offenders to detention without trial.
Levée en masse. Law of 23 August 1793, mobilizing the whole French nation for war. Subsequently used to denote the nation-at-arms in any country.
Lit de justice. Ceremonial meeting of the Parlement of Paris (q.v.) presided over by the King, seated on a *lit* or pile of cushions. On such occasions the Parlement had no right to remonstrate before registering edicts.
Livre (or franc). In 1789, roughly equivalent to 20p. There were 20 sous in a livre.
Lods et ventes. A feudal due levied on the sale of land.
Maîtres-ouvriers. Craftsmen in the Lyons silk industry who, though subject to the merchant–manufacturers, employed their own labour (*compagnons*).
Marc d'argent. A silver mark worth 52 francs. This was the annual amount that had to be paid in direct taxes in order to qualify as a deputy to the National Assembly by a law of December 1789. Following protests, the qualification was changed in August 1791 to one of 'active' citizenship.
Maréchaussée. Rural constabulary of the *ancien régime* in France
Maximum. There were two laws of the Maximum: that of May 1793, imposing a limit on the price of grain only; and that of September 1793, extending price controls to all articles of prime necessity including labour (*maximum des salaires*).
Menu peuple. The common people: wage-earners and small property-owners. See also *sans-culottes*.
Métayers. Sharecropping farmers, generally sharing their produce on a fifty–fifty (or less advantageous) basis with the landowner.
Mountain. Name acquired by the main group of Jacobin deputies led by Robespierre who, after their election to the National Convention in September 1792, sat in the upper seats of the Chamber.
Muscadins. Term applied by the *sans-culottes* to bourgeois citizens and middle-class youth in the period after 9th Thermidor. It suggests foppery and fine clothes.
Noblesse. French aristocracy or nobility, whose core was formed by the original *noblesse d'épée* (nobility of the sword), who derived their traditional privileges from military service to the Crown. More recent additions were the *noblesse de robe* (magisterial nobility), created by the sale of public offices, mainly since Louis XIV's time; and less commonly the *noblesse de cloche*, formed by the privileged holders of municipal offices.

Non-domiciliés. Persons living in hotels, lodgings or furnished rooms (*chambres garnies*) and, as such, generally omitted from the census and excluded from the franchise until June 1793.

Notables. Term applied to the more prosperous citizens, both bourgeois and former aristocrats, who came into power and favour under the Directory and at times remained so under Napoleon.

Ouvriers. Those working with their hands, whether petty manufacturers, independent craftsmen or wage-earners.

Pacte de famine. The policy, popularly ascribed to various governments under Louis XV and Louis XVI, charged with deliberately withholding grain from the market to force up prices and create famine.

Parlements. The most important of the French courts of ordinary royal jurisdiction intended mainly as High Courts of Appeal. Of the thirteen Parlements by far the most important was that of Paris, whose jurisdiction extended over a large part of the country and which, particularly under weak or indolent kings, had acquired the habit of remonstrating before consenting to register royal edicts – thus virtually usurping legislative powers.

'Patriots'. Name given to the radical party in England and Holland before the French Revolution and, during the Revolution, to its supporters and advanced reformers in every country (in the latter case, as an alternative to 'Jacobins'). Not to be confused with patriots (without quotation marks) as upholders of a national cause.

Pays d'élections. The majority of the French provinces of the *ancien régime*, in which there were no local assemblies to apportion taxes or to aspire to a limited form of self-government. See *pays d'états*.

Pays d'états. Provinces, mainly on the frontiers and recently acquired under the *ancien régime*, which had retained their traditional Estates, whose functions were strictly circumscribed but, on occasion, aroused hopes of a wider measure of self-government.

Plain (or Marsh). The non-committed centre party in the National Convention which, by withdrawing support from Robespierre in July 1794, helped to precipitate his fall.

Portion congrue. The salary paid by tithe-holding abbeys and chapters to parish priests not holding tithes in their own hands.

Prévôt des marchands. The senior magistrate of the royal government of the City of Paris prior to the Revolution.

Privilégiés. The French privileged orders, i.e. the clergy (though, generally, only the higher clergy) and nobility.

Rentiers. People living on fixed or unearned incomes, e.g. pensioners, stockholders.

Révolte nobiliaire (or 'aristocratic revolt'). Name given to the revolt of the nobility and Parlements against the monarchy in 1787–8, which served as a curtain-raiser to the Revolution of 1789.

Revolutionary Calendar. Introduced by the Jacobin Convention and in use from 22 September 1793 until the end of 1805.

Revolutionary government. Term applied to the strongly centralized government established by Robespierre, Saint-Just and their associates on the Committee of Public Safety after October 1793.

Revolutionary Tribunal. Court of justice, set up by the Convention in the crisis of March–April 1793, to try the enemies or suspected enemies of the Revolution.

Sans-culottes. An omnibus term (literally, those who wear trousers and not knee-breeches) sometimes applied to all the poorer classes of town and countryside; but, more particularly, to urban craftsmen, small shopkeepers, petty traders, journeymen, labourers and city poor. By extension, attached as a political label to the more militant revolutionaries of 1792–5 regardless of social origins.

Séance royale. The 'royal session' summoned by Louis XVI at Versailles on 23 June 1789 to hear his views on the issues dividing the three Estates.

Sections. The forty-eight units into which Paris became divided for electoral (and general political) purposes, in succession to the sixty districts (q.v.), by the municipal law of May–June 1790.

Señorios. Large landed estates held by Spanish grandees.

Sociétés populaires (or 'popular societies'). General term applied to the political clubs formed in the various Paris sections after the summer of 1791. Many were closed down in the spring of 1794, others after Thermidor (q.v.), and the rest in the early months of 1795.

States-General. Assembly of all three Estates convened by Louis XVI to discuss a constitution in May 1789.

Taille. The principal direct tax paid by all commoners (*rôturiers*) in France before the Revolution, usually levied on personal income (*taille personnelle*), more rarely on land (*taille réelle*).

Taxation populaire. Price control by riot – as in May 1775, January–February 1792, February 1793.

Terror. The term is used here not so much to describe a method as to define a period, September 1793 to July 1794, when the Jacobin government imposed its authority by varying means of compulsion – military, judicial and economic.

Thermidor. The month in the Revolutionary Calendar covering parts of July and August. In particular, applied to the two days in Thermidor (9th and 10th) of the Year II, which saw the overthrow of Robespierre and his associates. Hence, Thermidorians: Robespierre's immediate successors.

Third Estate (or *tiers état*). Literally, the representatives of the non-privileged of the three Estates summoned to attend the States-General (see above). More generally, it is used to denote all social classes other than the aristocracy, upper clergy or privileged magistrates – i.e. *menu peuple* as well as bourgeoisie.

Vainqueurs de la Bastille. Title given to the 662 persons who were able to establish their claim to have participated directly in the fall of the Bastille.

Vingtiéme. A tax on income levied on all except the clergy. Nominally a twentieth tax, it was more often extended to a tenth – or even, on occasion, to a quarter – of revenue.

Year II. The second year of the French Republic – i.e. from 22 September 1793 to 21 September 1794. Most often applied to the period of office of the great Committee of Public Safety (28 July 1793 to 28 July 1794).

Notes

1 Introduction

1 *Why Was There a Revolution in France?*

1 For Godechot see note 3 below and for Lefebvre and Mathiez see works cited in the text and notes to the next chapter. See also E. G. Barber, *The Bourgeoisie in Eighteenth-Century France* (Princeton, 1955), pp. 112–25; and F. Ford, *Robe and Sword: The Regrouping of the French Aristocracy after Louis* XV (Cambridge, Mass., 1953), *passim.*
2 For this paragraph and some of the facts and arguments that follow see my *Revolutionary Europe: 1713–1815* (London, 1964), chs 1–4, *passim.*
3 J. Godechot, *The Taking of the Bastille* (London, 1970), p. 51.
4 See, for example, C. B. A. Behrens, *The Ancien Régime* (London, 1971), p. 71; and, for a more comprehensive treatment, D. Bien, 'The Army in the French Enlightenment: Reform, Reaction and Revolution', *Past and Present*, 85 (1979), pp. 68–98; and also D. M. G. Sutherland, *France 1789–1815: Revolution and Counterrevolution* (London, 1985), pp. 9–21.
5 A. Cobban, *The Social Interpretation of the French Revolution* (London, 1964), p. 123.
6 For the above see C.-E. Labrousse, *Esquisse du mouvement des prix et des revenus en France au* XVIIIe SIÉCLE (2 vols., Paris, 1933), ii, pp. 637–42; and *La Crise de l'économie française à la fin de l'Ancien Régime et au début de la Révolution* (Paris, 1944), pp. ix–xli, 623.
7 For the best account of the 'aristocratic revolt' and its political consequences, see J. Egret, *La Pré-révolution française, 1787–88* (Paris, 1962); English trans., *The French Pre-Revolution, 1787–1788* (Chicago, 1977).
8 Godechot, *Bastille*, p. xxiv.
9 I have discussed this question in fuller detail in *Europe in the Eighteenth Century: Aristocracy and the Bourgeois Challenge* (London, 1972); see, in particular, the final chapter from which several of the preceding arguments are drawn.

2 Historians and the French Revolution

1 E. Burke, *Reflections on the Revolution in France* (London, 1790), *passim.*
2 For the view, however, that Cochin did not subscribe to the 'conspiracy' explanation of revolution, see F. Furet, *Penser la révolution française* (Paris, 1978); English trans. *Interpreting the French Revolution* (London, 1981; repr. 1985), esp. pp. 168–9.
3 For English translations see A. Thiers, *The History of the French Revolution* (London, n.d.); F. A. M. Mignet, *History of the French Revolution from 1789 to 1814* (London, 1915); Germaine de Staël, *Considerations on the Principal Events of the French Revolution* (3 vols., London, 1818).
4 Mignet, *History of the French Revolution*, p. 1.
5 F. Parkman, *Montcalm and Wolfe* (Toronto, 1964), p. 253.
6 J. Michelet, *Histoire de la Révolution française* (7 vols., Paris, 1847–53); English

trans. *History of the French Revolution* (3 vols., Chicago, 1967).
7 A. De Tocqueville, *The Ancien Régime and the French Revolution* (Oxford, 1933), p. 220.
8 *ibid.*, p. 186.
9 F. V. A. Aulard, *Histoire politique de la Révolution française* (4 vols., Paris, 1901); English trans., *The French Revolution: A Political History, 1789–1804* (4 vols., London, 1910), pp. 9–10.
10 J. Jaurès, Critical Introduction to the *Histoire socialiste*; cit. F. Stern, *The Varieties of History* (New York, 1956), p. 160.
11 A. Mathiez, *La Vie chère et le mouvement social sous la Terreur* (Paris, 1932).
12 G. Lefebvre, *Les Paysans du Nord pendant la Révolution française* (2 vols., Paris, 1924).
13 G. Lefebvre, *La Grande Peur de 1789* (Paris, 1932); English trans., *The Great Fear of 1789: Rural Panic in Revolutionary France* (London, 1973). See also 'Foules révolutionnaires', *Annales historiques de la Révolution française*, 11 (1934), 1–26.
14 A. Soboul, *Les Sans-culottes parisiens de l'an* II*: mouvement populaire et gouvernement revolutionnaire, 2 juin 1793–9 Thermidor an* II (La Roche-sur-Yon, 1958); English trans. (abridged), *The Parisian Sans-culottes and the French Revolution, 1793–4* (Oxford, 1964).
15 D. Guérin, *La Lutte de classes sous la première République: bourgeois et 'bras nus' (1793–1797)* (2 vols., Paris, 1946).
16 For Guérin, see *La Nouvelle Réforme* 2 (Jan.–Feb. 1956), pp. 195–217.
17 A. Cobban, *The Myth of the French Revolution* (London, 1955); *The Social Interpretation of the French Revolution* (London, 1964). See also, for more precise study, his *Aspects of the French Revolution* (London, 1968).
18 *Aspects*, pp. 172–3.
19 G. Taylor, 'Non-Capitalist Wealth and the Origin of the French Revolution', *American Historical Review*, lxxii (1966–7), 469–96; R. Forster, 'The Provincial Noble: A Reappraisal', *ibid.*, lxviii (1963), 681–91; E. Eisenstein, 'Who Intervened in 1788? A Commentary on *The Coming of the French Revolution*', *ibid.*, lxxi (1965), 77–103.
20 W. Doyle, *Origins of the French Revolution* (Oxford, 1980), pp. 212–13.
21 *ibid.*, pp. 2–3.
22 C. Mazauric, *La Révolution française* (Paris, 1970).
23 F. Furet and D. Richet, *La Révolution française* (2 vols., Paris, 1965–6); English trans., *The French Revolution* (London, 1970).
24 F. Furet, 'Le Catéchisme révolutionnaire', *Annales: Economie, Société, Civilisation* (March–April 1971), 255–89.
25 Furet, *Interpreting the French Revolution.*
26 This appears to be the old story of the 'mountain' and the 'mole-hill'. One can find plenty of examples scattered through the work of Soboul and Lefebvre to show that these two 'social interpreters', at least, were well aware of these distinctions as they were of the contradictory trends, and therefore lack of uniformity, within the French eighteenth-century bourgeoisie. For a more balanced and judicious examination of the evidence on both sides of the discussion, see G. Ellis, 'The "Marxist Interpretation" of the French Revolution', *English Historical Review*, xcii (1978), 353–71; and also J. M. Roberts, *The French Revolution* (Oxford, 1978), pp. 137–59.
27 *Interpreting the French Revolution*, pp. 1–28.
28 Yet he adds wisely: 'The fact is that scholarship, although it may be stimulated

by preoccupations stemming from the present, is never sufficient in itself to modify the conceptualisation of a problem or an event' (*ibid.*, p. 9).

29 Among these see (tentatively), Doyle, *Origins*, pp. 17–40; and (more explicitly) R. B. Rose in an unpublished paper entitled 'Reinterpreting the French Revolution: Cobban's "Myth": Thirty Years After'. See also, for a useful contribution to this discussion, M. Slavin, *The Revolution in Miniature* (Paris, 1986).

30 See Pierre Chaunu's Preface to F. Gendron, *La Jeunesse dorée* (Quebec, 1979), pp. 8–9.

31 See, in particular, the discussion programme 'Apostrophes' presented weekly on French television, channel 2.

II Opening Years

1 How the Revolution Began

1 C.-E. Labrousse, *La Crise de l'économie française à la fin de l'Ancien Régime et au début de la Révolution* (Paris, 1944), pp. 180ff.

2 D. Guérin, *La Lutte de classes sous la première République: bourgeois et 'bras nus' (1793–1797)* (2 vols., Paris, 1946), *passim.*

3 For this and much that follows, see my article, 'The Outbreak of the French Revolution', *Past and Present*, 8 (Nov. 1955), 28–42.

4 S. Hardy, 'Mes Loisirs, ou Journal d'événements tels qu'ils parviennent à ma connaissance', Bib. Nat. fonds français, nos. 6680–7, vols. 1–7, *passim.*

5 *Ibid.*, iii, 281; vi, 149–50, 266–7, 315, 413–14, 424–5.

6 *Ibid.*, viii, 58–109.

7 *Ibid.*, viii, 73.

8 *Ibid.*, viii, 154–5, 250.

9 *Ibid.*, viii, 168.

10 For historians' conflicting accounts of the causes of the industrial crisis of the 1780s, see C. Schmidt, 'La Crise industrielle de 1788 en France', *Revue historique*, lcvii (1908), 78–94; and L. Cahen, 'Une Nouvelle Interprétation du traité franco-anglais de 1786–7' *ibid.*, clxxxv (1939), 257–85.

11 Arch. Nat. H 1453; Hardy, 'Journal', viii, 262, 278.

12 For the latter, see G. Laurent, *Cahiers de doléances pour les États Généraux de 1789* (6 vols., Reims, 1906–30), iv, 94–5; G. Fournier, *Cahiers de doléances de la sénéchaussée de Marseille* (Marseilles, 1908), pp. 70, 228–34; G. L. Chassin, *Le Génie de la Révolution* (2 vols., Paris, 1863), i, 428–33.

13 A. Young, *Travels in France during the Years 1787–1788–1789* (New York, 1969), pp. 147–8.

14 J. Jaurès, *Histoire socialiste*, ed. A. Soboul (7 vols., Paris, 1968–73), i, pp. 177–8.

15 R. Dupuy, *La Garde nationale et les débuts de la Révolution en Ille-et-Vilaine* (Paris, 1972), pp. 55–67.

2 1789: The 'Bourgeois' Revolution

1 E. Eisenstein, 'Who Intervened in 1788?' *American Historical Review*, lxxi (1965), 77–103.

2 A. Cobban, *A History of Modern France* (3 vols, Harmondsworth, 1957), I. 140.

3 For a lively account, see P. Goubert and M. Denis (eds.), *1789: Les Français ont la parole: cahiers de États Généraux* (Paris, 1964).

4 From a variety of accounts of the 'municipal revolution', see the following (listed here in alphabetical order of authors and not in order of importance): R.M. Chase, *Bordeaux and the Gironde 1789–1974* (New York, 1968), pp. 15ff.; J. Egret, *La Révolution des Notables: Mounier et les Monarchiens 1789* (Paris, 1950), pp. 90–3; A. Forrest, *Society and Politics in Revolutionary Bordeaux* (Oxford, 1975), ch. 3; Lynn A. Hunt, *Revolution and Urban Politics in Provincial France: Troyes and Reims, 1786–1790* (Stanford, 1978), pp. 68–91; M. Lhéritier, *Les Débuts de la Révolution à Bordeaux* (Paris, 1919), pp. 73ff.; D. Ligou, *Montauban à la fin de l'Ancien Régime et aux débuts le la Révolution 1787–1794* (Paris, 1958), pp. 206ff.; C. Tilly, *The Contentious French* (Harvard, 1986), pp. 243–50; A. Young, *Travels in France during the Years 1787–1788–1789* (New York, 1969) esp. pp. 47–59; M. Vovelle, *The Fall of the French Monarchy 1787–1792* (English trans., Cambridge, Mass., 1984), pp. 106–7.

3 The 'Popular' Revolution

1 Lefebvre, *The Great Fear of 1789: Rural Panic in Revolutionary France* (English trans., London, 1973), p. 141.
2 A. Cobban, *The Social Interpretation of the French Revolution* (London, 1964), pp. 102–3.
3 For an interesting discussion of the whole affair by an English historian, see S. Herbert, *The Fall of Feudalism in France* (New York, 1969, reprint), *passim.*
4 S. Hardy, 'Mes Loisirs, ou journal d'événements tels qu'ils parviennent à ma connaissance', Bib. Nat. fonds français, nos. 6680–7, vols. 1–7, viii, 297–8.
5 *Ibid.*, viii, 299.
6 For a fuller account of the riots, see my *The Crowd in the French Revolution* (Oxford, 1959), pp. 34–44.
7 P. Goubert and M. Denis (eds.), *1789: Les Français ont la parole: cahiers des États Généraux* (Paris, 19), pp. 231–5.
8 See, *inter alia*, Cobban, *Social Interpretation*, pp. 95–9.
9 Arch. Nat. T 514[(i)]: *Noms des vainqueurs de la Bastille* (662 names).
10 C. Tilly, *The Contentious French*, (Harvard, 1986), pp. 231, 243–6; A. Young, *Travels in France during the Years 1787–1788–1789 (New York, 1969)*, pp. 151–3; M. Vovelle, *La Mentalité révolutionnaire*: *société et Mentalité sous la Révolution française* (Paris, 1985), pp. 73–5.
11 Hardy, 'Journal', viii, 478–80.
12 *Procédure criminelle instruite au Châtelet de Paris* (2 vols., Paris, 1790), i, pp. 117–32 (testimony of S. Maillard).

III Constitutional Monarchy

1 The 'Principles of '89'

1 In this short chapter I have followed fairly closely the arguments of G. Lefebvre in *The Coming of the French Revolution* (English trans., New York, 1947).

2 Constitution of 1791

1 R.R. Palmer, *The Age of the Democratic Revolution: A Political History of Europe and America, 1760–1800* (2 vols., Princeton, 1964), i, pp. 522–8.
2 S.E. Harris, *The Assignats* (Cambridge, Mass., 1930).
3 For relations between Church and state in pre-revolutionary France see, above

all, J. McManners, *French Ecclesiastical Society under the Ancien Régime* (Manchester, 1960).

IV The Struggle for Power

1 Fall of the Monarchy

1 See D. Greer, *The Incidence of the Emigration during the French Revolution* (Cambridge, Mass., 1951), and *The Incidence of the Terror during the French Revolution* (Cambridge, Mass., 1935).
2 *Marx–Engels Selected Correspondence, 1846–1895* (London, 1934), p. 458.
3 At this time commonly called Brissotins and, after September 1792, Girondins. For doubts about the wisdom of identifying them under either name as a distinctive political party, see M. J. Sydenham, *The Girondins* (London, 1961).
4 P. Caron, *Les Massacres de septembre* (Paris, 1935).

2 Girondins and Jacobins

1 Yet wage-earners and others living in furnished rooms appear to have been excluded from voting until the further 'revolution' of May–June 1793. Even after this, domestic servants (not properly considered as citizens) continued to be so.
2 For this point, see M. J. Sydenham, *The Girondins* (London, 1961), *passim*; and also Alison Patrick, *The Men of the First French Republic* (Baltimore and New York, 1972).
3 See A. Mathiez, *Girondins et Montagnards* (Paris, 1930).
4 For an original account and a detailed examination of the voting pattern within the Convention on Louis' trial and sentence of death, see Patrick, *The Men of the First French Republic*, pp. 83–107.
5 For the Declaration and Constitution of June 1793, see G. Lefebvre, *La Révolution française* ed. A. Soboul (Paris, 1951), pp. 350, 355–6. See also, for further details, J.H. Stewart, *A Documentary Survey of the French Revolution* (New York, 1957), pp. 113–15, 455–8.

3 Jacobins and *Sans-culottes*

1 M. Vovelle, 'Les Taxations populaires de février-mars et novembre–décembre 1792 dans la Beauce et sur ses confins', *Memoirs et documents*, xiii (Paris, 1958), 107–59.
2 A. Mathiez, *La Vie chère et le mouvement social sous la Terreur* (Paris, 1932), pp. 139–61.
3 R. B. Rose, 'The French Revolution and the Grain Supply', *Bulletin of the John Rylands Library*, xxxix.i (Sept. 1958), 171–87.
4 For a full study, see R. C. Cobb, *Les Armées révolutionnaires: instrument de la Terreur dans les départements avril 1793 – floréal an* II (2 vols., Paris, 1961–3).
5 H. Taine, *Les Origines de la France contemporaine: La Révolution* (3 vols., Paris, 1876), pp. i, 18, 53–4, 130, 272.
6 See p. 22 and note 23 to Part I, Chapter 2.
7 G. Ellis, 'The "Marxist Interpretation" of the French Revolution', *English Historical Review*, xcii (1978), 353–75. See also R. R. Andrews, 'Social Structures, Political Elites and Ideology in Revolutionary Paris, 1792–94', *Journal of Social History*, xix (1985–6), 71–112.
8 For my own treatment of the subject and the documentation used to support it,

see *The Crowd in the French Revolution* (Oxford, 1959), pp. 178–90. See also, for other interpretations in addition to those already cited in notes 5–7 above, A. Soboul, *The Parisian Sans-culottes and the French Revolution, 1793–4* (Oxford, 1964), pp. 22–54; M. Vovelle, *La Mentalité révolutionnaire: société et mentalité sous la Révolution française* (Paris, 1985), pp. 65–77; R. Cobb, *The Police and the People* (Oxford, 1970); G. Lefebvre, 'Les Foules révolutionnaires', in *Études sur la Révolution française* (Paris, 1954), pp. 271–87; O. Hufton, *The Poor in Eighteenth-Century France, 1750–1789* (Oxford, 1974), esp. pp. 355–61; *idem*, 'Women in Revolution, 1789–96', *Past and Present*, 53 (1971), 90–108; Andrews, 'Social Structures'; M. Salvin, *The Revolution in Miniature* (Paris, 1986); and see Bibliography.

4 'Revolutionary' Government

1 R. C. Cobb, *Les Armées révolutionnaires: instrument de la Terreur dans les départements avril 1793 – floréal an* II (2 vols., Paris, 1961–3), vol. ii.
2 For this point see A. Soboul, *The Parisian Sans-culottes and the French Revolution, 1793–4* (Oxford, 1964), pp. 45–50; and P. Sainte-Claire Deville, *La Commune de l'an* II (Paris, 1946), pp. 42–76.
3 See N. Hampson, *A Social History of the French Revolution* (Manchester, 1963), pp. 209–13.
4 C. Crane Brinton, *The Jacobins* (revised edn, New York, 1961), appendix II, pp. 46–72.
5 Soboul, *Parisian Sans-culottes*, p. 65.

5 Thermidor

1 *Tribun du peuple*, 5 Nov. 1795.

6 A Republic of 'Proprietors'

1 For a fuller discussion, see my 'Prices and Wages and Popular Movements in Paris during the French Revolution', in *Economic History Review*, vi.3 (1954), 246–67.
2 For a detailed account, see K. D. Tönnesson, *La Défaite des sans-culottes: mouvement populaire et réaction bourgeoise à Paris en l'an* III (Oslo and Paris, 1959).
3 So that whereas, in *1791*, a little under 4½ million males of twenty-five and above had the vote at the 'primary' stage, in *1795* 6 out of 7½ million males of twenty-one and above (note the more generous age qualification) had the vote at this stage. See J.-R. Suratteau, 'Travaux récents sur le Directoire', *Annales historiques de la Révolution française*, 224 (April–June 1976), 202.
4 For further details on the Constitution, see G. Lefebvre, *La France sous le Directoire (1795–1799)*, ed. J.-R. Suratteau (Paris, 1977), pp. 31–8.
5 *Ibid.*, p. 52.
6 For fuller, and more *positive*, accounts of the Directory's record, see Suratteau, 'Travaux récents', 181–214; and D. Woronoff, *The Thermidorean Régime and the Directory, 1794–1799* (Cambridge and Paris, 1984), esp. pp. 172–94.

V Napoleon

1 Rise to Power

1 For this chapter, as for my treatment and interpretation of the Napoleonic era

in general, I am greatly indebted to G. Lefebvre's *Napoleon* (Paris, 4th edn, 1953; also in English trans., 2 vols., New York, 1969). For further works on the period, see Bibliography.

2 See *Journal of the Private Life and Conversations of the Emperor Napoleon at Saint-Helena* (8 vols., London, 1823), esp. v, 265–7, and vii, 133–9.

2 Reforms in France

1 See I. Woloch, 'Napoleonic conscription: State Power and Civil Society', *Past and Present*, lll (May 1986), esp. pp. 126–7.

2 For the treatment of religion, irreligion and de-Christianization during the Enlightenment and revolutionary years, I refer the reader to the writings of Michel Vovelle, particularly to the following: *La Mentalité révolutionnaire: société et mentalité sous la Révolution française* (Paris, 1985); 'Le Tournant des mentalités en France, 1750–1789: la "sensibilité" pré-revolutionnaire', *Social History*, v (May 1977), 605–29; and *La Déchristianisation de l'an* II (Paris, 1976).

VI The Revolution and Europe

1 From Constituents to Directory

1 For a brief treatment of these earlier movements, see my *Revolutionary Europe, 1783–1815* (London, 1964), pp. 39–43, 45–6, 65. They can be followed more fully in R. Palmer, *The Age of the Democratic Revolution* (2 vols, Princeton, 1959–64); vol. 1, *The Challenge* (1959), vol. 2, *The Struggle* (1964).

2 The case has been argued, with different points of emphasis, in a number of contributions made since 1954 by R. R. Palmer and J. Godechot (for details see Bibliography).

3 E. Burke, *Reflections on the Revolution in France* (1st edn, London, 1790), pp. 36–7, 52–3, 55–9; *Life and Writings of Thomas Paine*, ed. D. E. Wheeler, (10 vols., New York, 1908), iv, pp. 7–9, 25–6, 51–60.

4 R. Herr, *The Eighteenth-Century Revolution in Spain* (Princeton, 1958), pp. 286–96.

5 See J. Godechot, *La Grande Nation: expansion révolutionnaire de la France dans le monde de 1789 à 1799* (2 vols., Paris 1956), ii, pp. 418–49.

2 Under Consulate and Empire

1 See F. Crouzet, *L'Économie britannique et le blocus continental* (2 vols., Paris, 1958).

2 For this chapter consult the maps of Europe and the French Empire at the beginning of the book.

3 The reader will note that I do not propose to follow the Napoleonic saga through the years of defeat and exile starting with what he called 'the Spanish ulcer' (1809) and ending with his death on St Helena in 1821. The reason is that virtually nothing of this account would be relevant to my central 'revolutionizing' theme in this part of the book. Inevitably, there are exceptions: the marriage to the Archduchess Marie Louise, which inaugurated the constitutional experiment – though hardly a 'revolutionary' one – of founding a Napoleonic imperial dynasty; more positively, the growth of nationalism which attended the decline of Napoleonic rule in Italy; and – perhaps most important of all, though impossible to gauge exactly – the Napoleonic Legend, with its blending of myth and reality,

which grew out of the St Helena exile. But the exceptions do not seem convincing enough to warrant the addition of a further chapter, and it is suggested rather that the reader might consult appropriate passages in Lefebvre's *Napoleon*, F. H. N. Markham's *Napoleon and the Awakening of Europe* (1954) or other titles listed in the Bibliography.

4 H. B. Hill, 'The Constitutions of Continental Europe, 1789–1813', *Journal of Modern History* viii (1936), 82.

3 Balance Sheet of Revolution, 1815–1848

1 See, for example, N. Hampson, *A Social History of the French Revolution* (Manchester, 1963), pp. 231–4.

2 The Soviet historian, Anatoli Ado, however, argues – against the generally received wisdom of Western scholars – that the comparative weakness of the French peasants in carrying through the bourgeois–democratic revolution in the countryside left the middle and small peasants exposed to feudal survivals in the nineteenth century that impeded their development as independent cultivators. (See A. Ado, 'The Peasant Movement during the French Revolution', doctoral thesis, University of Moscow, 1971.) Soboul, in reviewing the work, accepts the view: *Annales historiques de la Révolution française* 211 (Jan.–March 1973), 85–101. A symposium, held in Paris in October 1987, on 'The Revolution and the Countryside' has developed the argument further.

3 For the operation of this 'dual revolution', see E. J. Hobsbawm, *The Age of Revolution: Europe, 1789–1848* (London, 1962), pp. 168–81.

4 *Journal of the Private Life and Conversations of the Emperor Napoleon at Saint-Helena* (8 vols., London, 1823), vii, pp. 133–9.

5 For these developments, see W. H. Sewell, 'Property, Labor, and the Emergence of Socialism in France, 1789–1848', in J. Merriman (ed.), *Conciousness and Class Experience in Nineteenth-Century Europe* (New York and London, 1979), pp. 45–63; R. Bezucha, *The Lyon Uprising of 1834: Social and Political Conflict in the Early July Monarchy* (Cambridge, Mass., 1974); B. Moss, 'Parisian Workers and the Origins of Republican Socialism, 1830–1833', in J. Merriman (ed.), *1830 in France* (New York, 1975), pp. 203–21; G. Rudé, *Ideology and Popular Protest* (London, 1980), pp. 118–30.

6 For the latter, N. Liu, 'La Révolution française et la formation de l'idéologie révolutionnaire et républicaine chez ls Roumains', *Annales historiques de la Révolution française*, 265 (July–Aug. 1986), 285–306.

VII The Revolution and the Wider World

1 As a World-historical Event

1 W. E. H. Lecky, *A History of England in the Eighteenth Century* (7 vols., London, 1906), iv, pp 299–300.

2 The main stumbling block appears to have been the unacceptable demands made by the *chouans*' self-appointed spokesman, the ultra-royalist Comte de Puisaye. (See M. Hutt, 'Un Projet de colonie chouanne au Canada', in *Les Résistances à la Révolution* (Paris, 1987), pp. 444–5; for fuller details see note 8 to Part VII, Chapter 2.

3 J.-P. Wallot, 'Le Régime seigneurial et son abolition au Canada', *Annales historiques de la Révolution française*, 196 (April–June 1969), 343–71.

4 G. Rudé, *Protest and Punishment* (Oxford, 1978), pp. 49–51.

5 W. Smith, *Flags and Arms across the World* (with illustrations, London, 1980), *passim*.
6 Such flags include those of Portuguese Guinea, Ghana, Ethiopia and Sierra Leone (*ibid., passim*).
7 *Ibid.*, p. 130.
8 *Selections from the Prison Letters of Antonio Gramsci*, ed. G. N. Smith and Q. Hoare (London, 1971), p. 395.

2 Legacy and Tradition in France

1 G. Rudé, *Robespierre: Portrait of a Revolutionary Democrat* (London and New York, 1975), p. 88.
2 R. Huard, 'Marx et la Révolution française', *Cahiers d' histoire de l'Institut de recherches marxistes*, 21 (1985), pp. 35–6.
3 G. Chevalier, *Clochemerle* (Paris, 1934).
4 M. Agulhon, *La République au village* (Paris, 1970).
5 See p. 12 above.
6 See S. Mellon, *The Political Uses of History* (Stanford, Cal., 1958).
7 For a detailed and highly 'committed' account of the Barbie affair and its possible outcome, see E. Paris, *Unhealed Wounds: France and the Klaus Barbie Affair* (Toronto, New York, etc., 1985).
8 For the most up-to-date study of 'counter-revolution' and 'anti-revolution' in the revolutionary period, see the papers read by some fifty authors to the Colloquium at Rennes in September 1985, *Les Résistances à la Révolution*, ed. F. Lebrun and R. Dupuy (Paris, 1987).

Bibliography

In the massive bibliography of revolutionary and post-Napoleonic Europe the student is advised to tread warily and to seek constant guidance. Here, to save linguistic embarrassment, titles are cited in English and more rarely (where no English translation appears to be available) in French. First, the student may start by selecting one or more of the following general or introductory readings in the history of the Revolution:*

C. Crane Brinton, *A Decade of Revolution, 1789–99* (1944).
F. Furet and D. Richet, *The French Revolution* (English trans., 1970).
L. Gershoy, *From Despotism to Revolution* (1970).
L. R. Gottschalk, *The Era of the French Revolution: 1715–1815* (1929).
E. J. Hobsbawm, *The Age of Revolution: Europe 1789–1848* (1962).
G. Lefebvre, *The French Revolution* (English trans., 2 vols., 1963).
A. Mathiez, *The French Revolution* (English trans., 1927).
R. R. Palmer, *The Age of the Democratic Revolution: A Political History of Europe and America, 1760–1800* (2 vols., Princeton, 1964).
J. M. Roberts, *The French Revolution* (Oxford, 1978).
G. Rudé, *Revolutionary Europe, 1783–1815* (1964).
A. de Tocqueville, *The Ancien Régime and the French Revolution* (numerous editions in French and English).

For the background to revolution in both France and Europe, the following are recommended:

M. S. Anderson, *Europe in the Eighteenth Century, 1713–1783* (1961).
C. B. A. Behrens, *The Ancien Régime* (1971).
W. Doyle, *The Old European Order, 1660–1800* (Oxford, 1980).
A. Goodwin, *The European Nobility in the Eighteenth Century* (1953).
R. Herr, *The Eighteenth-Century Revolution in Spain* (Princeton, 1958).
O. Hufton, *Europe: Protest and Privilege, 1730–1789* (Glasgow, 1980).
R. Mousnier and C.-E. Labrousse, *Le* XCIIIe *Siècle: l'époque des 'lumières' (1715–1815)* (3rd edn, 1959).
G. Rudé, *Europe in the Eighteenth Century: Aristocracy and the Bourgeois Challenge* (1972).
E. Wangermann, *From Joseph* II *to the Jacobin Trials* (Oxford, 1959).
A. Young, *Travels in France during the Years 1787–1788–1789* (New York, 1969; and numerous other editions).
A. de Tocqueville (above).

To move closer to the Revolution itself: the 'twilight' period linking the 'aristocratic revolt' of 1787–8 and the revolutionary outbreak is admirably

* Where place of publication is added to the date it generally means that the work was published somewhere other than in the nation's principal city.

portrayed in its political aspects by J. Egret, *The French Pre-Revolution 1787–1788* (English trans., Chicago, 1977); and by A. Goodwin in 'Calonne, the Assembly of Notables of 1787 and the Origin of the "Révolte Nobiliaire"', *English Historical Review*, lxi (1946), 203–34, 329–77; but the social aspects remain to be more fully explored. The best work on the outbreak of the Revolution is still G. Lefebvre's *The Coming of the French Revolution* (English trans., Princeton, 1947). C.-E. Labrousse's thirty-page Introduction to his *Crise de l'économie française à la fin de l'Ancien Régime et au début de la Révolution* (1944) is also important. The 'municipal revolution' of 1789 in provincial France may be studied in some of the following: J. Egret, *La Révolution des Notables: Mousnier et les Monarchiens, 1789* (1950), pp. 90–3; A. Forrest, *Society and Politics in Revolutionary Bordeaux* (Oxford, 1975), ch. 3; L. A. Hunt, *Revolution and Urban Politics in Provincial France: Troyes and Reims, 1786–1790* (Stanford, Cal., 1978), pp. 206ff.; A. Young's *Travels* esp. pp. 47–59 (above); and (very briefly) in M. Vovelle's *The Fall of the French Monarchy, 1787–1792* (English trans., Cambridge, Mass., 1984), pp. 106–7. See also, for the outbreak of revolution, G. Rudé, 'The Outbreak of the French Revolution', *Past and Present*, 8 (Nov. 1955), 28–42.

Before coming to the Revolution's internal history, some mention must be made of the sometimes bitter debate that has divided historians and commentators on its origins, meaning and results. As this debate has been treated at some length in Part 1, Chapter 2 above, it will be presented here mainly by listing the names and written contributions of the major participants. As those writing in the late eighteenth and nineteenth centuries were little concerned with social and economic factors, we may divide them into four groups, purely in terms of ideology, as follows: (1) The out-and-out opponents of the Revolution, typified by Edmund Burke, whose *Reflections on the Revolution in France* first appeared in 1790, and H. Taine, author of *Les Origines de la France contemporaine: La Révolution* (3 vols., 1876). (2) The French liberal monarchists of 1815–30, who approved of the Constitution of 1791 but condemned the Revolution in its Republican and Jacobin phase. They included A. Thiers, whose *History of the French Revolution* (n.d.) saw early publication in London; as was the case with Germaine de Staël's *Considerations on the Principal Events of the French Revolution* (3 vols., London, 1815); and, a century later, with F. A. M. Mignet's *History of the French Revolution from 1789 to 1814* (1915). (For a discussion of these works and their political significance, see S. Mellon, *The Political Uses of History* [Stanford, Cal., 1958].) (3) The 'Whiggish' tradition, favourable to liberalism for an elite but suspicious of equality, associated with Tocqueville (see above). (4) The liberal–democratic school, founded by Jules Michelet with his *French Revolution* (1856), favourable to both democracy and liberty and, therefore, willing to embrace Republicans and Jacobins as the worthy heirs of the 'Principles of '89'. Such views, moreover, were broadly shared by the Republican–socialist Alphonse Aulard who, at the turn of the century, published his *French Revolution:*

A Political History 1789–1804 (English trans., 4 vols., 1910).

But social and economic factors and the serious study of the popular element – the peasants and *sans-culottes* – continued to be neglected. To repair this omission has been a major task of the historians of the twentieth century, starting with Jean Jaurès' *Histoire socialiste de la Révolution française* (first published in 1901, but not annotated until Soboul's seven-volume edition of 1968–73). Jaurès' initial explorations were carried much further by his successors: by A. Mathiez, in *La Vie chère et le mouvement social sous la Terreur* (1932); and, above all, in the work of Georges Lefebvre on peasants and revolutionary crowds, as in *Les Paysans du Nod pendant la Révolution française* (2 vols., 1924); *The Great Fear of 1789: Rural Panic in Revolutionary France* (English trans., 1973); and 'Foules révolutionnaires', first published in 1934 and reprinted in *Études sur la Révolution française* (1954). See also, for the first study-in-depth of the urban *sans-culottes* A. Soboul's *Les Sans-culottes parisiens de l'an* II (La Roche-sur-Yon, 1958), republished in an abridged English edition, *The Parisian Sans-culottes and the French Revolution, 1793–4* (Oxford, 1964).

The new direction given by the Jaurès–Lefebvre school to the study of revolutionary history has, partly owing to its often Marxist orientation, stirred up a hornet's nest of dissenting opinion. The first serious criticism of this new 'orthodoxy' (as it has been called by opponents) came from the left in D. Guérin's *La Lutte de classes sous la première République: bourgeois et 'bras nus' 1793–1797* (2 vols., 1946); but this amounted to comparatively little and ended in an early reconciliation (with Soboul in particular) as criticism, after some delay, developed from the right and centre. It began with Alfred Cobban, the English historian, in the mid-1950s and gradually was taken up by fellow 'revisionists' in the United States and France. For such dissenting views the reader is referred to the following authors: A. Cobban, *The Myth of the French Revolution* (1955), *The Social Interpretation of the French Revolution* (Cambridge, 1964), and *Aspects of the French Revolution* (1965); succeeded in the United States by E. Eisenstein, 'Who Intervened in 1788? A commentary on [Lefebvre's] *The Coming of the French Revolution*', *American Historical Review*, lxxi (1965), 77–103; George V. Taylor, 'Non-capitalist Wealth and the Origins of the French Revolution', *American Historical Review*, lxxii (1966–7), 469–96; D. Bien, 'The Army and the French Enlightenment: Reform, Reaction and Revolution', *Past and Present*, 85 (1979), 68–98; and, more guardedly, by R. Forster, *The Nobility of Toulouse in the Eighteenth Century* (Baltimore, 1960). In England Cobban was followed by C. B. A. Behrens, 'Nobles, Privileges and Taxes in France at the End of the Ancien Régime', *Economic History Review*, xv (1962–3), 451–75; and by W. Doyle in *Origins of the French Revolution* (Oxford, 1980). But the main indictment of the 'social interpreters' came from France: savagely from F. Furet in 'Le Catéchisme révolutionnaire', *Annales: Économie, Société, Civilisation* (March–April 1971); and, more mutedly, in his *Interpreting the French Revolution* (English trans., 1981). Meanwhile, the debate continues and is likely to do so through the Revolution's Bicentenary year.

For further work on the social background and social history of the Revolution the student is referred to E. G. Barber, *The Bourgeoisie in Eighteenth-Century France* (Princeton, 1955); F. Ford, *Robe and Sword: The Regrouping of the French Aristocracy after Louis* XV (1953); I. Cameron, *Crime and Repression in the Auvergne and the Guyenne, 1720–1790* (Cambridge, 1981); A. Davies, 'The Origins of the French Peasant Revolution of 1789', *History*, 49 (1964) 24–41; O. Hufton, *The Poor in Eighteenth-Century France, 1750–1789* (Oxford, 1974); S. Herbert, *The Fall of Feudalism in France* (London, 1921; reprinted in New York, 1969); and N. Hampson, *A Social History of the French Revolution* (Manchester, 1963)

The role of the common people in the Revolution has, since the pioneering works of Jaurès, Soboul and Lefebvre, been the subject of continuing study and also of continued controversy. For differing views, see Furet's *Interpreting the French Revolution* (above), Vovelle's *La Mentalité révolutionnaire* (1985), R. C. Cobb's *The Police and the People* (Oxford, 1970), O. Hufton's 'Women in Revolution, 1789–96', *Past and Present*, 53 (1971), 90–108; and see also R. J. Andrews, 'Social Structures, Political Elites and Ideology in Revolutionary Paris, 1792–94', *Journal of Modern History*, xix (1985–6), 71–112; and G. Rudé, *The Crowd in the French Revolution* (Oxford, 1959) and *Ideology and Popular Protest* (1980).

The study of the 'cultural' history of revolution is an even more recent development. For this see Vovelle's *Mentalité révolutionnaire* (above) and other of his works on irreligion and de-Christianization (both before and subsequent to the Revolution's outbreak) such as 'Le Tournant des mentalités en France, 1750–1789: la "sensibilité" pré-révolutionnaire', *Social History*, v (May 1977), 605–29; and *La Déchristianisation de l'an* II (1976). See also the seemingly macabre but highly readable *Great Cat Massacre* (Penguin, 1955) by Robert Danton; Mona Ozouf's 'Le Cortège et la ville: les itinéraires parisiens des fêtes révolutionnaires', in *Annales: Économie, Société, Civilisation*, 26 (1971), 689–916; and D. Mornet's classic, *Les Origines intellectuelles de la Révolution française* (1933).

Coming to the main stages of the internal history of the Revolution, the work of the Constituent Assembly is well summarized in P. Sagnac, *La Législation civile de la Révolution française* (1898); the ideas underlying the legislation of 1789–91 are discussed by E. Thompson in *Popular Sovereignty and the French Constituent Assembly, 1789–1791* (1952); and political movements of the time are treated by Mathiez in *Les Grandes Journées de la Constituante, 1789–91* (1913) and *Le Club des Cordeliers pendant la crise de Varennes et le massacre du Champ de Mars* (1910). The events of 1792 are related by Mathiez in *Le Dix Août* (1931) and by P. Carron in *Les Massacres de septembre* (1935). For the struggle between Gironde and Mountain in 1792–3, see the contrasting views of Mathiez in *Girondins et Montagnards* (1930), M. J. Sydenham in *The Girondins* (1961), and Alison Patrick in *The Men of the First French Republic* (Baltimore, 1973). For the work of the great Committee of Public Safety, see R. R. Palmer, *Twelve who Ruled* (1941); and, for an important part of its duties in 1794, A. Ording, *Le*

Bureau de police du Comité de Salut public (Oslo, 1935). For the relations between the 'revolutionary' government and the popular movement and sections in Paris, see Soboul's *Parisian Sans-culottes* (above); and for the operation of the Terror in the provinces see W. Scott, *Terror and Repression in Marseille* (1973) and, above all, R. C. Cobb's *Les Armées révolutionnaires: instrument de la Terreur dans les départments avril 1793 – floréal an* II (2 vols., 1961–3).

The post-Thermidorian period has, until recently, been rather sketchily – and unsympathetically – treated. For the year following Robespierre's fall see Mathiez' *La Réaction thermidorienne* (1929), Lefebvre's *The Thermidoreans* (English trans., 1964), and K.D. Tönnesson's study of the popular movements of Germinal–Prairial, *La Défaite des sans-culottes* (Oslo, 1959). For the later years see Lefebvre's *The Directory* (New York, 1964) and M. Lyons, *France and the Directory* (1975); and, for a more positive view of both Thermidorians and Directors, see D. Woronoff, *The Thermidorean Régime and the Directory, 1794–1799* (Cambridge and Paris, 1984).

From the vast storehouse of Napoleonic literature only a small sample will be offered here. Of biographies the following may be recommended: J.M. Thompson's *Napoleon Bonaparte: His Rise and Fall* (1952); and H. A. L. Fisher's old-fashiond but still readable *Napoleon* (1912). Opinions on Napoleon are discussed by P. Geyl, a critic, in *Napoleon For and Against* (English trans., 1949) and in D. Dowd's brief sketch, *Napoleon: Was he the Heir of the Revolution?* (1957). For the Continental System and England's counter-blockade, see F. Crouzet, *L'Économie britannique et le blocus continental* (2 vols., 1958) as well as pp. 342–76 of Lefebvre's *Napoleon* (English trans., 2 vols., 1969), a masterly portrayal of the Napoleonic era as a whole. For the 'revolutionizing' of Europe up to 1799 see J. Godechot's *La Grande Nation: expansion révolutionnaire de la France dans le monde de 1789 à 1799* (2 vols., 1956); for its continuation under the Consulate and Empire, see G. Lefebvre, *Napoleon* (1969), pp. 427–79; and for the constitutions that emerged through France's military occupation of the 'sister republics' and elsewhere, see H. B. Hill, 'The Constitutions of Continental Europe, 1789–1813', *Journal of Modern History*, viii (1936). And, for the development of a Napoleonic legend after the Emperor's exile to St Helena, the reader is referred to the would-be anonymous *Journal of the Private Life and Conversations of the Emperor Napoleon at Saint-Helena* (8 vols., London, 1923).

To continue with France's 'revolutionizing' of Europe both before and after Napoleon's fall: scholarly studies of this process in Scandinavia and Central Europe by K. Tönnesson, K. Benda and others have appeared in nos. 212 and 265 (1973 and 1986) of the *Annals historiques de la Révolution française*; while the French Revolutions of 1830 and 1848 (also, in major respects, projections of the Revolution of 1789) have been given scholarly attention in two books edited by J. Merriman of Yale: *1830 in France* (1975) and *Consciousness and Class Experience in Nineteenth-Century Europe* (1979).

The birth of a French working-class movement at Lyons is discussed by Robert Bezucha in *The Lyon Uprising of 1834: Social and Political Conflicts in the Early July Monarchy* (Cambridge, Mass., 1974). And, finally, the counter-revolution, which plagued the Revolution's National Assemblies as well as the Consulate and Empire, is studied in J. Godechot's *The Counter-Revolution, Doctrine and Action* (English trans., 1971) and, most recently and comprehensively, in F. Lebrun and R. Dupuy (eds.), *Les Résistances à la Revolution* (1987).

Index

Civil Constitution of the Clergy, 67–9